REVIEW IS INSIDE LAST PAGE

D1568592

Plants for
AMERICAN LANDSCAPES

Plants for
AMERICAN LANDSCAPES

NEIL G. ODENWALD, ASLA

CHARLES F. FRYLING, JR., ASLA

THOMAS E. POPE

Louisiana State University Press
Baton Rouge and London

Designer: Laura R. Gleason
Typeface: Sabon
Printer and binder: Sung In Printing

Library of Congress Cataloging-in-Publication Data
Odenwald, Neil G.
    Plants for American Landscapes / Neil G. Odenwald,
  Charles F. Fryling, Jr., and Thomas E. Pope.
        p.   cm.
    Includes bibliographical references (p.   ) and index.
    ISBN 0-8071-2093-6 (cloth : alk. paper)
    1. Landscape plants—United States. 2. Landscape plants—
  United States—Pictorial works. I. Fryling, Charles. II. Pope,
  T. E. (Thomas Everett), date. III. Title.
  SB435.5.034   1996
  635.9'0973—dc20   96-22844
                                               CIP

CONTENTS

ACKNOWLEDGMENTS

Writing this book has brought home to us that no man can be an island. To prepare a comprehensive book on plants, we needed the benefit of the experiences, resources, and support of many. Fortunately, gardeners and plant lovers are among the most caring and sharing people in the world. The authors have encountered tremendous generosity and kindness in the course of their work. Countless people have opened their gardens for photography and supplied us with valuable information on the regional suitability, adaptability, and performance of plant species and cultivars.

For sharing time and knowledge with us, we are especially indebted to Sadik Artunc, Edward Bush, Frank Chaffin, Miriam and Rex Davey, Marion Drummond, James Fowler, Don Fuller, Margie Jenkins, Mark Jenkins, Clinton Korfhage, John Korfhage, Joe Mertzweiller, E. N. O'Rourke, Don Reed, Lou Riddle, Gloria Sasek, Lawrence Sasek, Dan Scholz, Oscar Slade, Bruce Sharky, Lee Squires, Suzanne Turner, Mary Witt, Frank Zachariah, and Jim Zietz, and to the staffs of Ammon Landscape, Ammon Nursery, the Hilltop Aboretum of Louisiana State University, and Louisiana Nursery.

Many people have allowed us free access to their collections of photographs showing plants at strategic times and in memorable settings, among them Dick Ammon, R. A. Baumgardner, Van Cox, Max Z. Conrad, Dan Earle, Jon Emerson, Lester Estes, William Fountain, Charles Fritchie, Greg Grant, Linn Green, Herb Grove, Mark L. Kleiner, Alice Le Duc, Edward Missavage, Scott Ogden, E. Earl Puls, Benny J. Simpson, Art Van de Putte, and Wayne Womack. We are also grateful in this regard to Peter Hatch and the Thomas Jefferson Memorial Foundation, Eric Neuman and the staff at the National Arboretum, and Dean Norton and the Mount Vernon Ladies' Association, as well as to All America Selections. *Agricultural Research Magazine*, published by the United States Department of Agriculture, has provided the cold hardiness map.

We wish to thank Leslie Phillabaum, director of LSU Press, and the Press's staff for extending to us the invitation to write this book.

We are particularly appreciative of our families' love and support during the many months we spent on the volume. To Lucy Pope we are, in addition, deeply indebted for invaluable assistance with the preparation of the manuscript.

INTRODUCTION

Plants for American Landscapes combines the education and experience of the three authors over their lifetime careers. The volume represents more than a hundred years of training and work in the fields of landscape architecture and horticulture. Its aim is to help anyone interested in plants and gardening with information about the character, range of adaptation, and growing requirements of nearly a thousand of the most widely favored and dependable plants for American gardens.

The primary factors affecting plant growth and distribution are temperature, moisture, light, nutrients, and soil. With the exception of temperature, these factors may be altered or controlled to some degree in nearly all landscape settings. Consequently, the range of plant adaptation is largely a matter of cold hardiness. The hardiness zones cited in this book are from the United States Department of Agriculture Plant Hardiness Zone Map (Agricultural Research Service, Miscellaneous Publication Number 1475, January, 1990). But we have been content with recording general regional adaptation. We do not differentiate hardiness within zones, as the hardiness map does by dividing zone 8, for example, into areas *a* and *b*. It is important to keep in mind that within a region there are often microclimates that allow plants to survive in zones where they do not ordinarily succeed. The temperature within a large metropolitan area may be several degrees warmer than in the surrounding countryside. Large bodies of water moderate the temperatures of nearby areas. Near south-facing walls, temperatures are often a few degrees warmer, and northern exposures may be cooler throughout the year. In some cases, plants do not grow in an area because its high temperatures exceed the plants' tolerance. For instance, the Colorado blue spruce is not normally a success in zones 8 to 10.

The plant sizes we give are based on our experience in growing and observing plants. We also conducted an extensive review of the literature on plant performance. Stated dimensions of 20′ x 15′, for example, signify an average height of 20 feet and a 15-foot average spread. Optimum conditions may yield a larger plant, a stressful environment a smaller one. Many horticultural variables bear on plant size and development, the more obvious of them including soil preparation, fertilization, irrigation, pruning, mulching, and pest control.

Plants for
AMERICAN LANDSCAPES

Glossy Abelia
Abelia × grandiflora
Caprifoliaceae
6–8′ x 6′   Zones 5–9

A popular and easily grown semievergreen shrub, the glossy abelia produces clusters of fragrant white to slightly pink funnel-shaped flowers from May until killing frost. The small, fine-textured lustrous dark green leaves of summer turn reddish bronze in late autumn. Young growth is characterized by shiny red stems. The shrub grows best in a well-drained soil in a spot that receives at least a half day of sunlight. A late winter pruning is recommended to control size, remove winter-damaged parts, and maintain plant vigor. Later introductions vary in size, growth habit, flower color, and leaf texture and color. There are a number of dwarf cultivars, 'Creech's Dwarf' being one of the better. *A. chinensis* grows to seven feet and in the summer bears many large flower heads that butterflies love.

Abelia in bloom during the warm months

White Fir
Abies concolor
Pinaceae
35′ x 20′   Zones 3–7

White fir, an excellent conifer for the Midwest and East.

The white fir is an outstanding narrow-leaf evergreen for eastern and midwestern landscapes. Its best growth is in full sunlight where soils are deep, fertile, and well drained. A rigid conical form and blue to gray green foliage are distinguishing features. Expect moderately slow growth from this conifer. The tree can withstand urban conditions, including moderate heat, air pollution, and drought. A close relative, *A. fraseri*, the Fraser fir, is adapted to high altitudes and because of its form, dark green color, and foliage retention, is popular as a Christmas tree.

Flowering Maple
Abutilon pictum
Malvaceae
10–15′ x 8–10′
Zones 8–10

Close-up of the most common cultivar of the flowering maple.

A fast-growing semitropical perennial shrub, the flowering maple produces an abundance of large bell-shaped flowers. Cultivars have flowers that may be white, red, pink, yellow, or orange, and these are present from early spring until a killing frost. Most common is the rank-

---

For ascertaining the common form of common names, we have not relied on specialized references but have turned to standard dictionaries, particularly *Webster's Third New International Dictionary of the English Language, Unabridged.*

growing cultivar that produces orange blossoms with prominent red veins. This and other members of the species grow in a wide range of soils, even those which are poorly drained. They flower best in sunlight but will bloom reasonably well in shade. Even when freezes kill the upper portions, growth will normally return in the spring if the plants are heavily mulched. Some cultivars are treated as bedding annuals and are adapted to culture in hanging baskets. The flowers are among the best for attracting hummingbirds.

Acacia
Acacia farnesiana
Leguminosae
10–15′ x 10–15′
Zones 8–10

Yellow flowers appearing in early spring on an acacia, which Thomas Jefferson called "the most 'delicious' flowering shrub in the world."

Acacia is a tropical evergreen suitable where temperatures do not dip below 25 degrees Fahrenheit. Its shrublike form is oval to rounded, with multiple stems and thorny zigzag branches. The delicate foliage is blue gray, and there are clusters of bright yellow sweet-scented flowers. The plant is well adapted for dry sandy, alkaline soil. When planted in heavy, wet soil, it is short-lived.

Copper Plant
Acalypha wilkesiana
Euphorbiaceae
4′ x 3′   Zone 10

In full sunlight, the copper plant is widely planted for its striking foliage, which is predominantly red but mottled with shades of pink, white, and green. In frost-free areas it grows to heights exceeding eight feet. In colder climates it is used as a summer bedding plant or in containers. Vivid color and bold-textured foliage give it a commanding presence in the landscape, particularly in mass plantings.

Distinctive winter and spring foliage and flowers of bear's-breeches

Clump of copper plants on the River Walk in San Antonio

Bear's-Breeches
Acanthus mollis
Acanthaceae
2′ x 3′   Zones 9–10

The early Greeks so admired bear's-breeches that they sculptured its leaves on capitals of the Corinthian order. Carvings of the leaves also appear on fine furniture. Bold, deeply lobed leaves and imposing, statuesque four-foot flowering spikes make the plant a spectacular perennial in winter and spring. The upper segment of the flower has a strange hooded shape and is curved like a paw, ending in curved, clawlike spines. With the arrival of hot weather comes semi-dormancy. Satisfactory growth and performance can be expected under a broad range of soil conditions, from dry to slightly moist. The plant loves morning sun and requires protection from winter freezes.

THE MAPLES

Aceraceae

Maples constitute one of the largest groups of plants in the United States. There are over two hundred species nationwide, from large trees to shrubs. They are found in street plantings, in parks, as shade and accent trees, and in commercial forestry. Maples are fairly easy to grow in a well-drained soil and full sunlight or partial shade. All maples provide an outstanding display of autumn color, and some have colorful foliage even during the growing season. Most tend to have brittle wood and shallow roots. Some are relatively short-lived.

Southern sugar maple, an excellent maple for the Deep South.

Southern Sugar Maple
Acer barbatum
15' x 25'   Zones 7–9

The southern sugar maple is excellent for the Deep South, particularly coastal landscapes. It is distinguished from the better-known sugar maple that thrives farther north by a smaller size, smaller leaves, and adaptation as an understory tree. It grows in gardens with moist to well-drained soil. Its autumn color is noteworthy but does not rival that of maples grown in the North.

Box Elder
Acer negundo
40' x 30'   Zones 2–8/9

One of the most common maples in moist floodplains, the box elder grows in a wide range of soils. Fast growing, soft wooded,

Compound leaf of the box elder

and short-lived, it volunteers readily. Numerous large clusters of buff brown seed are a focus of interest in fall and winter. The tree is distinguished from other maples by its three- to five-leaflet leaves that resemble those of poison ivy. For quick shade there are few trees that match it. The

several cultivars that have been introduced are said to be superior to the native plant. 'Variegatum' is a selection with white variegated leaves; 'Flamingo' has pink coloration in the young leaves.

Japanese Maple
Acer palmatum
5–30' x 10–20'   Zones 5–8

The Japanese maple is one of the most beloved trees for accenting and embellishing the landscape. Of all the maples, it is the most exacting about situation. In the North it will perform well in full sunlight, but in the South it must be sheltered from hot sunlight and drying winds. Growth is relatively slow. Rich, well-drained soil and an annual application of all-purpose garden fertilizer will maximize growth. There are many selections, ranging from those reaching five feet or less to others capable of a mature height in excess of twenty-five feet. Leaf shape varies from fine and threadlike to coarse and deeply lobed. Leaf color ranges from green to deep burgundy, and leaf size from two inches to five inches.

Japanese maple at Williamsburg

Japanese maple's autumn color

Norway Maple
Acer platanoides
40' x 30'   Zones 4–7

Striking symmetrical form, dense, lustrous foliage, and rapid growth make the Norway maple a frequent choice for ornamental plantings, especially in urban settings. The tree is short-lived as a result of its susceptibility to verticillium wilt and anthracnose, two serious fungus diseases. In some places, trees seldom live beyond thirty years. The most popular selection from the thirty or more cultivars is

Deep burgundy foliage of the 'Crimson King' Norway maple.

Norway maple specimen in the Chicago Botanic Garden.

'Crimson King', by virtue of its season-long rich burgundy color and its commanding presence.

Red Maple
Acer rubrum
40–60' x 30'
Zones 3–8

Unsurpassed for a dazzling display of autumn color, the red maple is a premium shade tree. In autumn, the leaf color ranges

Outstanding autumn color of the red maple

from bright yellow to brilliant red. A medium to fast grower, the tree has dense foliage and a pyramidal form. It grows in a wide range of soils, from dry to moist. There are scores of cultivars with special features that include narrow, upright, and oval forms, unique foliage colors, and miniature sizes.

Red Swamp Maple, Drummond Red Maple
Acer rubrum var. drummondii
50' x 35'   Zones 8–9

Where soils are heavy and poorly drained in the Deep South, the red swamp maple makes an excellent shade tree. Notable among its features are showy red flowers, and fruit in late winter, when other deciduous plants are still dormant. Red leaf stems and silvery gray coloration on the underside of the leaves are

Red swamp maple in flower, an attractive lawn tree for the Deep South.

other distinguishing marks. The bark is silver gray. The tree is one of the few maples that have reliable fall color in the Deep South. It will grow on sites where water stands for lengthy periods.

Silver Maple
Acer saccharinum
50–70' x 35'   Zones 3–8

The silver maple is not one of the first choices among shade trees. Mature specimens are rare in the Lower South because of a host of diseases. Ice and windstorms often break the tree's limbs. Where the soil is dry and infertile, this vigorously growing tree deserves consideration. It offers ease of culture, a fast rate of growth, and good

Silver maple, a fast growing but short-lived tree.

autumn color. Its more deeply cut leaves and strong odor of crushed twigs distinguish it from the red maple.

Emerson

Sugar maple at Mt. Auburn Cemetery, Cambridge, Massachusetts.

Sugar maple foliage

Sugar Maple
Acer saccharum
50–70' x 35–50'   Zones 4–8

Among the sugar maple's advantages are beautiful fall coloring (shades of yellow, orange, and red), a pleasing growth habit, and little susceptibility to damage by insects and disease. Its upright oval to rounded form and high canopy make it one of the best of the large shade trees for planting in yards and parks. It is short-lived in the South, probably affected by the prolonged high temperatures. This species can live for over a century in the North, provided that it is not crowded or under stress. Normally a slow to medium grower, it is capable of rapid growth when planted in a fertile, well-drained soil in full sunlight. There are many cultivars, varying in form, growth rate, leaf color, and texture.

Common Yarrow
Achillea millefolium
Compositae
To 2′   Zones 3–9

Common yarrow's many flower colors.

The soft, fernlike yellow green foliage of common yarrow persists until a hard freeze. From late spring through early summer, compact flower heads rise above the foliage. At one time yarrow was almost always white or yellow, but hybridization has resulted in a broad palette of bold and pastel colors. Yarrow is not exacting in its soil preference, but it requires several hours of direct sunlight for acceptable growth and heavy flowering.

Sweet Flag
Acorus gramineus 'Variegatus'
Araceae
8–10″   Zones 6–9

Fine-textured, tufted foliage of the sweet flag.

Sweet flag is tolerant of a wide range of growing conditions but does best in fertile soil in a sunny or partially shaded spot. Its variegated foliage and compact tufted growth habit make it a good choice for containers, rock gardens, plantings of ground cover, and bog gardens. As with irises, new growth is from the tips of lead rhizomes, which must be dug and replanted every two to three years or the beds will thin in places.

Bromeliads
Aechmea species
Bromeliaceae
1–5′ x 1′   Zones 9–10

Bromeliads, members of a group of herbaceous plants native to tropical America, are sometimes called living vases, since their stiff, spiny leaves form a vase or funnel. Bold flowers in colors from red to yellow and blue are borne on spikes, panicles, or racemes above the foliage, usually in spring and summer. Many bromeliads are epiphytes: they grow on other plants but do not take nourishment from them. Others grow in a porous soil, and most will succeed only in full sunlight or partial shade. The epiphytes can be mounted on driftwood or exhibited on walls and fences.

Bishop's-Weed
Aegopodium podagraria 'Variegatum'
Umbelliferae
8–10″   Zones 3–8

Popular because it makes an excellent ground cover whether grown in poor or fertile soil, bishop's-weed has no particular light preference. The vigorous grower, which is often thought to deserve its name of weed, can spread as much as eighteen inches in a single growing season. For this reason it

Collection of bromeliads in the conservatory at City Park, New Orleans

Bishop's-weed, an easily grown herbaceous perennial ground cover

Bottlebrush Buckeye
Aesculus parviflora
10–12′ x 10–15′   Zones 4–8

In size a large, broad-spreading shrub or a small tree, the bottlebrush buckeye produces a mass of white bottlebrush-shaped flowers over a canopy of coarse-textured palmate leaves. Flowers continue over a relatively long period in midsummer, when few other large plants are in bloom. Singly grown specimens and mass plantings or shrub borders are equally appealing where there is ample space for the broad spread. Like other buckeyes, this species will grow in a wide range of conditions but does best in a fertile, well-drained soil and in full sunlight or partial shade.

may be advisable to contain it. Compound green leaves edged in white sparkle in the sun, but they are damaged by too much direct sunlight in warmer areas. Solid green leaves and shoots should be removed to prevent reversion to the highly invasive nonvariegated form.

Common horse chestnut, a long-lived flowering tree.

Horse chestnut flowers

Bottlebrush buckeye at Cave Hill Cemetery, Louisville, Kentucky

Common Horse Chestnut
Aesculus hippocastanum
Hippocastanaceae
75′ x 50′   Zones 3–7

The common horse chestnut is a handsome deciduous tree often seen in the eastern United States and widely planted throughout Europe and England. Large palmate leaves with five to seven leaflets are typical of the buckeye family. Prominent off-white flowers appear on one-foot candlelike panicles above the foliage in early summer. Of an upright oval form and ideal as a specimen, the tree should be reserved for open sunny areas where the soil is well drained.

Red Buckeye
Aesculus pavia
6–12′ x 6–15′
Zones 4–8

The red buckeye, seen widely through the South, can range in size from a small shrubby specimen, where the soil is dry and infertile, to a tree, in a moist, fertile

Red buckeye in early spring

soil. In a long series of interesting changes lasting from late winter through early summer, plants first produce prominent buds, then in spring develop delicate palmate reddish to copper-colored leaves. Next come handsome red flowers, which are followed by large nuts, each of them containing two chestnut brown seeds. Mature specimens have an interesting sculptural branching. The plant is ideally suited as a specimen or in a mass grouping in full sunlight or partial shade.

White-flowering lily of the Nile at the edge of a patio.

Blue-flowering lily of the Nile.

Lily of the Nile, Agapanthus
Agapanthus orientalis (africanus)
Amaryllidaceae
12–18′   Zones 8–10

A summer-flowering herbaceous perennial, lily of the Nile produces large rounded terminal clusters of up to a hundred blue or white funnel-shaped flowers on stalks to thirty inches above clumps of narrow, strap-shaped leaves. In warm areas it is planted in well-drained beds that receive full sunlight. In colder regions, it is a popular container plant. Flowering occurs over an extended period in early

summer. The plant can be used as an accent, as a blossoming selection for massing, or as a ground cover. 'Peter Pan' is a dwarf form, and 'Albus' is a white-flowering cultivar.

Century Plant
Agave americana
Agavaceae
6′ x 6′   Zones 8–10

The century plant is a prized succulent in Central America and South America. Parts of it are harvested for fiber, and the sap is distilled to make tequila. In warm, dry gardens in its native land it is a prominent ornamental. Broad, thick leaves with prickly edges form massive rosettes that eventually produce flowers, fragrant at night, on towering stalks capable of reaching twenty feet on mature plants. Once a plant flowers, it dies, but basal suckers normally form on it. The many cultivars include some that are very small. Foliage runs from dark olive green to gray, white, and yellow variegations. Since the plant must have full sunlight and a very dry, sandy soil, it is suitable for xeriscapes.

Century plant at the Alamo, in San Antonio

Variegated century plant, which does well in xeriscapes

Tree of heaven, which grows almost anywhere

Tree of Heaven
Ailanthus altissima
Simaroubaceae
25–50' x 20'   Zones 4–9

The tree of heaven is a rapid-growing, nearly indestructible deciduous tree observable in nearly every American center city. A prolific self-seeder, it is unfazed by the most adverse environments. It springs forth from cracked pavement and tiny slivers of soil between buildings, and in abandoned lots. Tall and slender, the tree is seldom given prominence in cultivated plantings, although it possesses the advantage of providing quick shade. It has prominent compound leaves to thirty inches long and produces an umbrella-like canopy and, during the summer months, showy terminal clusters of small green white flowers. It is tolerant of high levels of air pollution.

Ajuga spreading over a brick walk

Ajuga
Ajuga reptans
Labiatae
6"   Zones 3–9

Ajuga is a popular carpetlike ground cover suitable for small, well-tended plantings. A nonaggressive perennial, it is difficult to maintain in large plantings, for it does not compete well and weeds and grasses tend to invade its territory. Purple to green foliage is dense along prostrate (stoloniferous) square stems.

Blue violet flowers appear on six-inch spikes in spring and early summer. In the South, select a shaded, well-drained site. The plant will grow in considerably more sunlight in the northerly zones. It is susceptible to several stem and root fungi, but it is possible to keep problems in check by applying a fungicide drench several times during the summer. Fertilize sparingly in late winter. Several selections with varying foliage and flower coloration are available.

Five-leaf akebia, an excellent vine for garden structures.

Five-Leaf Akebia
Akebia quinata
Lardizabalaceae
20–40' vine
Zones 4–9

Native to Asia, five-leaf akebia has compound leaves the leaflets of which are between one and a half and three inches long. The blue green leaves give the vine a delicate quality in spring and summer. By selective pruning, this vigorous grower can be kept to trellises and fences and trained to cover utility poles. In spring it has clusters of small fragrant purplish flowers. Purple violet fruit follow in late summer.

Mimosa
Albizia julibrissin
Fabaceae
30' x 20'   Zones 7–10

Many predicted the demise of the mimosa when mimosa wilt, a soil-borne fungus disease, first attacked it. But the beautiful flowering tree has survived and is returning in significant numbers over much of the area to which it is adapted. Broad-spreading and deciduous, it grows in a wide range of soils, acid to alkaline and moist to dry, and makes a good specimen for seashore plantings. In late spring, fluffy light to dark pink flowers, two inches in diameter, develop in clusters at the tips of branches. Flowering may continue for six to eight weeks. The tree is fast-growing and drought-resistant, and it can survive temperatures down to 0 degrees Fahrenheit.

Broad-spreading canopy of the mimosa (right)

Broad, mounding clump of lady's mantle at the Arnold Arboretum, in Boston.

Lady's Mantle
Alchemilla mollis
Rosaceae
15–18″ x 24″
Zones 4–7

Lady's mantle thrives in a cool climate and a moist soil. In a hot or dry location it is necessary to place it in partial shade and in moist, fertile soil. It is a self-seeder and naturalizes to cover relatively large areas if not contained. Remove seed heads to encourage repeated flowering and reduce the plant's spread. Small yellowish green flowers borne in flat clusters from late spring into summer are frequent in fresh and dried arrangements. The large fan-shaped leaves have a silklike pubescence that holds glittering drops of dew and rain. In the northerly areas where the plant does best, it is used in mass groupings, as a ground cover, and in single clumps.

Tung Oil Tree
Aleurites fordii
Euphorbiaceae
30′ x 20′   Zones 8–9

The tung oil tree was once planted for the fine grade of oil that its nuts yield. A native of central Asia, the tree grows best in a sandy loam. White tubular flowers are borne in terminal panicles and have orange markings and maroon veins. The showy flowers, large in both size and number, appear in early spring before foliage growth. The large heart-shaped leaves, with a pair of basal glands, are dark green. In some autumns they turn bright orange to red. The tree seldom has a place in landscape developments, since the nuts are poisonous and create litter.

Tung oil tree foliage and nut

Powder-puff-like flowers of the mimosa

Golden trumpet, a yellow-flowering tropical vine

Golden Trumpet, Allamanda
Allamanda cathartica
Apocynaceae
10′   Zones 9–10

Outdoor use of the golden trumpet is confined to the coastal South, but it is a popular container plant throughout the nation. Beyond its zones of adaptation, winter protection is mandatory. The shrubby vine requires a fertile, sandy loam, warm temperatures, and full sunlight. Its golden yellow flowers are funnel-shaped and have a diameter of about three inches. Flowering is continuous while the plants are growing, but it is more abundant from late summer into fall, when vegetative growth slows.

Giant Onion
Allium giganteum
Alliaceae (Liliaceae)
3–4′ x 2′   Zones 5–8

The giant onion is one of a very large and complex group of plants, many of which are ornamental. Rounded umbels, five to six inches across, of pink to lilac flowers top three-foot stalks during spring and summer. The stalks rise from a basal mass of strap-shaped leaves, eighteen inches tall. When planted in a well-drained soil and full sunlight, this conversation piece is relatively easy to grow. Bulb rot can be a problem in poorly drained soil. *A.*

Large flower heads of the giant onion

sativum, society garlic, is a perennial with dark green leaves up to eight inches long and a quarter inch wide that bears clusters of small white to pink flowers in spring.

Alders
Alnus species
Betulaceae
40–60′ x 20–40′
Zones 3–8

Alders have some very desirable characteristics: an ability to grow in wet areas as well as dry, a tolerance of both

Leaves and woody seed cones of the speckled alder.

acidic and slightly alkaline soils, and with some, an ability to fix atmospheric nitrogen. Their fruit matures in autumn and is in small winged nutlets in egg-shaped, woody cones that persist well into the next growing season. *A. glutinosa,* a species from Europe, is a deciduous tree with dark green leaves up to four inches in both length and width. *A. rugosa,* the speckled alder or black alder, is a native species that makes a small tree or large shrub. *A. serrulata* has beautiful yellow brown catkins in early spring. Alders are not widely available but command consideration for landscapes where wet or poor soil makes growing other plants difficult. Available cultivars of the European species vary in growth habit and in leaf form and color.

Elephant Ear
Alocasia macrorrhiza
Araceae
4′ x 4′   Zones 8–10

Few plants have a more commanding presence in the garden than the elephant ear (see also *Colocasia esculenta*). Gigantic tropical leaves that can be four or more feet across are often the most visible accent foliage in a garden. In the South, the plant repeats year after year. Where the soil freezes, bulbs must be dug and stored after the first frost for replanting the next spring. The bulbs respond favorably to a very moist, fertile soil, and liberal applications of fertilizer during the summer months encourage the development of especially large leaves.

Variegated Shellflower, Variegated Ginger
Alpinia zerumbet 'Variegata'
Zingiberaceae
2–3′   Zones 8–10

The variegated shellflower is a herbaceous perennial of the ginger family that is grown for its showy variegated foliage. The clumped plant has leaves of dark green and yellow that can reach a height of two feet. It needs full sunlight or partial shade and grows best in a moist, well-drained soil with high organic content. Where not winter-killed, it may grow to eight feet or more, producing pendulous clusters of fragrant white flowers tinged with purple. The crinkled lip of the flower is yellow with red and brown variegation. The plant will withstand light frost, but cold-damaged parts should be removed in spring.

Variegated shellflower in Miami

Giant leaves of the elephant ear

Downy Serviceberry
Amelanchier arborea
Rosaceae
15–25′ x 10′
Zones 4–9

Flowers of downy serviceberry, an attractive small flowering tree.

A small deciduous tree or, more often, a multiple-trunked large shrub, the downy serviceberry has a wide distribution over the eastern United States. Other species, like its close relatives *A. laevis,* the Allegheny serviceberry, and *A. canadensis,* the shadblow serviceberry, perform equally well as understory growth in naturalistic settings where soils are moist, well drained, and acid. White flowers appear in pendulous racemes, two to five inches long, in spring. In early summer, mature specimens produce purplish black fruit, one-third inch in diameter, that both humans and birds seek out. The three-inch leaves render an excellent display of brilliant red autumn color. The winter bark is an interesting blue gray. There are more than a dozen cultivars, varying in size, form, leaf, flower, and autumn color. 'Pebina' and 'Smokey' are choice self-fertile selections.

Pepper Vine
Ampelopsis arborea
Vitaceae
15–20′ vine   Zones 7–10

Seldom observed in cultivation, the pepper vine grows naturally over anything in its path and often chokes out weaker plants. From late summer into autumn it produces an interesting, relatively fine-textured reddish to bronze foliage and clusters of shiny black porcelain-like berries. Worthy of more consideration than it receives as an ornamental that will give rapid coverage of garden structures and fences, the vine grows well in full sunlight to fairly heavy shade and adapts to nearly any soil from dry to very wet.

three inches in diameter in many shades of red, blue, and white appear during the cool months. Light freezes often kill back foliage and flowers, but both normally return in a few weeks. A mulch of leaves or pine straw will offer protection. A well-drained soil and sunlight, at least in the morning, are essential for good performance. For best results, tubers should be planted each autumn.

Pepper vine, rampant and invasive if growth is not curtailed.

Rosa-de-montana, a vine flowering through late summer

Anemone, with parsleylike foliage

Anemone
Anemone coronaria
Ranunculaceae
1′   Zones 5–8

A poppylike perennial that blooms with the earliest of the spring-flowering bulbs, the anemone continues in blossom until hot weather arrives. Clumps of finely divided foliage resembling parsley grow from small tubers planted in autumn. Single flowers, approximately two to

Rosa-de-Montana, Coral Vine
Antigonon leptopus
Polygonaceae
40′ vine   Zones 8–10

Rosa-de-montana, a popular perennial vine in the Deep South, is a native of Mexico. It dies back to the ground each winter but returns in early spring from large, fleshy tubers. In a matter of weeks the coarse-textured arrow-shaped foliage of a well-established vine can extend over several hundred square feet, including the fencing, garden pieces, porches, and other plants it uses for support. The hot pink tendril-laden, lacy flowers attract a lot of attention from midsummer through early autumn. Many insects, including honeybees, are attracted by the nectar. A white-flowering cultivar, 'Album', is available. Growth and management are relatively easy in a well-drained soil and full sunlight.

'Texas Gold' columbine, adapted to warm climates.

Columbines
Aquilegia species
Ranunculaceae
1–2′ x 1′   Zones 3–9

There are seventy or more species and many more cultivars of the columbine, which is a perennial of the buttercup family much acclaimed in the cooler regions of the United States. Some selections perform acceptably in warmer areas. Spring flowers come in many shades of white, yellow, pink, and purple and are easily identified by their hooked or straight swallowtail spurs on the back. The clumps of airy blue green compound leaves continue to add interest to the garden when the plant is not in bloom. Requiring a well-drained, moist soil, columbines perform best in full sunlight or partial shade. The Music Series encompasses the spectrum of rainbow colors. This perennial is particularly delightful viewed at close range.

Devil's-Walking-Stick
Aralia spinosa
Araliaceae
20′ x 10′   Zones 5–9

Woodland edges over much of the nation are home to the devil's-walking-stick, a small upright deciduous tree topped with an umbrella-like crown. Towering as a rule over young secondary growth, the tree produces bipinnate leaves up to four feet long during the summer. Off-white flowers are on prominent display from late summer to early autumn. In late autumn comes a more dramatic profusion of shiny black fruit on purple red stems. The clubby stems and twigs and even the backs of the leaves are heavily armed with spines. Excellent for naturalistic plantings, the tree can be a handsome single specimen or part of a mass arrayed to feature the tall, slender trunks.

Devil's-walking-stick, forming colonies with coarse-textured leaves topped by dramatic flower heads, along the Natchez Trace

Norfolk Island Pine
Araucaria heterophylla
Araucariaceae
3–25′ x 3–10′   Zone 10

Most people think of the Norfolk Island pine as a relatively small container-grown evergreen tree, to be placed indoors or on a patio. In the tree's native Australia, however, it grows to a height of over two hundred feet. Of a distinctive classical pyramidal form with stiff horizontal branching in tiers, the plant must be considered a tropical, because it cannot withstand temperatures below freezing. Branches sag from the horizontal after the tree reaches a height of about thirty feet. Plant in a well-drained soil and full sunlight, allowing ample space for growth and for viewing the unique form.

Norfolk Island pine, a tall-growing tree hardy outdoors only in zone 10, with a pair of arborvitae in the foreground.

Strawberry Tree, Arbutus
Arbutus unedo
Ericaceae
15–30′ x 15′
Zones 8–10

Mature fruit on the strawberry tree

Among lesser-known small evergreen trees and large shrubs, the strawberry tree is worthy of much more consideration for landscape use than it usually receives. Native of southern Europe, it does well in a relatively dry, well-drained location with full sunlight or partial shade. It cannot tolerate high humidity but is tolerant of a calcareous soil and coastal conditions. Among its admired qualities are dense dark evergreen foliage, an upright form, clusters of white to off-pink flowers like lilies of the valley, and prominent rounded, warted orange red strawberry-like fruit.

Abundant shiny red fruit of the Christmas berry, present for months

Christmas Berry
Ardisia crenata
Myrsinaceae
2–3′ x 1′   Zones 8–10

The shade-loving Christmas berry is a notable exception to the rule that plants that berry heavily do best in full sunlight. Seldom growing higher than three feet, the shrub produces clusters of showy red berries on bare stems just beneath its glossy dark blue green wavy-margined leaves. It can be striking in a ground cover of plants of varying heights but is equally effective as a single specimen along the shaded garden path. When planted in a soil with generous organic matter and leaf mulch, it is a prolific self-seeder. In general, ardisias are tender. If they freeze back to the ground in the climate zones of their adaptation, they normally return the following year. Do not expect many berries until plants are about three years old. There are cultivars that produce white berries, and others that produce pink.

Two cultivars of Japanese ardisia

Japanese Ardisia
Ardisia japonica
10–12″   Zones 8–10

For a ground cover that has near-perfect uniformity in height and spread, consider Japanese ardisia. Tolerating a small amount of morning sunlight, it grows best in shade, even heavy shade. It spreads rapidly by underground runners if the soil is loose, moist, heavily fortified with organic matter, and covered with a three- to four-inch mulch. A whorl of dark green leaves tops upright, slightly crooked woody stems approximately a foot tall. Orange red berries about the size of a pea are in the main hidden among the leaves. Popular cultivars include 'Gulf Stream', with white variegated foliage; 'Red Tide', with red-tinged variegated foliage; and 'Ito Fukurin', with silvery gray foliage that has thin white margins.

Red Chokeberry
Aronia arbutifolia
Rosaceae
6–10′ x 3–5′   Zones 5–9

A colony-forming deciduous shrub native to the eastern United States, the red chokeberry is suited to naturalistic landscapes involving soils from dry to moderately moist, as in bottomlands. The multiple-stemmed plants have upright to irregular open forms and brilliant red berries in late autumn. There is reasonably good fall foliage color, especially with the cultivars 'Brilliantissima' and 'Erecta', two selections that also produce large, prominent berries.

Red chokeberry, with small red applelike fruit and colorful autumn foliage.

Artemisias
Artemisia species
Compositae
3–4′   Zones dependent on cultivars

Artemisias, constituting a group of over two hundred tender to semiwoody aromatic perennials, are normally found in dry, well-drained, sunny landscapes. The frosty, silver-colored foliage offers a strong color contrast to the greens of most garden plants. Foliage runs from very fine to wide lobed, and form from mounding to rangy. Stems are felt-like. 'Silver King' and 'Valerie Finnis' are popular cultivars of *A. ludoviciana*. Among the common names for plants in the genus are dusty miller, southernwood, tarragon, white sage, and wormwood. Some members of the genus have medicinal qualities.

Clump of 'Valerie Finnis' artemisia in front of white cleome

Dwarf Bamboo
Arundinaria pygmaea
Gramineae
12–15″   Zones 8–10

Dwarf bamboo ground cover growing under windmill palm.

Dwarf bamboo is a low-growing, wide-bladed grass valued for its aggressive ground-covering potential in harsh, hot, dry places where more traditional ground covers may not fare well. It spreads rapidly by underground rhizomes and is well adapted to small plantings with barriers to keep it from spreading. Periodic grooming that includes ruthless clipping is necessary to maintain a refined appearance. *Sasa veitchii*, a dwarf bamboo with straw-colored edging that makes it appear variegated, is adaptable to zones 6–9.

Giant Reed
Arundo donax
Poaceae (Gramineae)
10–16′   Zones 7–10

A perennial grass native to the Mediterranean region, the giant reed presents a dramatic display of tall, somewhat woody leaning canes wherever it grows. Easily adapted to nearly any soil from wet to very dry, it performs best in full sunlight. The cultivar 'Variegata' has large white-and-green variegated leaves but loses much of its distinctive coloration in the summer, as the foliage matures. Large, prominent silky buff-colored plumes tower over the grassy mass in autumn. Although the grass is usually allowed free rein, regular management can keep clumps tidy and under control. For centuries, wood from the stems has been the source for woodwind reeds.

Variegated giant reed in a Louisiana garden

Butterfly Weed
Asclepias tuberosa
Asclepiadaceae
2–3′ x 2′   Zones 3–9

Present over a large area of the United States and among the nation's showiest perennials, butterfly weed creates a pageant of attractive flat-topped orange flowers on rigid stems in summer and early autumn. Unlike most wild flowers,

Naturalized colony of butterfly weed in an Arkansas setting

which spring up in large drifts, it typically grows in a single clump or at least in relatively small colonies. Because of a very long tuberlike taproot, it survives in extremely dry soil, but it must have sunlight most of the day. Butterflies are nearly always drawn to the plant. It is prized for garden, meadow, and roadside planting.

Pawpaw
Asimina triloba
Annonaceae
20–30′   Zones 5–8

Immature fruit and foliage of the pawpaw.

Although many have hummed the little jingle "Picking up paw paws, putting 'em in a basket," few are likely to recognize the pawpaw tree, a wonderful small deciduous understory tree native to the United States and widely distributed in forests and woodlands. It can be identified by its large, coarse slightly drooping leaves to six inches long and dark purple to burgundy bell-shaped flowers. In summer the pawpaw yields an edible fleshy three-lobed fruit, three to four inches across, with a custard flavor. Growth is often in clusters, because a large tree will send out suckers where the soil is moist and contains a generous amount of humus. 'Overleese', 'Taylor', 'Taytwo', and 'Mitchell' are cultivars that produce large, tasty fruit.

Asparagus Fern
Asparagus densiflorus
'Sprengeri'
Liliaceae
3–5′   Zones 9–10

Fernlike but not a true fern, asparagus fern is an exceptionally versatile perennial from the lily family. For many years it was seen primarily in hanging baskets and other containers. Now it has been adopted as a ground cover and put to a host of other uses where its beautiful lime green fine-textured foliage will be an asset. It is especially attractive planted high, for example, where the long, fluffy trailing branches are allowed to drape over the top of a retaining wall. Provide a fertile, well-drained soil and sunlight for several hours each day. The plant is tolerant of drought and salt. Applying fertilizer several times each summer will accelerate its growth.

Asparagus fern, a plant that performs well in hanging baskets and as a ground cover.

Ground cover of aspidistra beneath deciduous trees

Cast-Iron Plant, Aspidistra
Aspidistra elatior
Liliaceae
18–24″   Zones 8–10

The name of the cast-iron plant suggests that the perennial is very tough, as indeed it is. Still, the range of conditions under which it performs up to the high expectations of discriminating gardeners is relatively narrow. Provide shade most of the day, although it will fare quite well in winter sunlight beneath the canopies of deciduous trees. The soil should be moist and have a high humus content. When conditions are optimal, the bold, coarse-textured leaves can achieve a commanding presence in the shade garden. Periodic grooming—and cutting back all foliage every three or four years—keeps plants free of brown leaves. Otherwise, old plantings can look unkempt. Clumps spread slowly until they are well established, but then they expand rapidly. This member of the lily family is an excellent container plant. Resembling the cast-iron plant is *Curculigo capitulata*, palm grass or the pleated aspidistra, which has dull green pleated leaves to three feet long and six inches wide. A tropical herbaceous perennial, it requires abundant moisture and high temperatures but can withstand an occasional light freeze. It too makes an excellent container specimen.

Astilbe
Astilbe × arendsii
Saxifragaceae
3–4′ x 3′   Zones 4–8

Except in the coastal South, where astilbe cannot tolerate the heat and humidity, this summer bloomer is a greatly prized perennial, because of its flower panicles six to eight inches tall. White is the most common color, but shades of pink, lavender, and red are plentiful. Large compound leaves are produced on relatively tall, rangy stems. Both flowers and foliage can contribute a distinctive texture to the garden. The plant performs well in full sunlight or partial shade and in a moist, fertile soil.

Mass planting of pink astilbe in Vancouver

Variegated Japanese Aucuba
Aucuba japonica 'Variegata'
Cornaceae
4–6′ x 4′   Zones 6–8

Bold, leathery leaves splotched with yellow make the variegated Japanese aucuba a high-profile specimen in plantings protected from hot summer sunlight. In the Middle South, the female plants of several cultivars, especially the solid green, produce large bright red berries. The stiff stems and upright growth combine well with the green foliage of many other shade-loving plants. The plant must have a

'Picturata' aucuba in a protected position at the Fort Worth Botanic Garden.

'Gold Spot' aucuba, capable of brightening a shady spot in a garden.

porous, well drained soil, or it will be prone to disease and have a short life.

Groundsel Bush
Baccharis halimifolia
Compositae
10–12′ x 8′   Zones 4–9

One of the first shrubs to appear in open fields and cleared lands, the groundsel bush is a large native shrub with gray green willowlike foliage that is widely distributed over the United States. Not especially selective about where it puts down roots, it grows in places ranging from dry upland landscapes with alkaline soil to seaside marshes with high salt concentration. Female plants have large terminal panicles of white to greenish white flowers in mid- to late autumn. The large mounding form of irregular branches can make a handsome accent but can be equally effective in mass plantings on open, sunny sites. *B. pilularis* is a low-maintenance ground cover that grows to a height of thirty inches and a spread of six feet. It has small gray green leaves and a dense mass.

White flowers covering a female groundsel bush in autumn, with male plants displaying olive green foliage.

Hedge Bamboo
Bambusa glaucescens (multiplex)
Gramineae
10–15′   Zones 7–10

The bamboos constitute just a small part of the very large family of grasses, and of them hedge bamboo is noted for its massive clumping, different from the spread by aggressive underground stems of the running types. Once well established, hedge bamboo makes a dense, nearly impene-

trable thicket that is durable and virtually impossible to eradicate without heavy equipment. It is favored when there is a need for a forestlike mass of growth. Because of its enormous competitive root system and tall, leaning canes, other plants do not grow well near a mature stand. It grows in full sunlight to shade and tolerates most soils, except the extremely wet and poorly drained.

Hedge bamboo

Orchid Tree
Bauhinia purpurea
Leguminosae
20′ x 15′   Zones 9–10

Flowers and foliage of the orchid tree

Small and deciduous, the orchid tree can live for years. Its orchidlike flowers, three to four inches across, have five unequal petals, each narrowing to a claw. Autumn is the season of bloom for this tropical tree, with a few flowers unfolding in early winter. The yellow green foliage is compound, and the leaflets are split to resemble an ox hoof. A moist, well-drained soil and full sunlight or partial shade are required. The tree cannot withstand drought, a saline soil, or hot winds.

Wax-Leaf Begonia
Begonia semperflorens-cultorum
Begoniaceae
12–18″   Zones 9–10

One of over a thousand begonia species and cultivars, with the number constantly increasing, the wax-leaf begonia makes an excellent bedding plant for about eight or nine months of the year. The mounding plant has attractive

Wax-leaf begonias, staple summer bedding plants in all sections of the nation.

rounded to angular leaves variously colored from green to red and bronze. Flowers are single or double and, commonly, white, red, or pink. The plant blooms continuously from early spring until cold weather. It is an excellent flowering perennial for partial shade, but its soil must be well drained to prevent rot. It is widely grown as a container plant. Numerous "series" are available in the trade, and some of the preferred cultivars in those series are 'Memory', 'Musical', 'Spirit', and 'Whiskey'.

THE BARBERRIES

Berberidaceae

The barberries are much planted as ornamentals from zone 5 through zone 9. The more than five hundred members of the group have thorny stems, alternate leaves, and yellow internal wood. Especially effective in hedges and mass plantings, and sometimes as individual accents, the barberries require full sunlight and well-drained soil.

Berberis julianae, the wintergreen barberry, is an evergreen shrub growing to ten feet and producing shiny bright green leaves and prominent thorns.

Berberis × mentorensis, the mentor barberry, is a semievergreen shrub growing to five feet. It has prominent thorns and makes an excellent hedge. One of the best barberries for the Midwest, it withstands dry summers.

Wintergreen barberry, the hardiest of the evergreen barberries.

Mentor barberry in a hedge in Lexington, Kentucky

Founta

B. thunbergii var. **atropurpurea,** the purple-leaf Japanese barberry, grows to six feet or more in height and produces a vivid burgundy or wine-colored foliage. In the Lower South it is nearly evergreen, but in the North it loses all its leaves in winter, retaining attractive red berries. The dwarf form, 'Crimson Pygmy', grows only to about two feet and has a mounding form. 'Aurea', the golden barberry, has yellow foliage.

'Crimson Pygmy', a dwarf form of the purple-leaf barberry

'Aurea', a barberry with yellow foliage.

Purple-leaf barberry in Hershey, Pennsylvania

Bergenia
Bergenia cordifolia
Saxifragaceae
12–18″   Zones 4–8

The thick leathery, bold textured evergreen foliage of bergenia ideally suits it for use as a specimen perennial and as a ground cover in mass plantings. It grows best in the cooler regions of the nation in a fertile moist, well-drained soil and full sunlight or partial shade. Its special feature is prominent pink bell-shaped flowers on twelve- to fifteen-inch stalks in spring. Many hybrids and cultivars are available, with white, purple, or salmon flowers and with unusually large, variable-sized, or uniquely colored leaves.

Distinctive coarse-textured foliage of the bergenia.

Interesting exfoliating bark of the river birch.

Cluster of river birch on the bank of a sandy stream.

River Birch
Betula nigra
Betulaceae
40–60′ x 25′   Zones 4–9

Among the fastest growing of native American trees, the river birch adapts to a wide range of growing conditions. Successful in soil that is moist, fertile, and sandy as well as in soil that is relatively dry, it performs best in full sunlight but can also be grown close to large trees. A distinctive feature is the gray peeling, papery bark that exposes a cinnamon-colored inner bark. The thin arrow-shaped leaves and the upright form with twiggy growth are other identifying characteristics. This popular tree is subject to heavy infestations of aphids, and young trees may have to be sprayed a couple of times a year.

White Birch, Paper Birch
Betula papyrifera
50–60′ x 35′
Zones 2–6/7

Because of its beautiful chalky white, black-marked bark, the white birch may be the most photographed tree in the world. It performs best in colder areas where the soil is well drained and slightly acid. Having an upright form with

White birch with picturesque bark

Autumn color of the white birch

branches beginning near the ground, it is handsome as a single specimen and in tight clusters. Most often the tree is relatively short-lived. Its long-term survival is not dependable enough to make it the only species in a planting of trees. Another birch with equally impressive bark and a unique pendulous form is *B. pendula*, the European white birch. This grows under similar conditions in the upper regions of the United States.

European white birch, a cut-leafed, weeping tree.

'Tangerine Beauty' cross vine, a new cultivar

Cross Vine
Bignonia capreolata
Bignoniaceae
Vine to 60′   Zones 6/7–9

Climbing up the trunks and into the branches of trees or scampering up the walls of brick buildings, the cross vine has beautiful yellow-and-red funnel-shaped, two-lipped flowers that often go unnoticed until they drop to the ground. It can be handsome growing on garden structures. The drooping elongated two-stalked compound leaves cling to flat surfaces by two-branched tendrils. The vine grows in a wide range of soils.

Bougainvillea
Bougainvillea spectabilis
Nyctaginaceae
25–30′ vine   Zone 10

One of the most highly prized vines in its native South America as well as in other warm, arid parts of the world, the bougainvillea presents a spectacular display of intense color over long periods. Red is its most common color but it can also be purple, yellow, yellow orange, or salmon. The true flower is quite small and is nearly concealed by colorful bracts that people think of as petals. Slight water stress, a well-drained soil, bright sunlight, and a low rate of fertilization tend to force the plant into heavier flowering. It can be grown as a handsome vine covering garden structures but performs equally well as a container specimen. Although woody, the vine cannot tolerate temperatures much below freezing.

Paper Mulberry
Broussonetia papyrifera
Moraceae
25–30′ x 30′   Zones 6–10

Mockingbird dining on fruit of the paper mulberry.

Not a true mulberry, the paper mulberry was introduced from Asia for its promise as an abundant source of wood pulp for making paper. Because it suckers freely and is a prolific self-seeder, it has escaped its acreage of cultivation and is now widespread over much of the southern United States. On immature trees there are three types of leaves: three-lobed, two-lobed, and unlobed. A fine, pubescent textured surface covers both leaves and twigs. Very fast growing, the tree flourishes in nearly any soil, in shade and in full sunlight. In summer, the female tree produces many orange-seeded drupelets that protrude from marble-sized fruiting bodies. Except for messy fruit and large falling leaves, this species can make a reasonably satisfactory shade tree in some places, especially where others that are more desirable will not grow.

Spectacular display of bougainvillea in southern California

Angel's trumpet, a tropical with several cycles of exotic blooms.

Angel's Trumpet
Brugmansia arborea
Solanaceae
8–10′ x 8′   Zones 8/9–10

In a single season, the angel's trumpet, a broad-spreading, short-trunked, coarse-textured treelike

Pink-flowering angel's trumpet

tropical, produces mammoth exotic funnel-shaped blooms in several cycles from midsummer until frost. The flowers are most often white, but new cultivars are pink, salmon, yellow orange, and purple. Profuse flowering occurs when plants receive several hours of sunlight each day.

Yesterday, Today, and Tomorrow
Brunfelsia australis
Solanaceae
4–5′ x 3′   Zones 8/9–10

Yesterday, today, and tomorrow, the flowers of which open purple and change first to lavender and then to white.

Yesterday, today, and tomorrow is a showy evergreen shrub with fragrant spring flowers that are violet on opening, fading to lavender, then to white on the second day. The five-petaled flowers are two inches across. The shrub grows best in a rich acid soil and full sunlight or partial shade. The dull dark green leaves, to two inches long, are briefly lost in cold weather,

except in zone 10. Most suitable as a container plant in areas that receive killing frost, the shrub flowers well in containers only when pot-bound or crowded. Its form generally runs from open and irregular to dense.

Butterfly Bush, Fountain Buddleia
Buddleia alternifolia
Loganiaceae
10–12′ x 8′   Zones 5–9

If attracting butterflies is an objective, plant the butterfly bush. During its flowering period, from early summer or midsummer through autumn, butterflies will be numerous. The large mostly deciduous shrub has silvery gray willow-like tomentose leaves. Depending on the cultivar, the tall fountainlike stems support a profusion of drooping panicles of blooms in lilac purple, pink, or white. The shrub thrives in a fertile moist, well-drained location that receives full sunlight for most of the day. Provide ample space for the plant to display its beautiful, graceful form. Remove old, nonproductive canes in late winter, but retain much of the previous season's growth, since it is on it that flowers will form. *B. davidii*, orange-eye butterfly bush, another popular species, is not as hardy as *B. alternifolia*.

Butterfly bush

The many cultivars of *B. davidii* are widely grown for their showy flowers of deep purple ('Black Knight'), deep rose pink ('Charming'), white ('White Bouquet'), and red ('Royal Red'), which appear on new growth. For this species, cut back plants severely during late winter, before new growth begins.

THE BOXWOODS

Buxaceae

Boxwoods are among the longest-lived small to medium-sized evergreen shrubs. The classical, formal patterned gardens of the world normally include boxwoods in some form. They perform best in a fertile moist, well-drained soil and full sunlight or partial shade but acclimate to a broad variety of growing conditions. Before choosing a boxwood, it would be advisable to consult a plant specialist about the best selections for your area and conditions. Nematodes, root fungi, and stem rot can be troublesome.

Harland Boxwood
Buxus harlandii
2–4′ x 2′   Zones 7–9

Of all the boxwoods and their cultivars, the Harland boxwood appears to have the stiffest, most upright form. The emerald green leaves, compact oval form, and spatula-shaped

Broad, dense canopy and nearly bare base of Harland boxwood.

Orange-eye butterfly bush, which blooms on new growth

Boxwood parterre and numerous original boxwood hedges, mostly Buxus sempervirens *'Suffruticosa', in the upper, or pleasure, garden at Mount Vernon.*

Littleleaf boxwood parterre at Afton Villa, St. Francisville, Louisiana

Littleleaf boxwood at Colonial Williamsburg

leaves are identifying marks of the species. In comparison with other boxwoods, the Harland grows fairly slowly. Because of its form, it does not combine easily into a clean, uniformly clipped hedge. Each plant too clearly retains its shape.

Littleleaf Boxwood, Japanese Boxwood
Buxus microphylla
4–8′ x 4′   Zones 6–9

A native of Japan, the littleleaf boxwood is the most widely planted of the boxwoods in the Lower South. Its many cultivars come in a wide range of sizes and with varying growth characteristics and foliage colors. Typically, the distinguishing features are a light green foliage color and rounded leaves, some with a notched tip. Although well adapted to the South, the plant has foliage that can take on a brownish, burned color in a severe winter, which can cause severe injury. Popular cultivars include 'Winter Green', 'Koreana', 'Winter Gem', 'Japonica', and 'Green Mountain'.

English Boxwood
Buxus sempervirens
10–12′ x 8′   Zones 5–9

The English boxwood is the most popular boxwood in the United States. Performing best in cooler regions, it is widely used in clipped hedges that can provide strong geometry in formal plantings. It is equally handsome, however, as a large unpruned specimen. Its stiff, fragrant glossy dark blue green foliage can be fashioned into topiary. Cultivars include 'Angustifolia' and 'Arborescens' among the large treelike selections, and 'Inglis', 'Myrtifolia', 'Suffruticosa', and 'Welleri' among the smaller and slower-growing types.

Caladium
Caladium × *hortulanum*
Araceae
15–20″   Zones 9–10

A hybrid, the caladium is a
popular high-profile leafy tropical in the summer garden. Repeating only in warmer areas,
this tuberous perennial is usually treated as an annual. It
grows very little until the soil
warms and evening temperatures rise above sixty degrees
Fahrenheit. For best results, provide a well-drained, sandy loam,
and shade during the middle of
the day. In addition to ground
plantings, this tropical does well
in containers. The hybrids have
many leaf colorations, among
the most popular of which are white-and-green ('Can-
didum'), pink mottled with green ('Pink Cloud'), pink
('Pink Symphony'), and green with white ('June Bride').
Several dwarf forms are available in the trade.

Potted caladiums at Longue Vue Gardens, New Orleans

French Mulberry
Callicarpa americana
Verbenaceae
6–8′ x 6′   Zones 6–9

The French mulberry is a native deciduous shrub often
found growing along woodland edges and in open fields
after clear-cutting. It grows in soils ranging from alkaline

to acid, from dry to relatively
moist. In full sunlight it produces many berries, but it will
grow in partial shade. Leaf fall
occurs before the first frost,
exposing long radiating stems

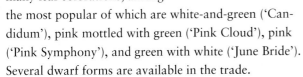

Native French mulberry

English boxwood at Cheekwood Gardens, Nashville

*Japanese mulberry, a species that fruits prolifically, in the Brooklyn Botanic
Garden.*

with tightly clustered rose to purple berries. The colorful
fruit seldom survives the foraging of birds. Although short-
lived, the shrub reseeds itself freely. 'Lactea', the white-
berrying selection, is somewhat less known than other cul-

tivars but often makes a stronger showing in shaded positions. *C. dichotoma* has clusters of small lavender pink flowers in summer and beautiful lilac violet fruit in early autumn. *C. japonica*, the Japanese mulberry, produces handsome bright violet-colored berries; it is best reserved for plantings in the cooler regions of the country.

Bottlebrush
Callistemon rigidus
Myrtaceae
6–8′ x 6′
Zones 8–10

Brilliantly colored flowers of the bottlebrush

Bottlebrush is a relatively cold tender evergreen shrub or small tree that grows best in a sandy, well-drained soil and full sunlight. Periodic winter-kill occurs outside the warm coastal regions. The plant's bright, showy red flowers are cylindrically shaped, like a bottle brush. They occur from late spring into summer. The leaves are narrow, rigid, sharp-pointed, and gray green. *C. citrinus*, the lemon bottlebrush, with lemon-scented foliage, is larger and treelike; *C. viminalis* has a weeping form and grows to a height of twenty feet.

Sweet Shrub, Carolina Allspice
Calycanthus floridus
Calycanthaceae
10–12′ x 6′
Zones 4–9

Sweet shrub, appreciated for its apple-scented blossoms in spring.

The sweet shrub is one of the pleasing but not so well known native deciduous shrubs of the southeastern United States. It possesses an upright multiple-stemmed form and produces relatively large leaves with prominent veins and bright yellow autumn color. Dark maroon brown to burgundy sweet-scented flowers appear just before and after full leaf in the spring. The fruit is pear-shaped or figlike in appearance. A mature specimen will sucker freely and eventually stand at the center of a small grove of canes. The cultivar 'Athens' has highly fragrant chartreuse yellow flowers in late spring and early summer.

Camellia
Camellia japonica
Theaceae
10–15′ x 8′   Zones 7–9

During the bleak days of winter, the camellia gives reassurance that there is life in the garden. It is a long-lived evergreen shrub that can endure for fifty years or more in a relatively fertile moist, well-drained acid soil with protection from noon sunlight. The countless cultivars include a broad range of flower colors, from white to pink, red, and rosy purple, including bicolors. Flowers may be single with prominent stamens or double with the petals concealing the stamens. Although the form and density of camellias are normally heavy, making the plants dominant as landscape specimens, there is considerable variation in foliage and form among the several species and many cultivars.

Display of several camellia flowers.

Red-flowering camellia in a specimen planting in Mobile, Alabama

'Shi Shi Gashira', a dwarf sasanqua camellia, usually with height and spread under four feet.

Mature specimens of regular sasanquas, which may grow to a height and spread of more than twelve feet.

Sasanqua Camellia
Camellia sasanqua
15–20' x 12'   Zones 7–9

Flowering in autumn and early winter, sasanqua camellias are evergreen shrubs appreciated for their abundance of blooms at a time of the year when most plants are going into dormancy. The old, standard cultivars can eventually become the size of trees. This camellia usually has dark blue green leaves that are smaller than those of *C. japonica*. Performance is best in a porous, well-drained acid soil in shade to nearly full sunlight. Depending on the cultivar, single or double flowers may be white, pink, lavender pink, crimson, or red. Dwarf, slow-growing selections are also popular, and they grow into dense, somewhat spreading shrubs.

Trumpet Vine
Campsis radicans
Bignoniaceae
20–30' vine
Zones 4–9

'Madame Galen' trumpet vine at Flat Rock, North Carolina.

Adapted to a wide range of growing conditions from full sunlight to shade that include nearly any soil, the trumpet vine is a native deciduous plant bearing clusters of brilliant orange red trumpet-shaped flowers during the warm months of the year. It climbs the trunks of trees and over the top of any other vegetation in its path. The cultivars 'Madame Galen' and 'Crimson Trumpet' are two exceptionally fine selections with handsome bright orange red flowers; 'Flava' has pure yellow flowers. Either the cultivars or the native species can be an ideal covering for garden structures.

Canna, an easy-to-grow summer-flowering perennial

Canna
Canna × generalis
Cannaceae
2–6′ x 3′   Zones 7–9

An all-time favorite perennial, the canna has gone through a lot of change over the past thirty years or so. Many people still admire some of the old large, standard selections, but there are also scores of new cultivars available today, some with variegated foliage. A few have reddish, wine-colored foliage, and some grow more compactly than the older types. Tall-stemmed gladiola-like flowers—pink, orange, red, yellow, or bicolor—tower over the large, coarse banana-like leaves. Always select a fertile moist, well-drained soil and full sunlight. Leaf-roller caterpillars often disfigure the foliage. Frequent spraying and grooming are required to maintain a clean, unblemished plant.

Variegated Japanese Sedge
Carex morrowii 'Aurea'
Cyperaceae
15–24″   Zones 5–9

Composed of grasslike tufted clumps of thin striped leaves, the variegated Japanese sedge is a striking herbaceous perennial worthy of consideration for gardens where detail is important. It will grow in full sunlight or partial shade under a wide range of conditions but performs best in a fertile moist, well-drained soil. Although nice in a clump by

itself, it is also effective in mass plantings, where its variegation can contrast with solid green foliage.

Natal Plum
Carissa grandiflora
Apocynaceae
2–5′ x 4′
Zones 9–10

Natal plum, which produces white flowers and edible red fruit.

Few plants have a more lustrous foliage than the Natal plum. Unfortunately, the interesting low-spreading, mounding shrub is suitable only where temperatures do not dip much below freezing. Fragrant white waxy star-shaped flowers and scarlet egg-shaped fruit are among its attractions. The assortment of handsome cultivars presents options concerning size, form, and flowering characteristics. Always provide full sunlight and a porous, well-drained soil.

Ironwood, American Hornbeam
Carpinus caroliniana
Betulaceae
20–30′ x 20′   Zones 2–9

Ironwood is a relatively small native deciduous tree normally growing along sandy streams and rivers but absent

Fine-textured, tufted foliage of the variegated Japanese sedge

Smooth, metal-like bark of the ironwood. **Inset:** *Foliage and fruit of the ironwood.*

Pecan
Carya illinoensis
Juglandaceae
75–100' x 50–60'
Zones 6–9

Among the tallest and most long-lived of deciduous trees on the North American continent, the pecan is widely distributed over much of the southeastern United States. Admired for its mammoth branches and large compound leaves, it is often grown for its delicious nuts. Plant the pecan where the dripping foliage cannot stain roofs, paving, or parked

from floodplains. The broad-spreading form with low horizontal branches and smooth, rippled musclelike slate gray bark make the tree worth exploring for landscape applications. Its leaves have prominent veins and provide reasonably good autumn color. It grows well in full sunlight and in understories to other hardwoods. The ironwood cannot tolerate alterations in the grade of the terrain near the spread of its roots. *C. betulus*, the European hornbeam, is used for screens and hedges and in groupings.

Typical southern pecan orchard in winter.

Pecan nuts and foliage

Pyramidal European hornbeam in Louisville, Kentucky

cars. The tree's widespread distribution attests to its adaptability to widely divergent growing conditions, but transplanting is difficult because of a very long taproot. For nut production, be sure to select cultivars that do well in your region. Some popular choices for the South include 'Candy', 'Choctaw', 'Elliot', 'Melrose', and 'Sumner'.

Foliage and silvery-colored bark of the shagbark hickory, Blue Ridge Mountain Parkway.

Shagbark Hickory
Carya ovata
75–100′ x 60′   Zones 4–9

Noted for a tall, straight trunk with shaggy silvery gray plated bark and brilliant golden yellow autumn color, the shagbark hickory is a native deciduous tree found growing in relatively dry upland soil over much of the United States. It has a large leaf with five leaflets that is somewhat similar to the compound foliage of other hickories and the pecan. Because of its huge size and slow growth, it is probably best reserved for large-scale plantings and other situations that can accommodate big trees. Other hickories that grow under similar conditions include *C. glabra*, the pignut; *C. cordiformis*, the bitternut; and *C. laciniosa*, the shellbark.

Cassia
Cassia corymbosa
Leguminosae
6–10′ x 6′   Zones 8–10

A somewhat upright, rangy shrub with thin stems, this cassia is one of a very large and complex group of legumes. It produces narrow dark blue green, nearly evergreen leaves in pairs, and sprays of yellow flowers at the end of long stems in summer and autumn. Slender cylindrical pealike seedpods that follow the flowers in late summer can give the plant a

Cassia, with arching branches terminating in yellow autumn flowers.

rather pendulous form. The shrub grows almost anywhere in its zones of adaptation, in full sunlight or partial shade and regardless of soil conditions. It is subject to winterkill but more often returns even after cold winters.

Golden Wonder
Cassia splendida
8–12′ x 8′   Zones 8/9–10

True to its common name, the golden wonder is a glorious spectacle for six weeks beginning in late October, when golden yellow flowers cover it. When most plants are going

Golden wonder in Charleston, South Carolina

into dormancy, this large, rangy tropical semi-evergreen shrub assumes an especially commanding presence. In other seasons it is not particularly interesting, and through most of the year it may go unnoticed. No one can miss a specimen, however, once it bursts into bloom. For best performance, provide a reasonably fertile moist, well-drained soil and full sunlight. The plant is subject to winterkill.

Chinese Chestnut
Castanea mollissima
Fagaceae
40–50' x 35'   Zones 4–8

The Chinese chestnut, a moderate-sized tree, is a widely accepted substitute for the American chestnut (*C. dentata*), which is nearly extinct owing to chestnut blight. It produces simple leaves up to two inches long with conspicuous serration along the edges and heavy venation. The whitish underside of the leaves has a soft, pubescent texture, and the stem coloration resembles cherry bark. Burrs two to three inches long split open to release two or three edible nuts, which appeal to humans and wildlife alike. As with all chestnuts, provide a well-drained acid soil and full sunlight. *C. pumila*, the chinquapin, is a close relative. It is a fairly low broad-spreading tree that produces clusters of burrs with edible small brown nuts.

Alley in south Florida lined with Australian pines

Chinese chestnut with foliage and male flowers

Australian Pine
Casuarina equisetifolia
Casuarinaceae
50–70' x 20'   Zone 10

Difficult to classify as friend or foe, the Australian pine is native to the country for which it is named. It is now common in the warm seaside areas of the United States. Very fast growing, it has feathery, scalelike olive green jointed leaves, somewhat similar to the horsetail rush's. It has escaped cultivation, and some consider it a pest. Others find considerable merit in the tree, because it can grow in salty seaside soil and help to stabilize sand dunes and prevent erosion. Although called a pine, it is not of the pine family.

Flowers and heart-shaped leaves of the 'Aurea' catalpa.

Southern catalpa, grown here as a specimen.

Southern Catalpa
Catalpa bignonioides
Bignoniaceae
30–50′ x 50′   Zones 6–9

A bold broad-spreading, coarse-textured deciduous tree, the southern catalpa, though not abundant, is scattered in landscapes throughout the South. Its northern, colder-growing relative, *C. speciosa*, is similar in many respects. Catalpas produce heart-shaped yellow green leaves measuring four to eight inches and white bell-shaped flowers spotted with purple. Seeds are enclosed in slender tubular bean-like pods twelve inches long that turn brown in autumn. The trees' leaves are a host for a particular caterpillar, the catalpa worm, which is a popular fish bait. Catalpas grow in a wide range of soils, from moist to dry, and prefer full sunlight. The trees can become somewhat untidy with advancing age.

Atlas Cedar
Cedrus atlantica
Pinaceae
30–50′ x 25′   Zones 7–8

The near-perfect pyramid of the Atlas cedar, formed by tiers of horizontal branches beginning at the ground, and its silvery-gray foliage make the popular conifer a strong focal point. As the tree gets older, it becomes somewhat more irregular in outline, however, and usually develops a relatively broad top. This narrow-leaf evergreen must have well-drained soil and full sunlight. It is one of the few cedars that will thrive in hot climates and withstand drought, and it performs best in the midrange of the United States. *C. deodara*, the deodar cedar, is similar in most respects, the primary difference being its long, horizontal branches with slightly pendulous tips, in contrast to the Atlas cedar's stiff branch tips. Presenting a Christmas-tree appearance, both cedars can serve as strong specimens. Each species has a number of cultivars with unique foliage colors and forms. Do not

'Aurea' deodar cedar, a golden-foliaged cultiva[r]

tiff, spiny foliage of the Atlas cedar

crowd cedars. Provide sufficient space for development of their classical form and beautiful silvery gray foliage. 'Glauca', with blue green foliage, and 'Glauca Pendula', with weeping branches, are two outstanding cultivars of *C. atlantica*.

Bittersweet
Celastrus scandens
Celastraceae
20–30′ vine   Zones 3–8

A highly prized native deciduous vine that produces bright orange red seeds in autumn, the bittersweet is prized for the holiday decorations obtainable by cutting its branches. The fast-growing vine thrives in nearly any soil and clambers over everything in its path to remain

Fruit and foliage of the bittersweet.

in open sunlight. The vine becomes especially showy after the first frost, when the leaves drop and the pods split, exposing the prominent berries that persist until birds eat them. Bittersweet cannot tolerate hot coastal climates.

Hackberry
Celtis laevigata
Ulmaceae
40–60′ x 30′   Zones 5–9

A fast-growing deciduous tree indigenous to much of the eastern United States, the hackberry will grow virtually anywhere. It thrives in adverse soil conditions from very dry to wet. Volunteers appear in surprising places, and thriving specimens appear on vacant lots and abandoned house sites in the center city. This pioneer species appears early along roadways and fences, and in cleared lands. The tree can be recognized at great distances by its relatively small, fine-textured yellow green leaves and rounded to upright canopy. It produces reasonably good autumn color. Many species of birds eat its small cream-colored one-quarter-inch nuts. The shallow fibrous roots are so compet-

itive that it is almost impossible to grow anything beneath the canopy of a large hackberry.

Buttonbush
Cephalanthus occidentalis
Rubiaceae
8–15′ x 8′   Zones 5–10

Given a little time, most ponds and streams will eventually have the buttonbush, an open, rangy deciduous shrub, along their edge. Seldom found in cultivation, it has leaves up to six inches long arranged in a whorled pattern, giving it a coarse texture overall. Rounded creamy white summer flowers about

Buttonbush flowers and foliage.

two inches in diameter are followed by hard rounded reddish brown fruit on long stems. The flowers attract many

Hackberry, with showy grayish white bark

35

insects, especially butterflies and honeybees. The shrub will grow with its roots submerged in water as well as in moist garden soil.

Prostrate-growing Harrington plum-yew

Harrington Plum-Yew
Cephalotaxus harringtonia
Cephalotaxaceae
4–6′ x 5′   Zones 6–9

Best suited to regions with moderate temperatures, the Harrington plum-yew is a broad-spreading evergreen shrub that closely resembles the true yew, *Taxus,* in its shiny dark green needle-like leaves. It is similar in form to a Pfitzer juniper and has lots of possibilities where a medium-sized shrub is needed in full sunlight or partial to fairly heavy shade. Provide a porous moist, well-drained soil for best results. A lesser known cultivar, 'Fastigiata', has an upright columnar form rising to ten feet.

Trunks of a large katsura tree at the Arnold Arboretum

Katsura Tree
Cercidiphyllum japonicum
Cercidiphyllaceae
40–50′ x 35′
Zones 4–8

Although not as well known as many other deciduous trees, the katsura tree has many qualities that make it a fine choice as an all-around shade tree. Best adapted to colder areas, it is most successful in a well-drained soil and full sunlight. The rounded redbudlike leaves emerge red and then change to their summer blue green. The tree produces excellent yellow to orange red autumn color. Given its clean appearance, ease of culture, and relatively fast growth, this Japanese and Chinese native deserves to be more widely planted.

Mature katsura tree

Leaves of the katsura tree, similar to those of the redbud and purplish when unfolding.

Redbud
Cercis canadensis
Leguminosae
20–30′ x 25′   Zones 5–9

The redbud is one of the all-time favorites among small flowering native trees. Among the first trees to bloom, it serves as a reminder that spring is close at hand. Thousands of tiny pealike rosy pink to magenta flowers cover the branches and twigs in late winter. Relatively large dull

White flowers of the 'Alba' redbud.

Redbud, a small flowering tree

Striking purplish foliage of the 'Forest Pansy' redbud

Night-Blooming Jessamine
Cestrum nocturnum
Solanaceae
6–8' x 6'   Zone 10

The night air is filled with a delightful fragrance when the night-blooming jessamine is grown in an enclosed space. Small greenish to off-white tubular flowers are produced in great profusion in the axils of its leaves. Not a particularly handsome shrub, the tropical is pleasant tucked into border plantings close enough so that the sweet-scented flowers can be enjoyed. Even in places where the plant does not freeze, it benefits from a vigorous grooming and pruning in late winter. Mulch the roots heavily in areas subject to freezes. Most will return the following year if the soil is not excessively wet and cold.

White berries of the night-blooming jessamine, a showy sequel to its small flowers.

Flowering Quince
Chaenomeles speciosa
Rosaceae
6–10' x 8'   Zones 4–8/9

Shrubs come and go in gardens, but the flowering quince is among the most long-lived and enduring of shrubs. It is not uncommon to find massive specimens that have lived for fifty or more years on old homesites. Given full sunlight and a porous, well-drained soil, there is not much that will do damage to the shrub. Flowers start appearing in late winter and continue for a couple of

Relatively old specimen of the flowering quince.

green heart-shaped leaves turn yellow in autumn. Not particularly choosy about where it grows, the tree performs best in a porous, well-drained acid soil in full sunlight to moderate shade. Root rot is a problem in heavy, clay soil. The cultivar 'Alba' has white flowers, and 'Forest Pansy' is more shrublike and produces purplish red foliage. 'Texensis', the Texas star redbud, is also shrubby, producing a large number of rosy pink flowers. *C. chinensis*, the Chinese redbud, is in every way more miniature, growing to only about eight feet. Multiple stemmed and shrublike, it is less hardy than *C. canadensis*, but otherwise its conditions for growth are the same.

months. Depending on the cultivar, flower colors can be white, pink, red, or salmon. The plant has sharp spines on the branches and small kidney-shaped leaves at the base of larger ones. Periodically remove old, large canes that do not flower, in order to maintain plant vigor. Leaf spot and leaf drop can cause a plant to be untidy for long periods.

Lawson False Cypress
Chamaecyparis lawsoniana
Cupressaceae
20–30′ x 15′   Zones 5–8

Best adapted to the parts of the nation with abundant moisture and moderate temperatures, the Lawson false cypress is a narrow-leafed evergreen that is gaining in acceptance. Its upright pyramidal form and bold shiny green frond-shaped, arborvitae-like foliage make it ideal as a specimen or accent tree and in mass plantings to provide privacy. A porous, well-drained soil and full sunlight are recommended for best performance. Several other species are notable for their more pendulous forms, especially *C. nootkatensis* 'Pendula' and selections from the *C. obtusa* group. *C. pisifera*, the Japanese false cypress, has a tall, slender pyramidal form to approximately seventy feet and forms a loose, open canopy as it ages. The branches are fine textured and somewhat feathery. It too has several popular cultivars.

Young Lawson false cypress, with a form like a Christmas tree

Hinoki False Cypress
Chamaecyparis obtusa
50–75′ x 10–20′   Zones 5–9

The closely pressed leaves of the hinoki false cypress are dark green and of two sizes. The smaller pairs are triangular, about a twenty-fourth of an inch long, with white X-shaped markings produced by a wax coating along the

Hinoki false cypress in Newport, Rhode Island

margins. The larger pairs are boat-shaped, one and a half inches long, with a blunt or pointed tip. This species forms a tall, slender pyramid with drooping, spreading frondlike branches. It grows best in a well-drained soil in full sunlight but protected from harsh winds. Several dwarf cultivars, among them 'Nana', are better choices for landscape projects, since they do not grow as large, often attaining no more than six feet in height.

'Nana', a dwarf cultivar of the hinoki false cypress.

Sawara false cypress, with golden foliage, in Hershey, Pennsylvania.

'Sun Gold', a popular Japanese false cypress

Japanese False Cypress
Chamaecyparis pisifera
Cupressaceae
50–70' x 10–20'   Zones 3–8

When young, the Japanese false cypress makes a handsome accent plant. It may lose some of its appeal as in time the lower branches die. The dark green leaves are similar to those of the hinoki false cypress, and the same growing conditions are required. The tree has a loose, open pyramidal form with numerous branches thickly covered with slender feathery sprays. Smaller cultivars are used in rock gardens and have foliage that may be silvery, blue green, or yellow.

Winter Sweet
Chimonanthus praecox
Calycanthaceae
8–12' x 8'   Zones 7–9

The winter sweet is a relatively large deciduous shrub with leathery dark green leaves to six inches. It is noted for its sweet-scented cup-shaped creamy white to light yellow flowers with deep purple maroon throats. A great winter-flowering shrub, it stays in bloom for a long period but is subject to injury in severe freezes. Winter sweet does well in full sunlight or partial shade and needs a porous, well-drained soil for best performance. Cut branches make attractive indoor arrangements at a time when few other plants are in bloom.

Chinese Fringe Tree
Chionanthus retusus
Oleaceae
30' x 20'   Zones 5–9

The Chinese fringe tree's thick lustrous dark green leaves persist into winter and are a rich yellow for two or more weeks before falling. Prominent snow white flowers at the end of new shoots are borne in panicles that are three inches tall and four inches across. Flowering comes later than for dogwood and other spring-flowering trees and is welcome in the midspring landscape. The bark is

Winter sweet bearing fragrant flowers in late winter

Chinese fringe tree, which does especially well in the heat of the Lower South.

Lacy flowers in pufflike clusters adorning a Chinese fringe tree in spring.

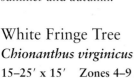

gray and generally tightly ridged or furrowed, and it peels when a specimen is a few years old. Dark blue fruit is present on the female plant in late summer and autumn.

White Fringe Tree
Chionanthus virginicus
15–25′ x 15′   Zones 4–9

A native small-flowering tree widely distributed over the eastern United States, the white fringe tree is conspicuous when it comes into bloom in early spring. The loose, delicate greenish white drooping panicles of fine, fleecy fringelike petals appear before the leaves. Sometimes multistemmed, at other times with a single trunk, the tree is usually shrublike for the

Delicate, frilly flowers of the white fringe tree

first five years or so. The overall texture is fairly coarse during the growing season, because of the six-inch leaves. As an understory species, the tree performs reliably in nearly any well-drained soil and in full sunlight or partial shade.

White fringe tree

Camphor Tree
Cinnamomum camphora
Lauraceae
40–50′ x 40′   Zones 9–10

The camphor tree is a rapid-growing evergreen tree from Asia that thrives in fertile moist, well-drained soil in full sunlight or partial shade. The glossy two-inch leaves, similar in appearance to those of the weeping fig, have a camphorlike odor when bruised. Green fruit, turning black in autumn, is about the size of a pea. It is eaten by many birds. Large populations of the tree have volunteered in warm regions of the nation, but the tree is subject to periodic severe freezes except in zone 10.

Citruses
***Citrus* species**
Rutaceae
10–20′ x 20′   Zones 9–10

Included in the citrus genus are several highly popular subtropical fruiting trees, including *C. aurantiifolia*, the lime; *C. limon*, the lemon, *Citrus* × *paradisi*, the grapefruit; *C. reticulata*, the tangerine and satsuma; and *C. sinensis*, the orange. Provide a well-drained soil, full sunlight, and a sheltered location in residential landscapes. The lustrous evergreen foliage ranges from one and a half to four inches

Foliage and berries of the camphor tree

Trunk of a mature camphor tree at Live Oak Gardens, New Iberia, Louisiana.

in length. Very fragrant waxy white flowers appear in early spring. Fruit size varies with the species, the fruit maturing in autumn and winter.

Fragrant white flowers of the yellowwood, abundant only every two or three years.

Van de Putte

Yellowwood
Cladrastis kentukea (lutea)
Fabaceae (Leguminosae)
30–40′ x 35′
Zones 3–7/8

The American yellowwood is an excellent medium-sized deciduous shade tree in the northern section of the United States. A slow-growing tree, it is notable for its attractive, fragrant creamy white wisteria-like flowers produced in panicles from ten to fourteen inches long in early summer. Often it does not flower until it is more than fifteen years old, and flowering typi-

weet orange in flower with mature fruit present

cally occurs only every second year. Large shiny dark green leaves that turn a bright yellow in autumn contribute toward making the tree a good choice for many plantings. The bark is smooth and gray, somewhat similar to the beech's. The tree grows in a wide range of soils from acid to alkaline, but the soil must be well drained.

Hybrid clematis with spectacular floral display.

'The President' hybrid clematis in the United States Botanic Garden, in Washington, D.C.

Close-up of the yellowwood's foliage

CLEMATIS SPECIES

Ranunculaceae

The clematis genus is large and complex, with scores of hybrids offered in the trade. Someone has called it the "queen of the climbers." Most other vines are aggressive and need a lot of pruning to control growth and spread, but the clematis is highly manageable. Members of the group thrive in a moist, well-drained soil and in full sunlight at least during the morning. They are popular on fences, arbors, trellises, and walls. For most of the hybrids, the vines and foliage are subordinate to the exquisite large, promi-

nent flowers. Some produce flowers on the previous season's growth, and others bloom on the current season's.

Jackman Clematis
Clematis × jackmanii
Vine to 15′   Zones 3–8

Hybrids of the jackman clematis are noted for their star-shaped flowers with diameters up to eight inches and colors of white, red, and purple. Most begin blooming in early summer, and the more vigorous have a few flowers into autumn.

Autumn Clematis
Clematis paniculata
Vine to 30′   Zones 5–9

Very different from the large-flowering hybrids, the autumn clematis is a vigorously growing twining semievergreen type that covers virtually everything in its path. It

Jackman clematis, among the easiest-to-grow and most floriferous of the many clematis selections, here growing in Fort Wayne, Indiana.

'Henryi' clematis, which produces many large white flowers

Mass of fragrant small white flowers on the autumn clematis

produces a mass of small white star-shaped flowers in August and September, with some vines flowering much later.

Clerodendron, Java Shrub
Clerodendron speciosissimum
Verbenaceae
10–12′ x 4′   Zones 9–10

A native of Java, the clerodendron is a semiwoody tropical with huge scarlet flowers during the summer months. The large heart-shaped leaves reinforce its strong presence in planting. Not particularly selective about where it grows, it finds any well-drained soil and either full sunlight or partial shade satisfactory. With a hard freeze the plant will die back to the roots, but usually it will return, especially if the roots are protected with a heavy mulch.

Striking flower color and coarse-textured foliage of the clerodendron

Sweet Pepperbush
Clethra alnifolia
Clethraceae
4–8′ x 6′
Zones 4–9

The sweet pepperbush is well adapted to moist acid soil and full sunlight or partial shade. The medium-sized upright-growing, multiple-stemmed deciduous shrub is appreciated for its

Foliage and white candlelike flowers of the sweet pepperbush.

sweet-scented creamy white flowers, which appear in summer on six-inch candlelike spikes above the foliage. Leaves of the plant have a rough upper surface with prominent veins. The cultivar 'Rosea' produces dark pink buds and light pink flowers. 'Hummingbird', a more dwarf, spreading selection, growing to only about three feet, displays an abundance of white flowers.

Black Titi
Cliftonia monophylla
Cyrillaceae
10–15′ x 8′   Zones 8–9

A large nearly evergreen shrub with its habitat in the relatively wet areas of the southeastern United States, the black titi is a little-known species but worthy of much greater use in plantings where native strains are desired. Slender trunks, shiny yellow green leaves, and compact, fragrant white or pinkish flowers in terminal racemes are among its characteristics. It is free of insects and diseases and grows virtually anywhere,

Black titi, with white flowers, at the Gloster Arboretum, in Gloster, Mississippi.

in full sunlight or partial shade and in a broad range of soils from wet and peaty to relatively dry. The nectar is attractive to honeybees.

Paired flowers of the Argentine trumpet vine.

Foliage mass and flowers of the Argentine trumpet vine.

Argentine Trumpet Vine
Clytostoma callistegioides
Bignoniaceae
20′ vine   Zones 8/9–10

The Argentine trumpet vine, a vigorous tropical evergreen, produces a mass of magnificent lavender trumpet-shaped flowers in spring, with a few appearing into summer. The shiny dark compound leaves formed in pairs attach to supports by long tendrils at the forks of the leaves. Although the vine grows fast, it is very manageable and makes a dense covering for fences, trellises, and arbors. Occasional pruning is recommended to remove old growth. The vine blooms best in full sunlight but will tolerate some shade.

plant in areas subject to freeze, this tender species really needs much more direct sunlight than is normally possible indoors. Its distinctive picturesque rounded form and handsome foliage make it a high-profile accent in landscape plantings.

Carolina Snail-Seed, Carolina Moonseed
Cocculus carolinus
Menispermaceae
Vine to 30′   Zones 6–8

The Carolina snail-seed, a wiry deciduous vine with shiny delta-shaped leaves, can go unnoticed for most of the year. It grows over nearly anything in its path, especially

Sea Grape
Coccoloba uvifera
Polygonaceae
15–25′ x 10′   Zone 10

Limited to tropical climates, the sea grape is a popular large shrub or small tree in southern Florida and other warm coastal areas. The large, rounded

Foliage and fruit of the sea grape

leathery leaves to eight inches across produce a general impression of coarse texture. Sometimes grown as an indoor

Carolina snail-seed, a high-climbing vine that produces abundant small red berries in autumn.

moderate-sized shrubs. In autumn, prominent red berries hang over much of the vine in dense clusters that can be as long as about six inches. Although seldom seen in cultivation, the plant has a lot of potential for landscapes where a clean, pest-free climber is imperative.

Laurel-leaf cocculus, grown for its attractive foliage and arching branches

Laurel-Leaf Cocculus
Cocculus laurifolius
10–15′ x 10′   Zones 9–10

A native of the Himalayas, the laurel-leaf cocculus is a mounding evergreen shrub with strong arching branches that produces large lustrous leaves up to seven inches long. It grows best in a well-drained soil and full sunlight but will tolerate partial shade. The shrub is widely planted close to the Gulf coast, but inland it is subject to damage by freezing. The beautiful foliage that appears polished makes it a handsome accent shrub or a good choice for mass plantings. It is particularly appealing on embankments and behind retaining walls, where the pendulous branches are on display to greatest advantage.

Croton, in one of many available colorations.

Croton
Codiaeum variegatum
Euphorbiaceae
3–8′ x 4′   Zone 10

Except in extremely warm tropical locations, the croton, in its many different variegated leaf markings and unusual leaf shapes, is planted in containers or in summertime beds. Standing out wherever it is used, it brings a strong accent to garden design, especially when combined with other foliage. Provide full sunlight to prevent leaf drop. It is possible to reclaim old, straggly plants by cutting back stems to about a foot above the soil line.

Elephant Ear
Colocasia esculenta
Araceae
4–6′   Zones 8/9–10

The mammoth size of the foliage of this elephant ear (see also *Alocasia macrorrhiza*) introduces a strong textural contrast into the garden. The bulbous perennial can serve as a single specimen or be grouped in mass plantings. Tolerant of most soils, it grows best in a very moist, fertile soil and responds favorably to applications of fertilizer during the growing season. In the North, the bulbs must be lifted and stored during the winter. In the South, they can remain in place. A heavy mulch will provide protection from severe freezes.

Small-leaf elephant ear, which grows well adjacent to a body of water but is hard to contain.

Coreopsis
Coreopsis auriculata
Compositae
To 15″   Zones 8–10

Coreopsis is a clump-forming perennial with bright yellow flowers that continue from early summer until midautumn. Provide full sunlight and well-drained soil. The plant will

'Early Sunrise' coreopsis, a yellow-flowering All America Selections winner.

tolerate a considerable amount of heat and relatively infertile soil. Excellent cultivars that are densely branched and produce large, two-inch flowers include 'Early Sunrise', a golden All America Selections winner, and 'Sunray', a bright yellow selection with double flowers. 'Nana' is a low-growing dwarf that makes an excellent ground cover in small plantings. *C. verticillata*, which is hardy in zones 3 through 9, grows one to two feet tall and prefers full sunlight or partial shade. 'Moonbéam' has large soft yellow double flowers, and 'Rosea' has finely cut foliage and pink flowers.

THE DOGWOODS

Cornaceae

North, south, east, or west—the dogwoods will surely play some role in nearly every serious gardener's landscape. From ground-covering creepers through intermediate-sized shrubs and on to large trees, they come in all forms with various special features. Unfortunately, some give satisfactory performance only within very narrow environmental ranges. When they are at home with preferred soil, climate, and exposure, they are easy to grow. In unfriendly environments, no tinkering with conditions will make them succeed. It is therefore imperative to match species to the conditions at hand.

'Argento-marginata' ('Elegantissima') white dogwood, the variegated summer foliage of which is followed in winter by red stems.

Tatarian Dogwood
Cornus alba 'Sibirica'
8' x 5'   Zones 2–8

The coral red stems of the Tatarian dogwood are striking in the winter landscape. Young plants have a distinctly erect form, but as plants age, they become somewhat arching, and loose and open in appearance. This deciduous shrub has a medium rate of growth and adapts to a fairly wide range of growing conditions but prefers a moist, well-drained soil and full sunlight or partial shade. Spring's yellowish white flowers in flat-topped clusters to two inches in diameter are followed by fall's bluish fruit.

Tatarian dogwood at the Arnold Arboretum

Rough-Leaf Dogwood
Cornus drummondii
20–30' x 15'   Zones 4–9

When attempts to grow other dogwoods fail, the rough-leaf dogwood will not disappoint. But it is not nearly so showy as many of the more popular garden species. This native dogwood is a pioneer species that appears immedi-

Autumn-fruiting rough-leaf dogwood

ately after lands are cleared. Liking heavy, wet soil, it springs up along roadside ditches and at the edge of wet woodlands. It produces flat clusters of greenish white flowers in spring after the leaves, though probably its showiest feature is the clusters of small chalky white berries in autumn. The autumn foliage is burgundy to purple.

Flowering Dogwood
Cornus florida
20–25′ x 15′   Zones 5–9

The flowering dogwood, a tree for all seasons, may be the most highly prized of all American small flowering trees. Although occurring over much of the eastern United States, it has highly specific requirements. To be successful, provide a moist, but well-drained, porous and acid soil. The tree prefers only morning sunlight, with protection from the hot noonday and early-afternoon sun. The large, showy white floral parts, which are modified leaves, that is, bracts, appear in spring before the foliage. Colorful foliage and clusters of red berries adorn the tree in autumn. Where the tree grows, it makes a beautiful specimen or an impressive understory planting to pines and other tall-growing trees. There are numerous white cultivars and several popular pink selections.

Pink-flowering dogwood

Flowering dogwood

Colorful autumn fruit and foliage of the flowering dogwood.

Mass planting of dogwoods at the Governor's Mansion in Columbia, South Carolina.

Kousa Dogwood
Cornus kousa
15–20' x 15'   Zones 5–8

A much-loved small flowering tree of colder regions of the United States, the kousa dogwood blooms in summer. Its flowers are small and inconspicuous, but each is surrounded by four white petal-like segments—modified leaves, or bracts—that taper to a point and are positioned close together atop strong

Close-up of flowers of the kousa dogwood

horizontal branches. The tree has distinctive stratified branching that extends nearly to the ground and creates a shrublike form. Flowering is over a prolonged period. Green raspberry-like fruit turns bright red in fall. This dogwood grows best in a well-drained acid soil and in full sunlight. Truly a specimen tree, it is a hit wherever it is grown.

Among the number of cultivars available, some have very large flowers or fruit and a few have pink to red flowers. Others have a weeping growth habit, and one produces yellow fruit. *C. kousa* var. angustata, the Chinese evergreen dogwood, is a hardy selection said to grow and flower well in the Deep South. It has white bracts that appear about a month after those on regular kousa dogwood, and the leaves may remain on the plant in winter.

Baumgardner

Fruit and foliage of the kousa dogwood.

Cornelian Cherry
Cornus mas
15–20' x 20'   Zones 4–8

A dogwood that performs best in colder climates, the cornelian cherry produces yellow flowers in spring before leafing out. The delightful small tree is named for the bright

Kousa dogwood in flower in a West Virginia garden

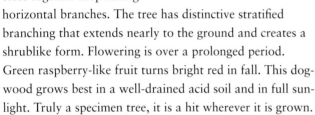

Cornelian cherry in fruit during late summer

Cornelian cherry cultivar with variegated foliage

Red Osier Dogwood
Cornus sericea
5–7′ x 4′   Zones 2–8

The red osier dogwood is a multiple-stemmed deciduous shrub that can put on a dramatic display in the winter garden. It produces fiery red stems and is a beautiful contrast to snow-covered grounds. In addition to the red winter stems, its summer foliage and light blue autumn fruit are

Red osier dogwood's stems in winter

attractive. Plant it in a moist, well-drained soil in full sunlight or light shade. The cultivar 'Flaviramea', the golden-twig dogwood, is similar but has yellow stems.

red cherrylike fruit that appears in late summer. The fruit can be used for jam. 'Alba' is a white-fruiting cultivar, and 'Flava' a yellow-fruiting. The cultivar 'Aureo-Elegantissima' has variegated foliage.

Pampas Grass
Cortaderia selloana
Gramineae
10′ x 10′   Zones 7/8–10

Pampas grass, with long tapering leaf blades up to seven feet tall, is highly visible in plantings. Even more prominent are the silky, silvery white flower plumes that appear from late summer into autumn. If this tough fountain-form grass is given well-drained soil and full sunlight, there is virtually nowhere in its zones of adaptation that it will not grow. Because it is nearly impossible to restrict its spread, it should be planted only where there is ample room for exhibiting it either as an accent or as a mass

Mass planting of pampas grass

49

planting. 'Monvin', sun-stripe pampas grass, is a cultivar with golden yellow variegated foliage and a lower growth habit, to only four or five feet.

Winter Hazel
Corylopsis glabrescens
Hamamelidaceae
7–12′ x 10′   Zones 5–8

Relatively common in winter gardens in the northern United States, the winter hazel is a large deciduous shrub producing fragrant yellow flowers from late winter through early spring, before the foliage appears. It is a close relative of the witch hazel and parrotia. Its large, coarse-textured leaves growing to a length of three inches turn a brilliant yellow in autumn. For best results, plant in a well-drained acid soil and in full sunlight or partial shade.

Broad-spreading branches of the winter hazel in flower

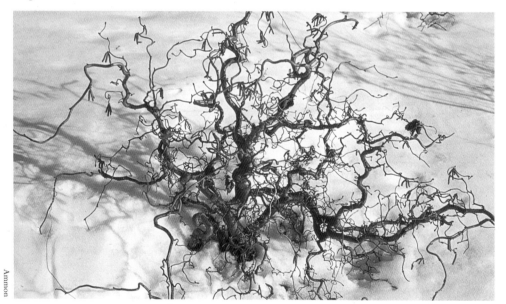

Sculptured branches of Harry Lauder's walking stick against snow

Harry Lauder's Walking Stick
Corylus avellana 'Contorta'
Betulaceae
10–12′ x 8′   Zones 4–8

Grown primarily for its interesting contorted, corkscrew-like branches, Harry Lauder's walking stick is a deciduous shrub that stands out in a garden. Pendulous catkins appear on the twisted branches in spring and add another detail to its unique profile. It is particularly popular with flower arrangers. Provide a well-drained soil and full sunlight, and give ample space so that a specimen will not be cramped.

Smoke Bush, Smoke Tree
Cotinus coggygria
Anacardiaceae
10–12′ x 8′   Zones 4/5–8

The smoke bush makes its most dramatic display in early spring, when it produces clusters of yellow green fringelike flowers that turn a smoky pinkish purple. Flower color can vary considerably by cultivar, but regardless of cultivar this plant makes a strong statement as a specimen or when massed in a shrub border. Several of the newer cultivars have interesting purple to purple green foliage. For best results, provide full sunlight and a porous, well-drained soil for this large deciduous shrub.

Cranberry Cotoneaster
Cotoneaster apiculatus
Rosaceae

3–4′ x 5′   Zones 4–8

Because of a broad spread and stiff branching, the cranberry cotoneaster is seen to best advantage in raised plantings and as a ground cover on slopes and embankments. The fine-textured dark green foliage, pink spring flowers, and handsome large cranberry red autumn berries enhance its appeal. Full sunlight and a porous, well-drained soil are essential for all the cotoneasters.

Cranberry cotoneaster in Cincinnati

Bearberry Cotoneaster
Cotoneaster dammeri
15–25″ x 5′   Zones 5–8

Bearberry cotoneaster is one of the highly popular ground-covering shrubs in the colder parts of the United States. Well adapted to dry, porous soils and full sunlight, it is carpetlike in growth. Its petite glossy, leathery leaves, white spring flowers, and bright red fall fruit make it an attractive ground cover for embankments, planters, and rock gardens and atop retaining walls.

Small fruit and foliage of the bearberry cotoneaster.

ink-flowering smoke bush at the National Arboretum, in Washington, D.C.

White-flowering cultivar of the smoke bush

51

Rock Spray Cotoneaster
Cotoneaster horizontalis
2–3' x 6'   Zones 4/5–7

Of the numerous cotoneaster species, the rock spray cotoneaster and its several cultivars are probably the most frequently planted. Its glossy dark blue green foliage, pink spring flowers, and dark cranberry-colored fall fruit, along with its classic fishbone layered branching, make it an irresistible selection among medium-sized shrubs. As with other cotoneasters, it is imperative to have a soil with fast drainage, and full sunlight. Leaf retention will vary by location. In more northerly zones it is nearly deciduous; in the Middle South it is mostly evergreen.

Rock spray cotoneaster covering a dry, rocky slope in North Carolina

Parney Cotoneaster
Cotoneaster lacteus
8' x 6'   Zones 6–8

Parney cotoneaster withstands both cold and drought and has good resistance to fire blight. A broadly arching evergreen shrub, it has white flowers in flat heads to three inches across, which appear in late spring. The red fruit is outstanding in autumn and persists through winter.

Parney cotoneaster, which grows well as far south as Memphis

THE HAWTHORNS

Rosaceae

Hawthorns grow over virtually the entire United States. In this very large and complex genus, there are many highly popular small ornamental flowering trees. These are among the easiest of American trees to grow, because of their adaptability to a wide range of soils from relatively heavy-textured and clayey to very dry acid to alkaline. The trees grow in full sunlight or light shade. Hawthorns are popular because of their relatively small, manageable size, heavy flowering, and beautiful orange red fruit in fall and winter. Their light, airy canopies cast very little shade; consequently many other plants can be grown beneath their branches. All are deciduous; most have some thorns, especially when young.

English Hawthorn
Crataegus laevigata
15' x 12'   Zones 4–7

The English hawthorn is valued for its outstanding display of flowers, with some cultivars and varieties being especially noteworthy. Single or double flowers that may be white, rose, or red appear in early spring. Fruit is showy in autumn, and color varies with the cultivar or variety, from yellow to scarlet to deep red. This hawthorn is a shrubby plant with low branching and a dense rounded top. As with other hawthorns, the smaller branches have thorns up to an inch long.

Parsley hawthorn with spring flowers and foliage, as well as, unusually, the previous year's fruit.

Parsley Hawthorn
Crataegus marshallii
10–20' x 15'   Zones 7–9

Deriving its name from its delicate, parsleylike leaves, the parsley hawthorn is a delightful small flowering tree that produces an abundance of flowers with an unpleasant odor in early spring and orange red fruit in autumn. It makes an excellent small specimen tree either single- or multiple-trunked. As the bark exfoliates, a copper color is revealed.

Mayhaw
Crataegus opaca
20' x 20'   Zones 7–9

With the slightest break in cold winter temperature, the mayhaw bursts into bloom. Showy white flowers with purple centers appear before nearly any

Fruit of the mayhaw, used for jelly

English hawthorn in the Royal Botanic Gardens, at Kew, London

other spring flowers on trees or shrubs. The miniature, nearly one-inch red applelike fruit is handsome, but this species is planted for the delicious taste of the fruit, which is used for mayhaw jelly. Special fruiting cultivars, like 'Super Spur', are being highly promoted in the trade.

Washington Hawthorn
Crataegus phaenopyrum
20–30' x 20'   Zones 3–8

The Washington hawthorn is among the showiest of the genus, with white flowers in spring and a spectacular display of clusters of quarter-inch red berries beginning in autumn and persisting into winter. Of an upright single-trunked form, the tree makes a profound impact in any landscape either as a specimen or in mass plantings. The cultivar 'Clark' can be chosen for an even more dramatic display of red fruit.

Green Hawthorn
Crataegus viridis
25–35' x 20'   Zones 5–9

Among the tallest of native hawthorns, the green "haw" produces white flowers in early spring that are followed by clusters of bright orange red fruit in fall. It is a tough tree and will grow under a wide range of conditions, even in extremely wet situations. Gray bark over cinnamon-colored inner bark and muscular-textured trunks add to the tree's appeal. The cultivar 'Winter King' is an especially fine se-

Washington hawthorn in flower at Niagara Falls

Fruit of the Washington hawthorn

Green hawthorn flowering in the Fort Worth Botanic Garden

Flowers of the green hawthorn

lection, producing a mass of large orange red berries. A single specimen of this cultivar in heavy fruit stands out from afar because of the contrast between the brilliant fruit and the bare tree.

Clump of old garden crinums

Crinums
Crinum species
Amaryllidaceae
2–5′ Zones 7–10

Approximately sixty species and hybrids of crinums have been cultivated in gardens. Among the most beautiful of spring- and summer-flowering perennials, they possess large, thick strap-shaped leaves and handsome funnel-like flowers that make a color and textural impact in the garden. Some have relatively soft, limp foliage; others have mammoth, turgid leaves. Clusters of white to rosy pink flowers, depending on the cultivar, are produced on tall, thick stalks that rise above the clump of foliage. Crinums

Southern swamp lily

should be planted in holes twelve to eighteen inches deep and heavily mulched to protect against summer's heat and winter's cold. Deep planting and mulching encourage the production of large bulbs. *C. americanum*, the southern swamp lily, grows in wet, boggy soil. *C. asiaticum* produces large clusters of fifteen or more white to pink flowers. *C. augustum* produces large bulbs and is popular in central and southern Florida. *C. bulbispermum* 'Roseum', the old milk-and-wine lily, is popular in southern gardens.

Brilliant red flowers of the 'Lucifer' crocosmia

Crocosmia, Montbretia
Crocosmia × crocosmiiflora

Iridaceae

2–3′   Zones 5–9

One of the most delightful of summer-flowering perennials—especially the cultivar 'Lucifer', with its fiery red gladiolus-like flowers—the crocosmia is becoming a very popular garden plant. The stiff sword-shaped leaves and bright-colored flowers make it a striking textural feature among other herbaceous bloomers. Provide a porous, well-drained soil and full sunlight for this corm-producing perennial. The foliage dies during the winter. Mulch with leaves or other organic matter to provide some winter protection in colder regions.

Japanese Cryptomeria
Cryptomeria japonica

Taxodiaceae

40–75′ x 30′   Zones 5–8

The Japanese cryptomeria is a delightful upright-growing conifer with emerald green awl-shaped foliage. It has a wide range of adaptation, provided that the soil is moist and well drained and the tree is planted in full sunlight. As with most conifers, this one has a rather tight, compact conical form when young and becomes somewhat more irregular as it ages. The tree can take on a bronzing color in the northern part of the nation, especially in open areas exposed to harsh winds. It is especially attractive as an accent tree, but it also makes an effective screen when used in mass plantings.

Screen planting of the Japanese cryptomeria at the National Arboretum

Spikelike foliage of the China fir

China Fir
Cunninghamia lanceolata
Taxodiaceae
25–60′ x 20′
Zones 7–9

The China fir is an extraordinarily impressive upright conifer with glossy dark green leaves, each terminating in a stiff, sharp point. It stands in striking contrast to most other garden plants in both form and texture. Unfortunately, the mature specimen has to be cleaned periodically of dead branches or it will have an untidy appearance. Provide ample space to display its strong form, and plant in a well-drained soil in full sunlight.

Mexican Heather
Cuphea hyssopifolia
Lythraceae
2′ x 2′   Zones 8/9–10

Mexican heather, a native of Mexico and Guatemala, is covered with small pink, purple, or white flowers for most of the year, particularly during the warm months. Very narrow foliage, to three-quarters of an inch long, is evergreen unless burned by subfreezing temperatures, but if it dies back to the ground, it generally returns from the root system. The plant also reseeds itself. It grows in a wide variety of soils but does best in a well-drained location in full sunlight. This perennial has a dense low, mounding form. The plant makes an excellent container specimen.

Mexican Cigar Plant
Cuphea micropetala
3–4′ x 3′   Zones 8/9–10

Mexican cigar plant in full flower in Texas landscape

Throughout the summer months, the Mexican cigar plant produces flowers that are yellow to orange, tipped with red. The tall, stiff stems of the hardy perennial are covered with colorful tubular flowers that hummingbirds find highly attractive. For any cuphea, provide a well-drained soil and full sunlight. In areas of periodic winterkill, cut stems immediately after the first light frost and mulch the roots with a heavy layer of leaves. *C. ignea*, the cigar flower, is similar but produces bright red tubular flowers. *C. hyssopifolia*, false heather, is a small, eighteen-inch shrublike perennial with tiny

Mexican heather, which flowers year-round where winters are mild, with dusty miller in foreground

57

leaves that produces pink to lavender flowers throughout the summer.

Italian Cypress
Cupressus sempervirens
Cupressaceae
20–40′ x 5′   Zones 7–9

The Italian cypress is a narrow-leaf evergreen that makes a strong impact because of its stiff vertical, columnar form. A prevalent tree in the warm parts of Italy, it is an exclamation point in landscape composition. It has a very limited growing range, because it cannot tolerate severe winters nor the hot, humid coastal South. It is absolutely essential that the soil be porous and well drained and that the tree be positioned in full sunlight. The cultivar 'Glauca' has blue green foliage, and 'Stricta' has a very thin upright form.

Pineapple Lily
Curcuma petiolata
Zingiberaceae
2–3′   Zones 9–10

A tuberous-rooted member of the ginger family, the pineapple lily produces large light green banana-like leaves to twenty-four inches. Somewhat hidden

Tall, columnar Italian cypress

Foliage and flowers of the pineapple lily

among the foliage are bright rosy pink petal-like bracts surrounding small pale yellow flowers. The subtropical perennial is an excellent coarse-textured plant for the shade garden. It performs best in moist, fertile soil that contains a generous amount of organic matter. *C. elata* has pale yellow flowers and leaves that are four feet long and a foot wide. Both it and the pineapple lily are easily harmed by freezing temperatures.

Broad-spreading rosette of the sago palm's dramatic dark green foliage

Sago Palm
Cycas revoluta
Cycadaceae
2–8′ x 8′ clump   Zones 8–10

A primitive plant native to Japan, the sago palm is a popular accent in southern gardens. Its broad, flat rosette of shiny, bright palmlike leaves, to five feet long, puts it in strong textural contrast to other ornamentals. It performs best in a fertile, well-drained slightly acid soil in full sunlight or partial shade. Although slow-growing, after ten to fifteen years it will produce a cluster of short, thick trunks, each terminating in a large rosette of foliage. Hard freezes damage the fronds. Periodic removal of old leaves is necessary to maintain an attractive specimen.

Mature sago palm in the Huntington Botanic Garden, in San Marino, California.

Quince
Cydonia sinensis
Rosaceae
10–20′ x 15′
Zones 5–9

Some references list the quince as *Pseudocydonia sinensis,* but here it is listed in its old classification. It is a pleasing small flowering tree that produces attractive pale pink flowers and

Sculptural, muscular branches of the quince.

Flowers of the quince

large pearlike fruit in late summer. The smooth muscular, sculptural lines of the trunks are somewhat similar to those of the crape myrtle, and it has attractive red autumn foliage. It is tolerant of a wide range of growing conditions but performs best in a well-drained slightly acid soil and full sunlight. The fruit of this species makes an excellent jelly.

Umbrella Plant
Cyperus alternifolius
Cyperaceae
3–6′ x 3′   Zones 8–10

A semitropical foliage plant used in garden design to add accent and enrichment, the umbrella plant has had a place in water gardens for hundreds of years. It grows in regular garden soil as well as with its roots submerged in water. Having a unique leaf structure, it produces a circle of whorled leaflets atop an unbranched tall green stem. Among the leaflets are rather inconspicuous creamy white flowers. *C. papyrus,* the bulrush, will grow in moist soil or shallow water. *C. haspon* 'Viviparus' is a dwarf selection that also grows in either soil or water.

Umbrella plant adjacent to a garden pool in south Florida

Bulrush, from which papyrus was made in ancient Egypt, here growing in Cypress Gardens, Florida

mature specimen. Long nodding racemes of creamy white flowers in early summer are followed by persistent yellow green to brown fruit in autumn and winter. Not temperamental, the delightful native will grow in almost any soil in full sunlight or partial shade. It can be a particularly interesting specimen adjacent to a small garden pond.

Scotch Broom
Cytisus scoparius
Fabaceae
5' x 7'
Zones 5–9

Flower and foliage of the sweet broom.

The Scotch broom is easy to grow in sunlight or partial shade where the soil is slightly acid and well drained. The salt-tolerant plant grows and flowers reasonably well in sandy and infertile soil. It is an excellent xeriscape specimen. A species that rarely lives for more than two years in the Deep South and up to five years in the Midwest, it flowers profusely with glowing yellow blossoms in spring and early summer and has angular green stems that are attractive in winter. The many cultivars from Europe have flowers of cream, yellow, pink,

Titi, Leatherwood
Cyrilla racemiflora
Cyrillaceae
10–25' x 10'   Zones 6–9

A large semievergreen shrub or small tree of the Middle South, the titi occurs naturally along the edges of swamps and streams. It produces a rather dense upright mass of branches and long, leathery willowlike leaves. Selective pruning causes it to exhibit the handsome branching of a

Fruit and foliage of the titi

Titi specimen

61

red, carmine, orange, or lilac. *Cytisus* × *spachianus*, the sweet broom, is not as large, has sulfur yellow flowers, and is widely available.

Variegated fragrant daphne on Clemson University campus.

Cluster of sweet-scented flowers on the fragrant daphne

Texas Sotol
Dasylirion texanum
Agavaceae
2–3′ x 4′   Zones 8/9–10

A plant of stemless rosette form native to northern Mexico and Texas, the Texas sotol is a relative of the yucca. Slender stiff leaves to a length of three feet with prominent marginal spines are arranged symmetrically around a basal crown. A dense panicle atop a fifteen-foot stalk puts on an impressive show. This accent

Fragrant Daphne
Daphne odora
Thymelaeaceae
3–4′ x 4′   Zones 4–7/8

No other garden plant has a scent quite like the fragrant daphne's. A choice slow-growing shrub with glossy narrow evergreen leaves to three inches long, it produces a low mounding to spreading form. The delightfully scented long-lasting pure white to purple spring flowers are crowded into terminal clusters. The plant has very exacting cultural requirements. Provide a fertile moist, well-drained neutral soil (pH 7.0) that contains a generous amount of organic matter. Filtered sunlight throughout the day is preferred. *D. cneorum* is a spreading shrub only about twelve inches high. *Daphne* × *burkwoodii* 'Somerset', the Burkwood daphne, is a desirable selection growing to four feet tall that produces creamy white flowers in clusters to six inches in diameter.

Dramatic tall seed head of the Texas sotol growing in the Big Bend National Park, Texas.

plant requires the same cultural conditions as the yucca and succulents: hot and dry porous, well-drained soil in full sunlight. It can be handsome in large containers as well as ground plantings.

Dove Tree, Handkerchief Tree
Davidia involucrata
Nyssaceae
25–35′ x 30′   Zones 6–8

flowers that resemble dangling handkerchiefs on a dove tree in San Francisco.

The dove tree, a relatively broad-spreading deciduous tree, is an object of conversation where it is grown because of its unusual floral display in late spring. The six- to eight-inch white dovelike or handkerchief-like bracts cover the flowers, in strong contrast to the four- to five-inch coarse-textured leaves. Primarily a specimen flowering tree in landscapes, it is especially appealing as a shade tree on relatively small sites, because of its moderate size. It may be slow to flower and may flower inconsistently from year to year. Provide a moist, well-drained soil, full sunlight, and open space for the relatively broad canopy.

Magnificent delphiniums at Levens Castle, in England

Royal Poinciana
Delonix regia
Leguminosae
20–30′ x 40′   Zone 10

Among the most showy of the tropical flowering trees, the royal poinciana produces a broad-spreading canopy of compound leaves, rendering it somewhat similar in form and foliage to the mimosa. It makes a dramatic display of bright orange red flowers with prominent filaments that can reach a length of about three inches. It must be grown in frost-free climates in a porous, well-drained soil.

Exotic flowers on a royal poinciana in Coral Gables, Florida

Delphinium
Delphinium × elatum
Ranunculaceae
4–7′   Zones 3–8

The delphinium, one of the most striking of flowering perennials in North America, has undergone extensive hybridization in creating today's beautiful selections in blue, white, purple, pink, and yellow. Towering above many other herbaceous plants, it flowers on tall spikes over a long period. The basal leaves are deeply cut into three major segments. This plant is best adapted to the cooler regions of the nation and performs best in a fertile, well-drained soil in full sunlight. Tall-growing specimens usually need staking.

Garden chrysanthemums covered with blooms in autumn

Garden Chrysanthemum
Dendranthema × morifolium
(Chrysanthemum × morifolium)
Asteraceae (Compositae)
12–30″   Zones 5–9

One of the most prized perennials of autumn is the garden chrysanthemum. Although it can be forced by florists at any time, it is photoperiodic, blooming naturally only when the nights are long. There are numerous kinds, from the low-growing, "cushion" and "button" hybrids with either single or double flowers to those with larger flowers that are taller and more upright in form. Besides single colors that include yellow, bronze, lavender, red, white, and pink, there are bicolors. Grow mums in full sunlight and in a well-drained soil. For low, compact plants, pinch the new growth back several times during the spring and summer, until mid-July. Dig and divide the clumps in early spring.

Deutzia specimen at Dumbarton Oaks, Washington, D.C.

Deutzia
Deutzia scabra
Saxifragaceae
6–10′ x 8′   Zones 4–8

The deutzia is a large, tough deciduous shrub. It is one of the persistent old, classic shrubs in American gardens. Blooming in midspring, somewhat later than most other spring-flowering shrubs, it produces clusters of white flowers along arching stems. Selective pruning is recommended to keep a mature specimen productive, but the plant should never be sheared. Allow ample

flowers of the deutzia

space for it to exhibit its long arching, ascending branches. This species works best when combined with other shrubs. The shrub grows in most garden soils in full sunlight or partial shade. *D. gracilis* 'Nikko' is a dwarf that produces a glorious floral display in spring. In the same species, the cultivar 'Summer Snow' has yellow-and-white variegated foliage.

Nikko' deutzia, a heavily flowering dwarf

porous, well-drained soil. Its sprawling, irregular mats of medium texture are useful for borders and rock gardens. Sometimes treated as an annual in cooler regions, the plant seldom lives more than two or three years even under good growing conditions.

Meadow pink, with tufted foliage resembling festuca

Meadow Pink
Dianthus myrtinervius
12″ x 12″   Zones 3–10

The meadow pink is a neglected dianthus that merits a place in a greater number of gardens. It is quite cold hardy, growing in the Far North, though it is also employed as a ground cover in Florida. The plant is evergreen and has very narrow silvery tufted leaves that can reach a length of ten inches. It may look like festuca at first glance. Light pink flowers approximately a half inch wide are most abundant in spring but also present in fall. This low grower does well in full sunlight or partial shade and has great heat tolerance.

Garden Pink
Dianthus deltoides
Caryophyllaceae
12″ x 6″   Zones 3–8

The garden pink has slightly fragrant carnation-like single flowers three-quarters of an inch in diameter. The colors run from white to light and dark rose and purple, and the flowers are usually spotted. Bloom begins in spring and continues through summer. The plant requires full sunlight or partial shade and a fertile,

Garden pinks in assorted colors

Cox

Flowers of the butterfly iris, exhibiting the basis for the name

Butterfly Iris, African Iris
Dietes vegeta
Iridaceae
24–30″ x 3′   Zones 8–10

A tight clump-forming perennial, the butterfly iris produces a mass of narrow sword-shaped leaves. White flowers marked with yellow or purple splotches are borne on long stems from spring through summer. Noted for a clean, attractive appearance, this iris is easy to manage. It stays in place, unlike many. The stiff dark green leaves are a good contrast to the softer foliage of most other herbaceous perennials. The plant grows in almost any garden soil and in full sunlight or partial shade. Removing old foliage is recommended, especially where the iris has sustained some freeze damage.

Japanese Persimmon
Diospyros kaki
Ebenaceae
40–60′ x 3′   Zones 8–9

The Japanese persimmon is very picturesque. Somewhat bonsai in appearance with its mounding canopy of short, horizontal slightly pendulous branches, it is an extremely popular fruiting tree in its native Japan and the Gulf South. It produces large coarse-textured rounded leaves. Globular orange red edible fruit three to five inches across ripen after the first frost, when the foliage drops. A heavily fruiting specimen can be extremely handsome silhouet-

ted against a blue sky in late fall. The tree grows in ordinary well-drained garden soil in full sunlight or partial shade, although fewer fruit will occur in shade. Among fruiting cultivars are 'Tanenashi', 'Eureka', 'Tamopan', and 'Hachiya'.

Common Persimmon
Diospyros virginiana
25–60′ x 30′   Zones 4–9

The common persimmon, an upright-growing native deciduous tree, is distributed over much of the United States. It grows in a wide range of soils, from heavy, wet,

Foliage of the common persimmon

Fruit of the Japanese persimmon, three to four inches in diameter, ready to eat when it is orange and soft.

Fruit of the Japanese persimmon silhouetted against the autumn sky.

Fruit of the common persimmon

and poorly drained to very dry. Its seedlings are among the first to appear on clear-cut land and along utility lines, fencerows, and highway rights-of-way. The female plant produces relatively large yellow orange fruit that is very astringent until it ripens fully after the first heavy frost. The large red to yellow leaves drop early exposing the colorful fruit. *D. texana,* the native Texas persimmon, a much smaller tree, produces attractive white peeling bark and black-skinned, dark-fleshed fruit.

Sky-Flower
Duranta repens
Verbenaceae
6–10′ x 5′
Zones 8/9–10

Small blue flowers and showy fruit of the sky-flower.

Not well known except in the warm coastal areas of the country, the sky-flower is an upright evergreen shrub that takes on a pendulous form when heavily laden with panicles of bright yellow berries from midsummer to early winter. The plant produces small baby-blue flowers at the terminal ends of its long panicles at the same time that it is setting fruit at their basal ends. Individual fruit, about a half inch in diameter, have the same color and texture as lemons. The flowers, and especially the fruit, are showy, but the plants are somewhat untidy and require periodic grooming to remove dead and unproductive wood. A hard freeze will kill the upper portions of a mature specimen. There are two new cultivars: 'Variegated Blue', with lilac blue

Simpson

The Texas persimmon's fruit, black at maturity.

flowers, and 'Variegated White', with white flowers. The green foliage of each of these is accented with soft yellow centers.

Russian Olive
Elaeagnus pungens
Elaeagnaceae
8–15′ x 10′
Zones 7–9

The Russian olive is a massive-growing evergreen shrub that produces long pendulous to rambling branches well beyond the dense foliage core. Having distinctive gray green leaves with silver-colored undersides, the fast-growing shrub is ideal for screening, for covering slopes and embankments, and for planting atop retaining walls. It grows in almost any soil unless it is poorly drained. Although the shrub prefers full sunlight, it accepts moderate shade. Highly fragrant buff-colored flowers appear in late autumn. There are numerous cultivars, with many sorts of yellow to white variegated foliage. *E. angustifolia,* also called the Russian olive, is a large deciduous shrub growing to fifteen feet and producing a yellow fruit coated with silvery scales. *E. multi-*

Russian olive as a young shrub

Russian olives pruned into trees at the Museum of Man and Nature, in Winnipeg.

flora, the gumi, is a relatively large shrub with silver-colored foliage that produces fragrant spring flowers and edible scarlet fruit on slender stalks in early summer.

Gumi at the Arnold Arboretum.

Russian olive cascading over a ten-foot retaining wall

Horsetail, which predates dinosaurs

Loquat, Japanese Plum
Eriobotrya japonica
Rosaceae
10–20′ x 15′   Zones 8–10

The loquat is a relatively small evergreen tree with a rounded to irregular form and large coarse-textured, leathery leaves to ten inches long. Fragrant creamy white flowers appear in late autumn or early winter. Yellow fruit to an inch in diameter matures in spring if winter freezes do not destroy it. The tree suits small spaces, but it is relatively short-lived. A member of the rose family, it is highly susceptible to fire blight. The tree must be in very well drained soil and preferably full sunlight, although it will tolerate some shade, especially during the afternoon. *E. deflexa*, the bronze loquat, is a large evergreen shrub to small tree on which the new leaves are a bronze color.

Flowers and bold, coarse-textured foliage of the loquat.

Horsetail
Equisetum hyemale
Equisetaceae
3–5′   Zones 7–10

Believed to have covered large portions of the earth as gigantic forests during the Carboniferous period, today the horsetail is little more than a garden enhancement. Despised by farmers who must constantly fight to keep it at bay, it can serve as a vertical contrast in landscapes as well as a container-grown specimen in water gardens. The plant "walks" rapidly and will spread into adjacent plantings in short order, requiring some method to keep it in bounds. Jointed olive green tubular stems rise straight up from underground stolons in large clumps. It is at home in any soil, and in sunlight or shade.

Loquat fruit, edible and used for jelly

Bloom of the coral tree in summer

Coral Tree, Crybaby Tree
Erythrina crista-galli
Leguminosae
8–20' x 8'
Zones 8/9–10

The coral tree, a large subtropical evergreen shrub to small tree, produces extremely unusual flowers. Tall stalks of bright red tubular flowers extend beyond the foliage in early summer, with intermittent flowering throughout that season. The plant is very coarse textured, because of the large compound leaves. There are prominent spines on stems, twigs, and backs of leaves. If the young, tender growth freezes, the dead and dying portions give the plant an untidy appearance unless it is pruned. Select a well-drained soil and full sunlight for best results, though the tree is tolerant of rugged environmental conditions within its zones of adaptation.

Silver-Dollar Tree, Eucalyptus
Eucalyptus cinerea
Myrtaceae
25–40' x 20'   Zones 8/9–10

Eucalyptus is a large genus comprising nearly seven hundred species and cultivars of the famous trees from Australia and Tasmania, among which the silver-dollar tree is highly variable in form. Normally it is an upright tree with irregular branching, but in the upper portion of its climatic range, it freezes periodically and grows multiple stems. Named for its rounded, coinlike leaves, there is no species that produces a more beautiful silver foliage than it. It requires full sun and a well-drained soil.

Foliage of the eucalyptus, popular as cut greenery.

Striking red flowers of the coral bean.

Coral Bean, Mamou
Erythrina herbacea
3–10' x 4'   Zones 8–9

The coral bean varies in performance. In warmer climates it becomes a relatively large, gangly woody shrub with very little dieback each winter. In colder and drier areas, where the plant is native, it produces a few tall flowering canes each year and dies back to the ground each winter like a herbaceous perennial. Its most striking characteristic is its bright red tubular, spurlike flowers produced on tall leafless stalks from late spring through midsummer. Beanlike pods six to eight inches long with constrictions at each seed appear in autumn. They split open, revealing bright red bony seed. The plant performs best in sandy, well-drained soil that is relatively infertile. If the soil is too rich, the plant produces only a mass of three-leaflet leaves.

Eucalyptus, large and gangly

Close-up of the sensational autumn foliage of the winged euonymus.

Strawberry Bush, Wahoo
Euonymus americanus
4–8' x 5'   Zones 6–9

The strawberry bush is a delightful upright-growing native shrub with thin green stems. It occurs as understory growth both singly and in colonies, because it spreads by underground stems. The thin, wiry green stems and small olive green leaves arranged in pairs give the plant a light, airy appearance in the forest. In autumn rounded, warty capsules resembling strawberries split open to reveal four or five prominent orange red seeds, which many forms of wildlife eat. The strawberry bush prefers a moist, well-drained soil of high organic content.

Fruit of the strawberry bush, resembling the fruit for which the plant is named.

Hedge of the winged euonymus afire in autumn in Louisville, Kentucky

Winged Euonymus
Euonymus alatus
Celastraceae
5–15' x 10'   Zones 3–8

The winged euonymus produces some of the most spectacular autumn coloration to be seen. Something of a sleeper and unnoticed most of the year, the dense deciduous shrub comes forth in late autumn with brilliant scarlet foliage. Often used as screening in privacy hedges or as a single specimen plant, it has interesting branching. Corky wings develop along the stems and are especially visible in winter, when the plant is leafless. For success with this species, select a well-drained soil and preferably full sunlight, although reasonably good growth with autumn color is possible in partial shade.

Spreading Euonymus
Euonymus fortunei
2–4' x 5'   Zones 4–9

For large masses of ground cover, the cultivars of the spreading euonymus are excellent. Because the plant sports readily, a lot of variation and many cultivars have resulted, with the primary differences being in leaf color, height, and spread. The plant is well adapted to open terrain in full sunlight and is suitable on slopes and embankments, atop retaining walls, and in other situations where large rambling plants are needed for a textural contrast. Some of the most popular selections are var. coloratus, the purple-leaf

Ground cover of the spreading euonymus

Variegated Euonymus
Euonymus japonicus
3–6′ x 3′   Zones 6–9

Flashy foliage of the golden euonymus

Among the available selections of the variegated euonymus are some of the showiest of all ornamental shrubs. All are prone to powdery mildew and heavy infestations of scale insects if they are not sprayed frequently, however. The shrubs should be planted in moist, well-drained soil where they receive full sunlight for most of the day. Some of the most popular cultivars are 'Argenteo Variegata', the silver queen euonymus, a tight, upright-growing cultivar with dark green, white-margined leaves; 'Aureo Marginata', the golden euonymus, upright in form with dark green, yellow-margined leaves; and 'Aureo Variegata', the gold spot euonymus, tightly upright with dark green leaves that have yellow blotches in the center.

euonymus, with a prostrate form and plum-colored winter foliage; var. radicans, the big-leaf wintercreeper, with large glossy foliage; 'Emerald 'n' Gold', a low-growing cultivar with dense erect branches and leaves with white margins; and 'Emerald Beauty', a cultivar growing to five feet and producing pink capsules that split to reveal orange red berries.

Silver queen euonymus as a container plant

Joe-Pye Weed
Eupatorium purpureum
Compositae
6–8′ x 4′   Zones 4–9

Joe-Pye weed is a native roadside perennial that, having been domesticated, is now highly visible in midsummer landscapes. Full sunlight and abundant moisture are required for best performance. The green canelike stems bear coarse-textured leaves with serrated margins that measure to ten inches in length. This clump-forming species is an effective accompaniment to grasses and other perennials and is appropriate for naturalistic settings. In mid- to late summer there are showy mauve purple

Joe-Pye weed, a native perennial that can be grown over much of the country, here in western North Carolina.

Large, floriferous specimen of Exochorda giraldii *var.* wilsonii, *the Wilson pearlbush.*

Pearl-like buds and flowers of the pearlbush

Pearlbush
Exochorda racemosa
Rosaceae
5–10′ x 8′   Zones 4–8

The pearlbush is a popular large upright-growing shrub in the more northerly regions of the United States. Its somewhat fountainlike spreading branches are covered with clusters of white flowers produced in three- to five-inch racemes in late spring. As an individual specimen, the plant is not a standout except when flowering. It is probably best used in combination with other plants. For greatest success, select a well-drained slightly acid soil in full sunlight or partial shade. The removal of old, nonproductive canes will improve the overall appearance, keep the plant thrifty, and extend its life.

panicles up to fifteen inches in diameter. Cut tops back in winter, and divide established clumps in early spring on a three year rotation.

American Beech
Fagus grandifolia
Fagaceae
50–75′ x 50′   Zones 3–9

Among the most prized of native trees, the American beech is a long-lived deciduous tree that occurs naturally along sandy streams and woodland bluffs in moist, well-drained acid soil. It is highly sensitive to any alteration of grade in the surrounding terrain, to soil compaction, and to changes in the water table under the tree canopy. The beech cannot tolerate harsh growing conditions. Smooth gray bark, shiny

Wavy-edged leaves and mature nuts of the American beech at the Dawes Arboretum, in Newark, Ohio.

dark green foliage that turns bronze in autumn and lasts into winter, and near perfect symmetry of form distinguish this wonderful dense shade tree. Wildlife consumes its small three-angled nut enclosed in a prickly husk.

European Beech
Fagus sylvatica
40–50′ x 40′   Zones 4–7

A beloved tree in its native Europe, the European beech makes a stunning specimen. With branches growing near the ground on a short trunk, the tree has near-perfect form. It requires a well-drained acid soil and enough open space in full sunlight to exhibit its grand features. The cultivar 'Atropunicea', the copper beech, has purple leaves and receives much acclaim in the northern part of the United States. Another cultivar, 'Purpurea-Pendula', produces purple foliage on strong pendulous branches, making it an even more dramatic specimen in the landscape than the copper beech.

Columnar, pyramidal European beech.

Copper beech specimen in Minnesota

Fatshedera, Tree Ivy
× *Fatshedera lizei*
Araliaceae
To 15′   Zones 8–10

The fatshedera results from a highly unusual cross of plants of two unlike genera, *Hedera* and *Fatsia*. Taking on the characteristics of both its parents, English ivy and fatsia, it is half vine and half shrub. Fastened to a wall or other flat surface, the large dark green ivylike leaves make a striking coarse-textured display. The vine does not attach by itself to surfaces like ivy, but must be held in place. If unattached, the tree ivy rambles and produces a shrublike form. Highly susceptible to the same root fungi that attack English ivy, the plant must be grown in a porous, well-drained soil. It does best with morning sunlight but will tolerate some shade.

Large leathery, ivylike leaves of the fatshedera espaliered on a brick wall.

Fatsia, Japanese Aralia
Fatsia japonica
Araliaceae
4–8′ x 4′   Zones 8–10

Large leathery deeply lobed leaves mark the fatsia, a heavy, medium-sized evergreen shrub. A mainstay in shade gardens of the south, the shrub is very manageable and provides year-round coarse foliage texture in the landscape. Round creamy white flowers appear in late autumn, and large branched clusters of black fruit in spring. Very intolerant of heavy, wet soil, the plant needs soil that is moist, porous, and well drained. It prefers morning sunlight, with protection from the hot noonday sun.

Silvery foliage of the mature pineapple guava contrasted with the Japanese plum and turf.

Unusual but little-appreciated flowers of the pineapple guava at the Hilltop Arboretum of Louisiana State University.

Pineapple Guava
Feijoa sellowiana
Myrtaceae
6–10′ x 8′   Zones 8–9

Although a very successful large evergreen shrub in the Middle South, the pineapple guava is not widely grown. The dark blue green leaves with silver undersurfaces are in strong color contrast to most other plants. The shrub is

Commanding coarse-textured foliage of the fatsia

ideal for privacy screening or planted as individual specimens on sites large enough to accommodate their great height and spread. Dull white flowers with rosy red stamens appear in spring, and oval to oblong fruit, edible except for the skin, matures in fall. The fruit has a pineapple-like flavor; pollination and fruit-set are reportedly best on sites with relatively low humidity. The shrub needs full sunlight and will tolerate most soils, provided that they drain well. Older plants have beautiful reddish-colored trunks.

THE FERNS

Polypodiaceae

Ferns are flowerless plants that produce true roots from a rhizome, bear leaves, and reproduce from spores borne on the lower sides of the leaves, or fronds. Over ten thousand species are known to exist worldwide. The greatest number and diversity are in humid forested tropical areas. Hardy ferns, particularly native species, will grow in American gardens. Most ferns are shade lovers, and many will grow in very low light intensities. In the landscape, a moist organic soil that is fairly well drained is ideal. The division of clumps should be carried out in late winter or early spring, just before new growth begins.

Maidenhair Fern
Adiantum capillus-veneris
To 18″ Zones 7–10

The maidenhair fern is a clump-growing species with fine-textured compound leaves. The ginkgo- or fan-shaped leaflets are yellow green on glossy purple to black stems. The plant is widely used in containers in colder regions, and outdoors it may be killed back to the ground. *A. pedatum*, the

five-finger or American maidenhair fern, grows in zones 3–8.

Holly Leaf Fern
Cyrtomium falcatum
2′ x 3′ Zones 8–10

The holly leaf fern's dense low, mounding clumps of coarse-textured arching evergreen fronds up to thirty inches long and eight inches wide have segments to four inches long. The fern makes an excellent ground cover and is useful as an understory plant with old, reclaimed shrubs such as camellias, sweet olives, and hollies.

Holly leaf fern, an evergreen for southern gardens.

Boston Fern
Nephrolepis exaltata 'Bostoniensis'
To 40″ Zones 9–10

The Boston fern is an evergreen species widely used in hanging baskets and other containers, but it also performs well as a ground cover in warmer regions. The graceful, arching bright yellow green fronds form dense masses of fine-textured foliage. Unsightly old foliage should be cut back just as new growth begins in spring.

Hardy five-finger maidenhair fern

Boston fern, hardy outdoors only in the Deep South

Cinnamon Fern
Osmunda cinnamomea
To 3'   Zones 3–8

The cinnamon fern is
named for the
cinnamon-colored fuzz
that covers the young
fiddleheads of the large
deciduous perennial. It is
a slow spreader, but
often a single clump can
be a handsome detail in
a garden.

*Cinnamon fern, which unfurls its
lacy green umbrella foliage in early
spring after a long winter's sleep.*

Royal Fern
Osmunda regalis
To 6'   Zones 3–9

The royal fern, a hardy native deciduous fern, has a clumping habit and is slow to multiply. It forms a dense mass of
rich green upright-arching fronds to eighteen inches in
width. The terminal portions of the fertile fronds are
brown. A single clump can stand alone as a striking accent
plant. This fern has good autumn color.

Leatherleaf fern, a tropical fern widely used for cut foliage

Leatherleaf Fern
Rumohra adiantiformis
18–30″   Zones 8/9–10

Hardy in zones 9 and 10 and the lower part of zone 8, the
leatherleaf fern has triangular leathery evergreen fronds to
thirty inches long and fifteen inches wide. Its dark green
color and coarse texture are striking in naturalistic settings
and in detail plantings. The same characteristics make the
fern an outstanding container plant. Its long-lasting cut foliage is used extensively in the florist trade.

royal fern, a large hardy fern growing in humus-rich soil

Bracken Fern
Pteridium aquilinum
To 4' x 3'   Zones 3–10

The bracken fern is a large fern with airy foliage growing
over most of the eastern United States. It is easily transplanted and spreads rapidly to form colonies of durable,
hardy, perennial foliage that may become untidy if not
groomed periodically. The rhizomes are carcinogenic.

Bracken fern

Cedar Fern
Selaginella pulcherrima
To 15″   Zones 8–10

The cedar fern is not a true fern but belongs to the family Selaginellaceae. Its appearance is fernlike, however, and it has the same growing requirements as ferns. The foliage is like the arborvitae's, and it is branched to form a dense olive green mat. The plant makes an attractive ground cover in shaded spots, but it is also planted in containers, because of its distinctive foliage.

Australian Tree Fern
Sphaeropteris cooperi
20′ x 30′   Zones 9/10–10

The Australian tree fern is treelike in size. It is a commanding plant admired for its large ascending yellow green fronds. Although reliably hardy only in zone 10, it is commonly grown as a container plant in other areas, where it can be given protection during the winter. It can tolerate sun during the morning hours but needs shade during the hotter part of the day.

Australian tree fern, used indoors as a container specimen where it is not hardy.

Cedar fern, an excellent ground cover in shady areas such as this, at Rosedown plantation, near St. Francisville, Louisiana

Marsh fern growing in the Atchafalaya Basin, in Louisiana

Marsh Fern
Thelypteris palustris
30–40″   Zones 8–10

The marsh fern is a deciduous fern distinguished by its large graceful, arching chartreuse fronds. It is a fast spreader and forms a natural ground cover in woodland settings. That effect is often reproduced in shade gardens, where the light yellow green coloring provides a strong contrast to dark green foliage.

Common Fig
Ficus carica
Moraceae
12–15′ x 15′   Zones 8–10

The fig is a tasty fruit that is very easy to produce in the Lower South, and the common fig tree is a deciduous tree with a broad-spreading to rounded form that requires a considerable amount of growing space. The large three- to five-lobed leaves and heavy, thick stems give the tree a coarse texture overall. The tree's sweet-flavored fruit matures in early summer. The tree per-

forms best in deep, fertile moist but well-drained soil in full sunlight or partial shade. It does particularly well on the north side of a building, where the soil is moister. In the upper part of its range of adaptation, it is periodically killed back to the ground by freezes. Popular cultivars include 'Brown Turkey', 'Celeste', 'Magnolia', 'Mission', and a new introduction, 'LSU Purple'.

Common fig, a source of delicious fruit in early summer

Embellishment of a wall by creeping fig in Charleston, South Carolina

Same Charleston wall from the opposite side

Creeping Fig
Ficus pumila
50–60′ vine   Zones 8–10

The first year it sleeps, the second year it creeps, and the third year it leaps—those are the facts about the growth of the creeping fig. Select this clinging vine only after knowing its power should it go unattended. With careful management, it can be kept under control, but that means removing large pieces every year. Beginning as a flat mat against a wall or other such surface, with time the vine will grow thicker than the wall. Leaves are small on the young plant, but as it matures it produces very large coarse-textured leaves, as well as fruit on shoots growing at right angles to the flat surface. Walls that have had the vine growing on them are difficult to clean, root residue persisting long after the plant has been removed.

Chinese Parasol Tree
Firmiana simplex
Sterculiaceae
20–40′ x 15′   Zones 8–10

With tall, erect smooth green trunks and three- to five-lobed leaves ten to twelve inches across, the Chinese parasol tree produces a large rounded, umbrella-like

Chinese parasol tree in flower, erect in form and with coarse-textured foliage, towering over a planting of Pfitzer juniper.

canopy. It can be planted in unusually tight places. In an area five feet by five feet, one to three trees can be planted to let the trunks provide strong vertical lines in the landscape. The tree is seldom grown as a single specimen but is normally part of a cluster. Deep rooted, the species tolerates drought well. The tree is very susceptible to scale insects, however, and these are best controlled with a systemic insecticide.

Forsythia, Golden Bells
Forsythia × intermedia
Oleaceae
6–10′ x 8′   Zones 5–8

One of the earliest of spring-flowering deciduous shrubs, the forsythia makes a dramatic show in the late-winter landscape before most other plants break dormancy. The multiple-stemmed broad, mounding form makes the plant an excellent accent shrub, or it can be used in mass plantings. Popular with florists, it is often cut for indoor forcing of the buds. Plant in a well-drained soil and full sunlight. To keep a specimen thrifty and producing many flowers, periodically remove old, nonproductive canes at ground level. That will force the shrub to grow new flowering stems. Some references list fifteen or more cultivars, varying in size, color and type of flower, and leaf characteristics.

Kumquat

Fortunella japonica

Rutaceae

8–15′ x 6′   Zones 9–10

A citrus that can withstand freezing temperatures better than most, the kumquat is a delightful large, dense evergreen shrub to small tree, similar to cherry laurel. It produces small edible rounded or oval yellow orange fruit in late autumn. The fruit can hang on the plant through the winter and usually gets sweeter the longer it stays there. In areas where the species will not freeze, it can be chosen over many of the more traditional hedge plants to provide privacy. Not particular about soil, it grows best in a well-drained location and full sunlight but will produce a fair amount of fruit in partial shade.

Kumquat hedge in a New Orleans landscape

Fothergilla

Fothergilla major

Hamamelidaceae

5–6′ x 5′   Zones 4–8

Adapting well to naturalistic settings, the fothergilla, a multiple-stemmed deciduous shrub, blends well with other plants rather than serving as an accent. Not particularly well known, as a result of its rather low profile during most of the year, it comes into its own in early spring with fragrant white flowers on two-inch stalks. The blooms, with prominent stamens, appear

Honey-scented flowers of the fothergilla resembling bottle brushes.

Forsythia surrounded by a naturalized planting of spring bulbs.

Forsythia flowers

before the foliage and are somewhat like miniature bottlebrush flowers. The leaves, which are rather large and rounded to oval, provide an excellent display of yellow, orange, and scarlet color in early autumn. Provide a well-drained acid soil and full sunlight or partial shade.

Franklinia
Franklinia alatamaha
Theaceae
12–20′ x 10′   Zones 5–8

Not frequently encountered but a very famous tree, the franklinia was discovered in the wilds of Georgia by John Bartram in the 1760s. He transplanted trees from a large native stand on the Altamaha River to his Philadelphia garden. No plants have been found in nature since the late 1700s. Clusters of small greenish white pearl-like buds are followed by beautiful white flowers to three inches across. The flowers have a light, delicate fragrance, and the leaves are approximately six inches long and provide some autumn color. The tree, similar to the sweet-bay magnolia, should have a moist, well-drained acid soil and full sunlight or partial shade.

Autumn color of the green ash.

Compound leaves of the green ash.

Green Ash
Fraxinus pennsylvanica
Oleaceae
40–60′ x 40′   Zones 3–9

A large native deciduous tree widely distributed on the North American continent, the green ash is an excellent shade tree. It is upright oval in form, with shiny dark green compound leaves to ten inches in length. The leaves turn a rich yellow in autumn. Because the numerous winged seeds can be a nuisance, many people choose one of several seedless cultivars for landscapes. The tree tolerates a wide variety of soils, from rather wet and heavy to dry. Allocate a considerable amount of space when positioning. Several popular cultivars are 'Emerald', 'Marshall Seedless', and 'Summit'. A very similar and equally good ash is *F. americana,* the white ash, which also has outstanding autumn color but may be a bit more temperamental about where it grows. It too is large, and there are many cultivars from which to choose.

Prominent magnolia-like flowers of the franklinia, on a tree growing at the North Carolina State Arboretum, in Asheville.

flowers up to four inches in diameter. The flowers are set among large shiny dark green leaves on a large mounding shrub. The shrub performs best in a well-drained acid soil in morning sunlight. Unfortunately, it is plagued by whitefly, scale insects, and sooty mold fungus. Periodic spraying is required to ensure survival. Cultivars with superior flowering and foliage characteristics include 'August Beauty', 'Mystery', 'Veitchii', and 'Aurero-Marginata', the last with white variegation in the foliage. *G. thunbergia*, the hip gardenia, has fragrant flowers in late spring and fruit, or hips, that turn red in fall and remain on the shrub into winter.

Arizona ash as a shade tree

Arizona Ash
Fraxinus velutina
30–40′ x 30′   Zones 7–9

The acceptability of the Arizona ash depends on the region for which it is intended. For dry, arid landscapes where few other trees perform well, it can be a good fast-growing shade tree. But in areas with moist, fertile soil, it can be very short-lived and require high maintenance. If other possibilities exist, it is doubtful that this ash should be planted to any great degree. For its first ten years it can perform reasonably well, but with aging it suffers severe dieback and develops competitive roots near the surface of the soil. It is also very susceptible to infestation by mistletoe. Few plants will grow below the heavy, dense canopy of this ash.

Gardenia, Cape Jasmine
Gardenia jasminoides
Rubiaceae
5–10′ x 6′   Zones 8–9

In the South, the gardenia is one of the all-time favorite evergreen shrubs. A mainstay in old gardens, it is best known for its highly fragrant creamy white late-spring to early-summer

Large gardenia specimen with a multitude of flowers

Close-up of fragrant white satiny flowers of the gardenia.

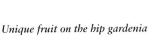

Unique fruit on the hip gardenia

Prostrate-growing dwarf gardenia

Dwarf Gardenia
Gardenia jasminoides 'Radicans'
2′ x 3′   Zones 8–9

With a low, prostrate form and small shiny, fine-textured leaves, the dwarf gardenia is effective as a ground cover when massed on three-foot centers. It is particularly attractive in planters and where the low, creeping branches can drape over retaining walls and other edges. Numerous small flowers to two inches in diameter nearly cover the plant in late spring and early summer. Like the regular gardenia, the dwarf has flowers that are fragrant, sometimes to the point of being offensive. The dwarf tends to be somewhat less hardy than the larger plant. It grows best in a well-drained acid soil and with morning sunlight, preferring to be protected from the hot noonday sun. This cultivar has the same insect and disease problems as the regular gardenia, and it can be killed by root-knot nematodes.

Huckleberry
Gaylussacia dumosa
Ericaceae
4–8′ x 5′   Zones 7–9

It is a puzzle why a native that has as many outstanding characteristics as the dwarf huckleberry is not more popular in contemporary gardens. The open, airy deciduous shrub with small lustrous leaves produces many pinkish white bell-shaped flowers in late winter and early spring, before the leaves appear. Flowers are followed in May by

edible shiny black fruit, about a quarter inch in diameter. A superior understory species, the plant grows well in a humus-rich acid soil. Even in shade it produces beautiful red foliage in early winter. As a specimen gets larger, it becomes more picturesque, with handsome sculptural trunks topped with fine-textured foliage.

Black fruit of summer following late-winter and early-spring huckleberry blooms.

Carolina Yellow Jessamine
Gelsemium sempervirens
Loganiaceae
15–20′ vine   Zones 7–9

A semievergreen native vine, the Carolina yellow jessamine is a prolific grower and produces fragrant bright yellow funnel-shaped flowers over an extended period from late winter into early summer. The thin, wiry stems and dense foliage can cover a garden structure like a fence or arbor relatively quickly. The vine appears to bloom best if growth is restricted. Provide a moist, well-drained acid soil, and this, the state flower of South Carolina, will bloom fairly well in partial shade. In its native habitat, the "jasmine" climbs into trees and over smaller plants on woodland edges, forming a beautiful tracery of foliage and yellow flowers. 'Pride of Augusta' is a beautiful double-flowered cultivar.

Early spring flowers of the Carolina yellow jessamine

Fan-shaped foliage of the "living fossil," the ginkgo.

Earle

Specimen ginkgo in autumn color at Magnolia Vale, Natchez

Ginkgo, Maidenhair Tree
Ginkgo biloba
Ginkgoaceae
40–75' x 40'   Zones 4–9

In a poll to determine the most cherished tree in the world, and the tree bringing together the best combination of features in a single species, the ginkgo would surely rank high if not first. Its classical fan-shaped leaves turn an incomparable brilliant golden yellow in late autumn. The tree is easy to grow and maintain, provided that it is given a well-drained soil and full sunlight. Its only negative may be its relatively slow growth rate. The pyramidal form of the young tree becomes somewhat more irregular with age. Stout branching and the short budding spurs present a beautiful silhouette in the winter landscape. There are numerous cultivars. Most are male, since the fruit the female tree produces has a foul odor. Some of the cultivars with interesting forms are 'Autumn Gold', 'Fastigiata', and 'Princeton Sentry', along with 'Pendula', a weeping selection.

Byzantine Gladiolus
Gladiolus byzantinus
Iridaceae
2–3'   Zones 8–10

Byzantine gladioli, which will persist in gardens for years without care.

The dark green sword-like leaves of the Byzantine gladiolus are capped with magenta flowers at the same time that most iris are in bloom. Flowers are borne on a spike, typical of gladioli. Each of the three lower flower segments has a narrow creamy white line down its center. The frost hardy foliage is present from January until it dies down in summer. This species, cultivated in Europe for hundreds of years, thrives in a variety of garden soils and grows well in full sunlight or partial shade. The plant multiplies to form large clumps and will endure for years with little or no attention. Corms should be planted in fall, and small corms (cormels), which will take three years to flower, may be planted concurrently to add foliage. 'Alba' is a rare, white-flowering cultivar.

Honey Locust
Gleditsia triacanthos
Fabaceae (Leguminosae)
30–75' x 40'   Zones 4–9

The native honey locust, with its light, airy umbrella-like canopy of fine-textured compound leaves and vicious thorns, is a parent to numerous varieties and cultivars. Al-

Soft, graceful foliage of the thornless honey locust var. inermis.

though the native makes an attractive specimen and will grow nearly anywhere, its thorns are too dangerous for most plantings. Cultivars have been widely planted in plazas, parking lots, parks, and playgrounds, and along streets. These have beautiful forms, and their sizes are manageable for small spaces with less than ideal growing conditions. The most popular thornless selection is var. inermis. The cultivars include 'Majestic', 'Moraine', and 'Shademaster', as well as 'Sunburst' and 'Summergold', two that have bright yellow in their new foliage.

Loblolly Bay, Gordonia
Gordonia lasianthus
Theaceae
20–30' x 15'   Zones 8–10

Loblolly bay

Upright and columnar in form, with a rather loose, open canopy, the loblolly bay is a native evergreen tree somewhat similar to the sweet-bay magnolia and closely related to camellias. It frequently grows in moist

Lawn specimen of the Moraine honey locust at the Morton Arboretum, near Chicago.

Golden-colored foliage of a 'Sunburst' honey locust in California

sandy, peaty acid soil adjacent to rivers and streams in the South and the Southeast. The leaves, two to five inches long, are lustrous dark green above and a much paler green below. Beautiful white cup-shaped flowers with yellow centers are scattered over the tree from late spring into summer.

THE ORNAMENTAL GRASSES
Gramineae

Ornamental grasses have gained popularity in the landscape for several reasons. Seasonal interest, ease of cultivation, freedom from plant pests, wide adaptation to soil, temperature, and water availability, and distinctive flower and foliage characteristics all help explain the appeal of perennial grasses. Unlike lawn grasses, which spread by stolons or runners, ornamental grasses are for the most part clump-forming. Enjoy the new spring growth, the summer foliage, and the flowers in autumn and early winter, and then, just before new growth begins, remove the previous season's growth and fertilize with an all-purpose garden fertilizer. Grasses require full sunlight for best performance, but a few do passably in light shade. They are an excellent choice for xeriscapes, the trend toward which will bring wider acceptance of them, but some are adapted to moist or wet soil.

The grass family comprises over seven thousand species. It is the most important group of plants of all, because members of the family include the cereals—like rice, wheat, corn, rye, and oats—that are the mainstay source of food for humans and livestock. Grasses used in landscapes are herbaceous perennials capable of imparting interest through size, form, color, or texture. They have ephemeral qualities that bring variety, richness, and seasonal change to the garden.

The ornamental grasses vary from low, tufted clumps under six inches to giant selections that grow to twelve feet or more. The larger growers are effective for screening and embellishing sizable spaces, the smaller ones for adding subtle detail to a planting. Some are used as ground covers for soil stabilization.

Most grasses are not particular about soil, so long as it is well drained. They are carefree plants, requiring no maintenance beyond cutting back old growth before new growth begins in spring. They are environmentally friendly.

Feather Reed Grass
Calamagrostis acutiflora 'Stricta'
To 7'   Zones 5–9

Feather reed grass is outstanding for its formal vertical contribution to the landscape. It bears feathery blossoms in summer that are striking when silhouetted against a sunlit sky. The tan stems, leaves, and seed heads are attractive in winter.

A rooftop garden of ornamental grasses at the Hansa Museum, in Berlin

Feather reed grass

Ravenna grass, here at the Brooklyn Botanic Garden, growing to a height of ten feet, with flower panicles up to two feet long.

Ravenna Grass
Erianthus ravennae
To 12′   Zones 6–9

Ravenna grass, a reedlike grass with panicles of silvery seed heads to two feet long, is impressive in fall and winter landscapes. The tall, slender reeds last over winter. The grass grows in full sunlight and can survive arid conditions.

Festuca
Festuca ovina glauca
8–10″ x 12″   Zones 4–8

Festuca is a tufted grass to eight inches tall with rolled, threadlike silver to sapphire blue foliage. Small flower spikes rise above the foliage. It is particularly well adapted to harsh, dry sites and is often used in rock gardens and xeriscape plantings. *F. cinerea* 'Elijah Blue' has outstanding powder blue needle-thin foliage that keeps its looks through most of the year.

Green

Japanese blood grass, here the lower-growing brilliant red clump among a collection of other grasses.

Japanese Blood Grass
Imperata cylindrica var. rubra
18–24″ x 12″   Zones 6–9

One of the most unusual of the ornamental grasses, Japanese blood grass produces narrow blood red leaves that can be a striking accent alongside other plants. It is particularly effective in mass groupings. The cultivar 'Red Baron' is promoted in the trade for the intensity of its red color.

Festuca, a good xeriscape plant, in an Arizona landscape

Maiden Grass
Miscanthus sinensis '*Gracillimus*'
4–5' x 5'   Zones 4–9

Sometimes referred to as the queen of ornamental grasses, maiden grass has graceful narrow arching, channeled leaves to a quarter inch wide. The flower heads are branched and resemble a feather duster, and the flowers are silvery airy, silky plumes on five-foot stems that are very prominent in autumn and survive into winter. A clump resembles in miniature the more common pampas grass. The cultivar 'Silberfeder' is a larger-growing variegated selection with seven-foot beige flowering plumes. Another cultivar, 'Zebrinus', also grows to seven feet but has variegated foliage with horizontal whitish gold bands and an upright form. 'Autumn Light' is a low-growing type that has narrow leaves and produces an abundance of flower heads.

Specimen clump of maiden grass in early autumn

Variegated Japanese Silver Grass
Miscanthus sinensis '*Variegatus*'
4–8' x 6'   Zones 5–9

Among the large variegated perennial grasses, variegated Japanese silver grass has a mounding habit with foliage that is relatively broad and creamy white on both sides of a silver white midrib. Beige to tan branched flower heads appear in autumn and continue on the plant into winter.

Variegated Japanese silver grass at the Biltmore Estate, in Asheville, North Carolina.

Porcupine grass with interesting golden bands in the leaf

Fountain grass

Purple Fountain Grass
***Pennisetum alopecuroides* 'Purpureum'**
4′ x 3′   Zones 6–9

Purple fountain grass is a distinctive reddish purple. Clumps have an upright form and relatively compact growth. Because of the grass's form and color, it is capable of a strong impact when combined with other plants. The flowers resembling bottle brushes that appear from late summer into autumn are secondary to the colorful foliage.

Fountain Grass
Pennisetum alopecuroides
5′ x 3′   Zones 6–9

Fountain grass, which grows in clumps to a height of five feet, has upright-arching leaves. Fuzzy flower heads, to two feet above the leaves, resemble those of the bottlebrush. The coppery tan to reddish flowers occur from late summer through autumn. Chinese pennisetum, or rose fountain grass, is a showy ornamental with slender two-foot leaves, and silvery rose flowers from July through September.

Purple fountain grass

Rose fountain grass

Flower and foliage of the silk oak on the UCLA campus.

Silk Oak
Grevillea robusta
Proteaceae
30–75′ x 30′
Zones 9–10

Not a true oak, the silk oak is a subtropical evergreen tree with soft, fern-like compound leaves that are deep green with a silvery cast. The tree's form is upright to pyramidal, with strong horizontal branches. In addition to the distinctive foliage, there are large flat-sided bright yellow orange racemes that appear in early spring. A desirable shade tree along the warm Gulf Coast, this species is sometimes planted indoors farther north. The tree must have a well-drained soil and full sunlight. Root rot occurs in heavy, poorly drained soil.

Kentucky Coffee Tree
Gymnocladus dioicus
Fabaceae (Leguminosae)
50–75′ x 40′   Zones 4–8

The Kentucky coffee tree is a popular shade tree in the more northerly parts of the United States. Large compound leaves to approximately thirty inches long and twenty-four inches wide on strong ascending branches and a full, dense canopy make this a desirable specimen tree. Fragrant greenish white flowers occur in early summer, followed by seedpods ten inches long in autumn. The mature tree has a distinctive brown coarse-textured, scaly ridged bark. There is good growth in a wide range of soils, including dry and chalky, but performance is best in one that is fertile, moist, and well drained.

Foliage of the Kentucky coffee tree

Kentucky coffee tree, an outstanding large shade tree for northern landscapes.

Carolina Silver Bell
Halesia carolina
Styracaceae
25–40′ x 30′   Zones 4–8

Present over a wide area of the eastern United States, the Carolina silver bell is a delightful small flowering tree. Relatively large leaves that are thin and translucent, white bell-shaped flowers, a manageable size, and easy culture make the tree worthy of a much larger role in contemporary landscapes. It is handsome as a lawn or patio specimen or in front of evergreens that can provide a strong color contrast to the white flowers. It grows best in a fertile moist, well-drained acid soil in full sunlight or partial shade. In its native habitat, it often grows along small rivers and sandy streams.

Young specimen of the Carolina silverbell.

Bell-shaped flowers and immature foliage of the silver bell.

Ammon

Mountain silverbell's pink flowers

Silver Bell
Halesia diptera
35′ x 20′   Zones 7–9

Native to the Middle South region, the silver bell is a very dependable small flowering tree that makes a terrific patio or lawn specimen. Just before the large, thin leaves of relatively coarse texture appear, the tree is covered with a mass of white bell-shaped flowers. Although often recommended for locations where soil conditions are too stressful for dogwoods, the silverbell is outstanding in its own right. It grows relatively fast, is highly tolerant of a wide range of soil conditions, and produces a pleasing yellow autumn color in the Lower South. It occurs naturally along small sandy streams and on slopes.

H. monticola, the mountain silver bell, is a native that grows two or three times as large as either the silver bell or the Carolina silver bell and has larger flowers and seeds. The cultivar 'Rosea' has pale pink flowers. This species grows best at high altitudes.

Witch Hazel
Hamamelis × intermedia
Hamamelidaceae
20′ x 15′   Zones 5–8

There are a large number of cultivars of this hybrid witch hazel, a cross between *H. japonica* and *H. mollis*. Vigorous growers, deciduous upright spreaders, the loosely branched plants flower in January in the South and in mid-March farther north, depending on the cultivar. Red fall coloration is generally more pronounced in the red-flowering selections. 'Arnold Promise' has large, deep fragrant yellow flowers in early spring. 'Diane' has copper red flowers and a rich orange red autumn color.

Chinese Witch Hazel
Hamamelis mollis
10′ x 10′   Zones 5–8

Broad-spreading form of the Chinese witch hazel.

The Chinese witch hazel is a large deciduous shrub with dull green semi-heart-shaped leaves that can be six inches long and almost as wide. Fragrant yellow strap-shaped flower petals, five-eighths of an inch long, appear in late winter and continue for two or more weeks. Leaves turn a crisp yellow in autumn. The shrub has an oval to rounded outline with spreading branches. It is appreciated for flowering when other plants are still dormant. Growing well in full sunlight or partial shade, it needs a well-drained organic soil. A few cultivars are available that have larger flowers with different shades of yellow and vary in growth habit. 'Brevipetala', 'Early Bright', 'Goldcrest', and 'Pallida' are four that are good.

Ammon

'Arnold Promise' witch hazel flowering in early March, with snow on the ground.

92

Vernal Witch Hazel
Hamamelis vernalis
10–12' x 10'   Zones 4–8

A large, broad-spreading deciduous shrub with coarse-textured leaves to five inches long, the vernal witch hazel does not command much attention until it begins to flower in late winter or early spring. Blooming before most woody plants come out of dormancy, it has yellow flowers with thin curly, ribbonlike petals that punctuate the late-winter landscape. Mass plantings can serve as privacy screens, but the shrub is equally effective as an accent. Unpruned, it has very interesting sculptural branches. It performs well in full sunlight, though also in considerable shade as understory growth, and it produces beautiful yellow foliage in autumn. It is tolerant of a wide variety of soils, from moist to relatively dry.

Spectacular late-winter flowers of the vernal witch hazel

Witch Hazel
Hamamelis virginiana
20–25' x 15'   Zones 4–9

A large deciduous shrub to small tree, this native witch hazel has coarse-textured oval leaves to five inches long. The irregular open horizontal branches have a sculptural quality and are lined with mustard-yellow flowers the

ribbonlike petals of which unroll outward as they open in late autumn. The flowers, possessing a mild spicy fragrance, continue for several weeks. At about the same time the blooms appear, the rich golden yellow

Common witch hazel, which drops its yellow leaves when it blooms in late autumn.

leaves drop. The plant is one of the last natives to make a strong showing in early winter. It grows in a wide range of soils, from the relatively heavy, moist, and clayey to the dry and sandy. It is a good choice for both naturalistic settings and conventional plantings.

Fire Bush
Hamelia patens
Rubiaceae
4–6' x 5'   Zones 9–10

The fire bush, a rapid-growing perennial, is an excellent bedding plant for color during the hot months of the year. Once it starts blooming after a rather slow beginning very much like that of the hibiscus, bright orange red tubular flowers continue to appear until cold weather arrives. In the northern range of the subtropical shrublike plant's adaptation, it normally dies back to the ground after the occurrence of freezing temperatures, but it returns from the roots the following spring. Even where it is warmer, annual grooming is necessary to keep the plant thrifty and floriferous. Select a site with full sunlight and a well-drained, porous soil.

Tubular red flowers of the fire bush

93

Algerian Ivy
Hedera canariensis
Araliaceae
8–10″ x 40′   Zones 8–10

Distinguished by big dark blue green heart-shaped leaves with long reddish-colored leaf stems to a length of eight inches, Algerian ivy is a popular ground cover where a coarse-textured plant contrasting with turf is wanted. It is widely used to cover steep slopes, embankments, and other sizable areas in the warm, dry regions of the country, particularly California. Not as cold hardy as English ivy, it grows best in a porous, well-drained soil in partial shade, although it will take full sunlight where the humidity is relatively low. In the warm, humid South, it is susceptible to a root fungus and should be used with great reservation in large projects.

English ivy

English Ivy
Hedera helix
6″ x 50′   Zones 5–9

English ivy is in all likelihood the most widely used ground cover in the United States. As a substitute for turf in covering large areas, it does not have an equal. Grown in both full sunlight and shade in the North, it needs protection from the hot noonday sun in the Lower South. The dark blue green lobed leaves to about four inches in width make a dense evergreen blanket. Unlike many other vines, English ivy is controllable and will not normally overpower other plants in a ground cover. Spring-flowering bulbs and other herbaceous plants can be interplanted with it for seasonal interest. In the South,

Large mass of coarse-textured Algerian ivy in San Francisco

English ivy as a ground cover for a large area

Lenten Rose
Helleborus orientalis
Ranunculaceae
15″ x 15″   Zones 3–8

The Lenten rose is a cool-season perennial that produces large coarse-textured, leathery leaves divided into five to seven segments. Nodding cup-shaped greenish purple to rosy pink flowers appear in late winter or early spring, depending on location. Well adapted to naturalistic settings with shaded garden paths, this perennial is a wonderful surprise plant, starting active growth in early winter. It does particularly well in soils with a high organic content. *H. niger,* the Christmas rose, is however, it is very susceptible to a root fungus that takes a heavy toll on many plantings. There are numerous cultivars, with varying leaf shapes, that are popular for ornamental plantings, especially in containers. 'Variegata' is one of the best, with petite variegated leaves.

Lenten rose's unusual flowers in late winter or early spring.

Butterfly Ginger, Butterfly Lily, Ginger Lily
Hedychium coronarium
Zingiberaceae
4–6′ x 3′
Zones 8–10

The tall stiff, leaning stems of the butterfly ginger have foliage radiating from them and, on top, clusters of sweet-scented white flowers with large and small lobes in the shape of butterflies. Flowering occurs from mid-summer until cold weather arrives. With time, the subtropical herbaceous perennial forms heavy clumps of canes with coarse-textured leaves. It grows well in a moist soil and full sunlight or partial shade. A heavy feeder, it grows much faster when fertilized at least every spring. Mulch roots in the Upper South.

Tropical foliage and flowers of the butterfly ginger

very similar. It has palmately compound dull green leaves. Nodding cup-shaped flowers are greenish white. The Christmas rose blooms slightly earlier than the Lenten rose.

Day Lily
Hemerocallis fulva
Liliaceae
1–2′ x 1′   Zones 4–9

One of the best of all perennials, the day lily has been around as long as there have been gardens—according to records, going back at least as far as the birth of Christ. Clumps of long, narrow green keeled leaves give rise to widely expanded funnel-shaped flowers on tall stalks. Highly variable according to cultivar, with single or double

flowers in bright colors—orange, yellow, red, pink, brown, green, or combinations—they can flower from midspring until frost. Because of the relative ease of their hybridization, it is not unusual to have several hundred selections introduced in a year. The plant is best adapted to well-drained soils in full sunlight, but it tolerates a wide range of growing conditions. Lift, divide, and replant in autumn.

Red Yucca
Hesperaloe parviflora
Agavaceae
2–4′ x 3′   Zones 8–10

The red yucca, a stemless clump-forming perennial, is

Day lily flowers, a bright spot in spring and summer gardens.

'Persian Market' hybrid day lily in the Missouri Botanic Garden, in St. Louis.

Red yucca in Balmorhea, Texas, a plant that blooms in spring and summer

often part of warm, dry, airy landscapes. It produces tall, somewhat thick silvery gray twisted grasslike leaves to more than three feet in height. From the center arises a stalked flower head bearing many dark red bell-shaped florets of considerable durability. Growing in dry, porous soils where cacti are found, the plant is often an accent in rock gardens. It is popular in xeriscapes. *H. parviflora* var. *engelmannii* has bell-shaped flowers up to an inch long.

Mounding clump of 'Palace Purple' alumroot in the Chicago Botanic Garden.

Alumroot
Heuchera micrantha
Saxifragaceae
18–24″ x 15″   Zones 4–8

The alumroot is a much-favored mounding herbaceous perennial in the cool regions of the nation. It produces a low clump of heart-shaped, geranium-like leaves of varying colors, depending on the cultivar. Arising out of the foliage are several twelve- to fifteen-inch stalked airy panicles of white, pink, or ruby red flowers. The plant is often grown for its richly colored leaves, primarily in shades of purple, and from ivylike to crinkly. It grows best in a well-drained soil and full sunlight in the North but is better adapted to the shade garden in the Middle South. *H. americana*, the American alumroot, is a better selection for the South.

Native Red Hibiscus
Hibiscus coccineus
Malvaceae
4–8′ x 4′   Zones 6–10

Solitary bright red funnel-shaped flowers to about five inches across are produced on long stems by the native red hibiscus, a relatively large deciduous shrub. Plants are often sprawling and rangy with several stems. The leaves are

palmately shaped, with three, five, or seven jagged segments. In the upper range of the plant's adaptation, freezing normally kills what is above ground. In the Lower South, no more than the tender shoots may be killed in most years. This hibiscus needs periodic grooming or it will become large and unattractive. It grows in a wide range of soils, from dry to wet and marshy. For best flowering, provide six to eight hours of sunlight daily during the growing season.

Texas star native red hibiscus, with the promise of many more to come from buds.

Halberd-Leaved Mallow, Soldier Mallow
Hibiscus militaris
6–8′ x 5′   Zones 6–10

A native of marshes and other wet spots like roadside ditches, the halberd-leaved mallow has large, prominent funnel-shaped flowers in white to dark pink, with a maroon throat. Flowers usually begin white and turn pink later in the day. Plants are open and single stemmed but produce many flowers from midsummer until cold weather.

Single-flowering halberd-leaved mallow.

Often it is the primary flowering perennial in extremely wet areas. *H. moscheutos* 'Southern Bell' is a perennial with large flowers up to eight inches across.

Large flowers of the 'Southern Bell' mallow

darker pink by late afternoon, when they begin closing. Hard freezes kill plants back to the ground, but most return the following spring. Often seen in old center-city gardens, this hibiscus can be a very showy autumn-flowering accent provided that it is given a well-drained soil and full sunlight.

Chinese Hibiscus
Hibiscus rosa-sinensis
5–10′ x 6′   Zones 9–10

Suitable as a permanent plant outdoors only in warm climates, the Chinese hibiscus is a prized fast-growing tropical for the summer and autumn months. The large glossy green leaves make a nice

Chinese hibiscus

background for the showy, bright funnel-shaped flowers in white, yellow, orange, pink, coral, and red. There are also bicolors and variegations. Flowers may be single, semi-double, or double. This hibiscus blooms best if the soil is not too fertile and there is slight moisture stress; otherwise it continues to grow and produces few flowers. The plant is effective in beds for temporary color or in containers that allow it to be brought indoors to escape freezing temperatures.

Old-fashioned, much-loved althea

Confederate Rose
Hibiscus mutabilis
10–15′ x 10′   Zones 8–10

Likely the largest ornamental hibiscus, the Confederate rose can grow over ten feet in a single season. More treelike than shrublike, it usually produces many long, thick radiating stems from a central crown. Late in the season, prominent, heavy double flowers appear at the end of the stems. The flowers start out white in the morning and turn

Althea, Rose of Sharon
Hibiscus syriacus
8–12′ x 6′   Zones 5–9

The althea is a long-lived deciduous shrub that blooms profusely from summer into autumn. Having an upright form with several small vertical trunks, the shrub can be tucked into a relatively small space. Its main appeal is the showy broad, funnel-shaped flowers the color of which depends on the cultivar. Old-fashioned altheas were primarily

Double flowers of the Confederate rose

lavender, white, or pink, with single or double flowers, but many selections are available today in other colors. Tolerant of a wide range of soils from relatively heavy to dry, this hibiscus blooms best in full sunlight but will tolerate shade for several hours each day, especially in the afternoon. Among new cultivars are 'Diana', with white flowers; 'Helene', with white flowers that have burgundy centers; and 'Minerva', with lavender flowers.

Amaryllises
Hippeastrum species
Amaryllidaceae
2'   Zones 8–10

Amaryllises are bulbous perennials that produce broad, thick strap-shaped leaves to two feet tall. Emerging in early spring from the center of the pairs of arching leaves are bright-colored funnel-shaped flowers on thick

Mass planting of amaryllises

stalks fifteen to eighteen inches tall. Variable in color, the blooms include the standard whites, reds, and pinks. There are also many new introductions every year. Bulbs should be set with the tip right at the surface of the soil. In areas where severe freezing occurs, mulch bulbs heavily with leaves or pine straw, but remove the mulch in early spring when flower buds begin to form. The plants perform well in a fertile moist, well-drained soil in full sunlight or partial shade. Under satisfactory conditions amaryllises multiply nicely in place, producing colonies of bulbs.

Close-up of hosta flowers on plants growing in the Queen Elizabeth Garden, in Vancouver.

Hostas, Plantain Lilies
Hosta species
Liliaceae
2' x 2'   Zones 3–9

One of the most admired perennials, hostas are low-growing plants with broad heart- to lance-shaped leaves. In summer, from the centers of the dense mounding foliage clumps rise tall stalked terminal clusters of white, blue, or lilac hyacinth-like flowers. Tolerant of a wide range of soil conditions, the plants prefer a moist, well-drained soil heavily fortified with organic matter and mulched in winter. In the North, they grow well in full sunlight, but in the South they perform best when shielded from direct sunlight. They are effective both in mass plantings that create ground covers and in single clumps along paths in the woodland garden. *H. sieboldiana* 'Elegans' has large blue green leaves and is often used as an accent plant. There are numerous species and cultivars, with new selections being offered annually. The cultivar 'Honeybells' has light green leaves, with fragrant lavender flowers in late summer; 'Royal Standard' has dark green foliage, with white flowers in late summer; and 'Gold Crown' has a tight rosette of thick yellow-edged leaves.

Border of hostas in western North Carolina

Dutch hyacinth

Dutch Hyacinth
Hyacinthus orientalis
Liliaceae
6–8″   Zones 5–7/8

Grown from a bulb, the Dutch hyacinth produces a cluster of strap-shaped leaves from which in early spring appear stiff, erect bloom spikes of sweet-scented flowers. Bell-shaped single or double flowers with wide-spreading lobes come in colors that include pink, white, red, purple, violet, and yellow. The bulbs repeat and naturalize well in the North and Middle South but normally have to be planted anew each year in the Gulf Coast region because of the mild winters. In the Lower South, they require forty days of cold storage—for example, in the crisper section of the refrigerator—before being planted in December. The main requirement for spring-flowering bulbs in general is a well-drained soil with several hours of sunlight each day.

THE HYDRANGEAS
Hydrangeaceae (Saxifragaceae)

Large, showy flowers in late spring, in summer, and into early fall, along with coarse-textured foliage and interesting bark, make hydrangeas an asset to many landscapes. They may be used as single plants or in groups. Growing best in partial shade, they are ideal for planting on the north side of a building. Well-drained, moist soil is necessary for best growth and flowering. Pruning of established plants should be done yearly to maintain the desired size and improve the quality and quantity of blooms. Because flower buds form on growth made by these deciduous plants during the previous season, pruning should take place as soon as the major blooming cycle is completed. Later pruning removes flower buds, leading to a sparse display, or none, during the following bloom season.

Climbing Hydrangea
Hydrangea anomala **subsp.** petiolaris
Vine to 80′   Zones 4–7

Sometimes planted as a ground cover or a low-growing shrub, the climbing hydrangea is spectacular as a flowering vine. It ascends trellises, arbors, trees, and walls without tying or fastening, often reaching a height of over fifty feet. Given its rich green foliage, its fragrant white flowers in late spring and early summer, and its exfoliating bark in fall and winter, the vine holds interest most of the year. Do not expect rapid growth for the first two years, but once established, the plant makes superb growth annually.

Smooth Hydrangea, Mountain Hydrangea
Hydrangea arborescens
3–5′ x 4′   Zones 4–8

Native to the eastern part of the United States, the smooth hydrangea early in summer has flat white

Smooth hydrangea, with its small, delicate flowers.

Climbing hydrangea in Grosse Pointe Farms, Michigan

Very large, showy flowers of the 'Annabelle' smooth hydrangea in midsummer.

flower heads two to six inches across that remain as dried seed heads through autumn and winter. Growth is irregular, and the deciduous plant is broad-creeping with many curving non-branching stems. It is excellent for planting on rocky slopes. The cultivar 'Annabelle', discovered in Anna, Illinois, is the most resplendent of this species. Few plants surpass its beauty and showiness, with huge pure white flower heads, rounded and up to a foot in diameter, appearing on established plants. Flowering starts in June and then increases in July and August, when the blooming peak is reached. Plant in partial shade or full sunlight and in moist, well-drained soil.

Common Hydrangea
Hydrangea macrophylla
4' x 6'   Zones 7–9

Flowering freely in shade or partial sun, the common hydrangea, a native of Japan and China, prefers moist, well-drained soil that is fertile. Large flower heads may be flat or round, in white, blue, or pink, depending on variety and soil acidity. Flowers are blue when the soil is acid (pH of 6.0 or less), and pink when it is alkaline (pH of 7.0 or more). To make the soil more acid, add sulfur; to make it more alkaline, add lime. Only a soil test can determine the amount to add. It generally takes two years to effect a color change. Color in the white-

'Blue Wave' lacecap hydrangea at Martha's Vineyard.

Common hydrangea, which adds color to the late-spring and summer landscape

flowering cultivars does not vary with soil pH. Remember that hydrangeas grow best in organic soil. Heavy mulches conserve moisture during summer and reduce winter damage to the crown and roots. Cultivars with flat heads—'Mariesii', 'Variegated Mariesii', and 'Tricolor'—have an outer ring of large, showy sterile florets surrounding a center mass of small fertile, seedlike florets. The dwarf cultivar 'Pia' grows from one to two feet high and has long-lasting showy rose pink flowers regardless of soil pH.

'Variegata' lacecap hydrangea

Panicle Hydrangea
Hydrangea paniculata
15–25' x 10'   Zones 3–8

One of the most pleasing and sensational of midsummer-flowering shrubs is the panicle hydrangea. The cultivar 'Grandiflora', known as the Peegee hydrangea, has flower clusters up to eighteen inches long and twelve inches wide that cover the entire top of the plant. The flowers, which last into autumn, are first white, then gradually become coppery pink. After the plants is established, a judicious pruning after flowering will result in larger blooms. The flowering is more abundant on plants mulched with compost or well-composted cow manure. Apply the mulch after growth starts. For best performance, grow the plant in partial shade or full sunlight.

Mature specimens of the oak leaf hydrangea

Mammoth specimen of the Peegee hydrangea in a Pittsburgh garden

Oak Leaf Hydrangea
Hydrangea quercifolia
6–12' x 8'   Zones 5–9

Perfectly at home in moderate shade, the oak leaf hydrangea is an outstanding native deciduous shrub that will grow and flower surprisingly

Autumn foliage of the oak leaf hydrangea

well in almost full sunlight when provided with a well-drained humus-rich soil and ample moisture. Large conical heads of pure white flowers appear in late spring and early summer. They generally turn rosy red, then tannish brown, and remain on the plant for several months. They are excellent for dried arrangements. The large leaves, resembling oak leaves, have rich autumn shades of red and purple. Old plants may become quite large, but pruning to maintain a desired size may be done immediately after flowering. The exfoliating coppery-colored bark is an additional asset. Among cultivars that have larger and showier flowers are 'Harmony', 'Roanoke', and 'Snow Flake'.

Caribbean hymenocallis, which grows well in sandy beach gardens of the Gulf Coast.

Spider lily growing at water's edge in the Atchafalaya Basin

selection that has beautiful reddish flowers. It grows along the Gulf Coast and over much of Florida.

Hypericum, Saint-John's-Wort
Hypericum calycinum
Hypericaceae (Guttiferae)
18″ x 24″   Zones 5–8

Hypericum is a sprawling to mounding shrub with ascending branches that produces prominent bright yellow three-inch flowers with showy center stamens from June to September. Depending on the severity of the win-

Hypericum's flowers and foliage in Seattle

ter, this hypericum can be nearly evergreen in the lower portion of its range of adaptation. Because it flowers on new wood, untidy plants can be cut back freely to keep them thrifty and to maintain a more dense, compact form. Select a well-drained soil and full sunlight or partial shade for best results. The shrub can be used as a single small-scale specimen but is equally effective as a ground cover in a mass planting.

Spider Lily, Swamp Lily
Hymenocallis liriosme
Amaryllidaceae
2′ x 2′   Zones 7–10

The spider lily, a native bulbous perennial, grows over a large part of the southeastern United States. There are about thirty related species and hybrids that may be grown successfully in the garden. This species thrives in low, poorly drained soils, such as that along roadside ditches and in low bog areas and other wetlands. Normally, the plant naturalizes and forms colonies at drainage ways. Six to eight white spiderlike flowers with yellow throats are supported on thick stems originating in a clump of shiny bright green sword-shaped leaves. The center floral parts are united by a saucer-shaped membrane. Blooming is over a several-week period in spring. This bulb will grow in containers or in the shallow water of garden pools. *H. latifolia (caribaea)* is a large-growing

Hypericum ground cover at Sapphire Lakes, North Carolina

103

Mounding specimen of shrubby hypericum

Shrubby Hypericum, Shrubby Saint-John's-Wort
Hypericum prolificum
1–3′ x 3′   Zones 4–8

The shrubby hypericum is a relatively large-growing member of its genus producing bright golden yellow one-inch flowers from June until mid-August. It is a dense, mounding shrub with stiff upright stems. Growing in a wide range of soils from dry to moist and in full sunlight or partial shade, it can be a very effective summer-flowering shrub when few other plants are in blossom. *H. frondosum*, the golden hypericum or golden Saint-John's-wort, is somewhat similar but is more spreading and mounding to three feet tall. Flowers up to three inches in diameter have prominent stamens, and the foliage is shiny. *H. patulum*, the goldencup Saint-John's-wort, also grows to about three feet tall. It has bright yellow flowers to two inches in diameter. The cultivar 'Hidcote' is reported to produce three-inch yellow flowers on new wood each summer.

THE HOLLIES

Aquifoliaceae

The hollies are found worldwide. Both native and introduced species are among the most prized of American ornamentals. Plant form varies tremendously—from low, spreading shrubs to medium-sized trees. Adaptability is equally diverse, from requiring hot, dry, sandy, fast-draining soil to tolerating relatively wet, heavy, poorly drained clay. Although most hollies grow best in full sunlight, some do well in partial shade.

Bright red berries are one of the chief attractions of holly. Most individual plants bear either male or female flowers, however, and only the female produce berries—and they only upon receiving pollen from male flowers. Thus, only if plants of both sexes are grown fairly together are berries produced. A few Asian selections, like the Burford holly, will set fruit without pollination and fertilization. Wildlife, especially birds, thrive on the bounty of the fruit.

Many of the hollies have rich glossy evergreen foliage that holds appeal in itself. A few are deciduous, in late autumn exposing the heavy fruit completely. Many choice ornamental species and their cultivars have one or several spines on the margins of their leaves, though not all plants with marginal leaf spines are hollies.

Most members of the genus are highly tolerant of a wide range of growing conditions. But, typically, hollies perform best in a fertile moist, well-drained soil that is slightly acid and in full sunlight.

English Holly
Ilex aquifolium
10–20′ x 8′
Zones 6–8

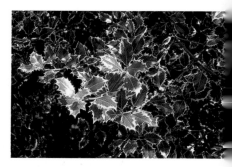

Variegated cultivar of English holly

A native of Europe, this English holly is an evergreen holly of cool climates. It possesses a dense upright, pyramidal form with lustrous green triangular leaves that have spines. The female plant produces reddish orange berries on the previous season's growth. It makes an outstanding freestanding specimen and is equally effective in mass plantings that provide screening and privacy. There are numerous cultivars, with more than fifty having cream or yellow variegation. Although the English holly is not well adapted to the Lower South, a cross of it and *I. cornuta*, the Chinese holly, in a relatively new introduction, 'Nellie R. Stevens', has given southerners a superb and very durable evergreen with glossy dark green foliage and an abundance of large red fruit. The foliage is ideal for indoor holiday decorations.

Foster's Holly
Ilex × *attenuata* 'Fosteri'
10–20′ x 6′   Zones 7–9

A cross between two fine natives, American holly and cassine holly, the Foster's holly has narrow rich dark green leaves with prominent spines on the upper half of the leaves. It is upright in form, and with advanced age it can be pruned to form a small specimen evergreen tree. It produces prominent red berries in late autumn and is one of the best hollies for cut greenery in the Lower South. The cultivar 'Savannah' is outstanding for growth and fruit production.

'Savannah' holly specimen in the city of the same name

Cassine Holly, Dahoon Holly
Ilex cassine
15–20′ x 10′   Zones 8–9

Cassine holly adapts easily to both relatively heavy, wet soil and dry soil. Its leaves are much more yellow green than the typical holly's, setting it in contrast to most other plants in the garden. The weight of its plentiful orange red berries sometimes bends the branches. A fine cultivar, 'Myrtifolia', is similar in most respects but has unusually narrow leaves.

Leaves. Far left: *deciduous holly.* Top row, left to right: *Chinese holly, convex-leaf holly, American holly.* Middle row: *Foster's holly, Japanese holly, cassine holly.* Bottom row: *yaupon, Helleri holly, rotunda holly.*

Chinese Holly
Ilex cornuta
7–9′   Zones 7–9

Not only is the Chinese holly widely planted as a large nearly tree-form evergreen but it has importance as a parent to numerous fine ornamental cultivars. The plant has lustrous leaves with very prominent sharp convex and concave spines. Three-eighths-inch orange red berries hang in heavy clusters. Among the species' most admired cultivars are 'Carrisa', 'Dazzler', 'D'Or', and 'Needlepoint', as well as 'Burfordii' and 'Rotunda', listed below. The scale insect can be very troublesome on all the Chinese hollies. Annual spraying may be necessary for control.

Burford Holly
Ilex cornuta 'Burfordii'
10–25′ x 15′   Zones 7–9

One of the first Chinese hollies to be introduced into the United States, the Burford holly can grow into a mammoth upright or oval shrub or small tree in a relatively short time. It produces lustrous cup-shaped dark blue green foliage, usually with only one spine on each leaf, at the tip. The orange red three-eighths-inch clustered berries are produced thickly enough that they can cover nearly the entire plant, concealing the evergreen foliage. Sometimes in late autumn and in winter the berries' weight bends the branches. This holly is effective as a hedge or barrier, but pruning is difficult because of the plant's size. Old specimens are often reclaimed as small accent trees. *I. cornuta* 'Burfordii Nana', the dwarf Burford holly, can itself grow to more than ten feet if not pruned. Its leaves are smaller, and it tends not to produce as many berries, which are smaller as well.

Magnificent specimens of the Burford holly in Norwood, Louisiana

Cedar waxwings enjoying the fruit of the 'Lord' holly.

Rotunda Holly
Ilex cornuta 'Rotunda'
2–5′ x 5′   Zones 7–9

With foliage very similar to that of its parent, the Chinese holly, the rotunda holly is a fast-growing mounding shrub with dense, spiny yellow green leaves. For a barrier shrub, there is probably no better choice. The stiff spines are so inescapable that maintenance can be a serious problem. The plant seldom produces berries. Another Chinese holly cultivar is 'Lord', which can become a tree thirty feet tall. It has dull green leaves without spines, and the female plant produces a large number of small orange red berries.

Japanese Hollies
Ilex crenata cultivars
2–6′ x 4′   Zones 5–9

This species comprises several popular Japanese hollies. All members of this group are extremely sensitive to soil moisture, requiring a porous, well-drained soil. They will not survive in water-logged soil. If necessary to achieve proper drainage, raise the beds in which they are planted. Usually the berries of these hollies begin green but turn black in late summer and early autumn. New growth is yellow green and turns silvery gray as it matures. Most cultivars are slow-growing in comparison with other hollies.

I. crenata 'Compacta', the dwarf Japanese holly, is a dense, compact medium-sized evergreen shrub that grows eventually to about five feet tall. Its foliage is dark blue green and similar in size and shape to that of the boxwood.

I. crenata 'Convexa', the convex-leaf Japanese holly, is a relatively tight, rounded to oval shrub to five feet tall. Its fine-textured leaves are small, oval, and dark blue green, and they have recurved margins, giving the foliage a somewhat cup-shaped appearance.

I. crenata 'Helleri', the Helleri holly, is probably the lowest-growing of all the holly species and cultivars. At maturity it seldom exceeds a height of two feet, achieving its maximum only after ten years or more. The petite dark blue green leaves are similar to the yaupon's but are smaller and have a minutely saw-toothed margin.

Deciduous Holly, Possum Haw
Ilex decidua
20′ x 15′   Zones 5–9

The deciduous holly goes virtually unnoticed until late autumn, when it drops its foliage and reveals an abundance of orange red fruit on bare gray branches. A small tree, it

Deciduous holly with bright red fruit, which remains for months

can grow almost anywhere. It is seen as a single specimen or in colonies in lowland swamps, in hedgerows, along highways, and at woodland edges. This holly can have multiple, shrublike stems or a single trunk. Only the female plant produces berries, and females are many fewer than males. The dull green leaves are thin and membranous, with toothed margins that are often ragged or damaged. An especially handsome selection is 'Longipes', which produces small hanging cherrylike berries on unusually long, two-inch, stems.

Berries and large, coarse-textured foliage of the luster-leaf holly in the Biedenharn Garden, in Monroe, Louisiana.

Unique black fruit of the native inkberry

Inkberry, Gallberry
Ilex glabra
4–8' x 5'   Zones 5–9

A native holly often found growing in large colonies in sandy, acid soil and even bogs, the inkberry has an upright irregular form. Its small gray green leaves are crowded along the stems. Berries to a third of an inch in diameter turn black in late autumn, at maturity. This holly appears to have considerably more specific requirements concerning its siting than most hollies. It is indigenous to wet, boggy areas and to pinelands and prairies. Because it spreads by stolons, that is, underground stems, there are usually several clumps forming a thicket. 'Ivory Queen' is a white-fruited cultivar growing as high as eight feet.

Luster-Leaf Holly
Ilex latifolia
15–30' x 20'   Zones 7–8/9

Producing bold, nearly exotic foliage, the luster-leaf holly is a large coarse-textured shrub that grows into a moderate-sized tree after twenty years or more. The lustrous thick, leathery evergreen leaves, to nearly seven inches long, are probably the largest on any holly grown as an ornamental.

The leaves are somewhat similar to the camellia's and rhododendron's. The dark green foliage contrasts with the clusters of large, prominent red berries nesting in the axils of the leaves on female plants. The leaves are large and widely spaced so that there is a somewhat open canopy. This holly is a parent to an extremely well accepted large-growing holly, 'Emily Bruner'. 'Mary Nell' has a pyramidal habit and spiny lustrous dark green leaves. In autumn there is a bountiful crop of large bright red berries.

Very cold hardy 'Blue Prince' Meserve hybrid holly

Meserve Hybrid Hollies
Ilex × meserveae
8–15' x 8'   Zones 4–7

The Meserve hybrid hollies are extremely cold hardy. They are crosses between the English holly and *I. regosa*. The growth habits of the cultivars vary, with many being very compact. Lustrous dark green foliage and large red or yellow fruit are characteristic. 'Blue Angel', 'Blue Boy', 'Blue Maid', 'Blue Stallion', 'China Boy', 'China Girl', and 'Golden Girl' are some cultivars currently available.

American Holly
Ilex opaca
25–40' x 25'   Zones 5–9

An evergreen tree that is a sentimental favorite over much of the eastern United States, the American holly grows in a wide range of soils, from the heavy clay at the borders of swamps and bogs to the dry, well-drained soil of rolling terrain. The dense conical form of the yellow green foliage becomes more irregular with advancing age. The short gray trunk, with stiff horizontal branches, produces leaves with anywhere from one to five spines. The female of this long-lived species produces bright red berries an eighth of an inch across in autumn. Cultivars offered in the trade may have superiorities over the parent. Among the cultivars widely sold are 'Bountiful', 'Callaway', Greenleaf', and 'Howardii'.

Classical conical form of the American holly in a Kentucky landscape.

Winterberry, Black Alder
Ilex verticillata
8–15' x 10'   Zones 4–8/9

The winterberry is esteemed for its unusually large and striking orange red berries, up to three-eighths of an inch in diameter. The berries are particularly spectacular after the foliage drops. The large upright single- or multiple-stemmed shrub produces coarse-textured light green leaves with heavy imprinted venation. Among cultivars, 'Winter Red' is one of the best.

Wintergreen

Multitude of small red fruit produced on the female yaupon tree.

Yaupon
Ilex vomitoria
10–25' x 8'   Zones 6–9

Among the most widely observed hollies in the southeastern United States, the yaupon, an upright-growing evergreen, is often seen in multistemmed colonies, in clipped hedges, or as a single specimen. The female plant produces an abundance of translucent red berries an eighth of an inch in diameter. The species' very small dark blue green leaves are thick, with saw-toothed margins. This holly does well in alkaline soil as well as in the acid soil that most other hollies prefer. *I. vomitoria* 'Pendula', the weeping yaupon, is similar but has strong drooping branches that hang close to the main trunk. It loses some of its harshly pendulous lines as it matures and becomes more irregular in form. The fruiting on the female of the weeping yaupon is as heavy as, and possibly even more picturesque than, that on the regular female yaupon.

Dwarf yaupon hedges with center circle of English boxwood at Rosedown plantation

Dwarf Yaupon
Ilex vomitoria 'Nana'
2–6' x 5'   Zones 7–9

A smaller form of the regular yaupon, the dwarf yaupon has dark blue green leaves and a dense, mounding form. One of the most dependable of all medium-sized hollies, it does not produce berries, since cuttings for propagation are generally taken from male plants. Calling it a dwarf can be misleading, for without frequent pruning it will grow to six feet or more in height. It lends itself to frequent pruning and is often used as a boxwood substitute where boxwood does not grow well. The dwarf yaupon succeeds equally well in full sunlight or considerable shade, the difference having little effect on its form or density. It will also tolerate the wet conditions that many other evergreens cannot.

Spring flowers of the starbush, with previous year's foliage.

Starbush, Florida Anise
Illicium floridanum
Illiciaceae
6–12' x 6'   Zones 8–9

The starbush is a large coarse-textured evergreen shrub that is not especially well known but is present throughout the southeastern United States. In full sunlight it takes a dense upright form, and in heavy shade, where it grows equally well, it is more open and airy. The large smooth, leathery leaves are aromatic, having an aniselike fragrance. The shrub is particularly content in naturalistic settings with deciduous trees, where soils are moist, slightly acid, and well drained. As understory growth, it produces dark maroon red many-petaled, star-shaped flowers from early spring to early summer. These are nearly two inches in diameter and are followed by thick green star-shaped fruit. The cultivar 'Alba' has white flowers. *I. parviflorum*, the Japanese anise, is similar, but it will grow into a tree

White-flowering starbush

over twenty feet high and produces yellow green flowers. *I. anisatum* produces off-white flowers and has aromatic smooth, leathery leaves to four inches long. *I. henryi*, the Henry anise, is an evergreen shrub growing to approximately twelve feet and producing leathery glossy dark green leaves up to six inches long and two inches wide. Its twenty-petaled flowers in late spring are pink- to dark crimson and to an inch and a half in diameter. This species is adapted to zones 7–9. It grows well in shade.

Indigo, Indigofera
Indigofera kirilowii
Leguminosae
2–3′ x 3′   Zones 6–9

The low-growing "half shrub" that the indigo is has leaning thin, twiggy stems and leaves composed of many tiny yellow green leaflets. Grown primarily for its dainty wisteria-like pendulous rosy pink spring flowers, it seldom stays exactly where it is planted but spreads by underground stems. Its airy look is welcome among dark green ground covers, where both the summer foliage and the light tan-colored deciduous stems of winter contrast pleasingly with the background planting. Indigo favors a moist, well-drained soil heavily fortified with organic matter. It grows well in morning sunlight and partial shade during the remainder of the day.

Delicate, fine-textured foliage and wisteria-like flowers of the indigo

Mass planting of the indigo, a tall, loose-growing deciduous ground cover

THE IRISES

Iridaceae

The irises are valued as garden perennials. Varying within the genus in foliage, flowers, and cultural requirements, they are grown for the most part because of their attractive flowers atop thick stalks. Still, the foliage of many provides excellent lasting greenery in herbaceous plantings. Most form clumps with relatively stiff sword-shaped leaves varying in height from a few inches to nearly five feet. In the main, irises grow best in well-drained soil and flower best in full morning sunlight. Overfertile soil will produce heavy foliage at the expense of flowers. Light applications of fertilizer each year to plants in sandy, infertile soil seem to yield the best results.

Dutch iris

Japanese iris

Japanese Iris
Iris ensata (kaempferi)
2′ x 2′   Zones 4–8

The Japanese iris is an import that produces branched flowering stems and sword-shaped leaves with thick midribs. Broad, flat flowers to six inches across come in purple, blue, and lavender pink, with prominent darker veins. This iris grows best in a moist acid soil heavily fortified with organic matter.

Dutch Iris
Iris × hollandica
2′ x 1′   Zones 6–8

The Dutch iris produces several solitary flowers on tall stalks originating from the center of soft silvery gray reed-like leaves. Among popular colors are lavender, blue, dark purple, white, yellow, and bronze. There are also bicolors. Under ideal conditions, the plant will multiply and mass in

Bearded Iris
Iris × germanica
15–18″   Zones 3–9

The bearded iris is likely the most popular iris grown in the United States. Clumps of its relatively short silvery blue stiff, fan-shaped leaves hold interest in the herbaceous garden from spring to fall. Plantings of "white flags" in old gardens have sometimes endured for more than a century. Today there are exotic large-flowering types in white, yellow, blue, and purple, and in mixed colors. This iris grows well in the kind of soil that most irises prefer. Among the new cultivars are "rebloomers," plants that bloom in spring, summer, and fall.

Bearded iris in New York's Central Park

beds with well-drained soil in morning sunlight. In view of the relatively low cost of bulbs, however, this iris is often planted only for one season's color and not kept in place from year to year. The foliage is not the major asset it is with many of the other members of the genus.

Bog planting of Louisiana irises

Close-up of Louisiana iris flowers.

Louisiana Iris
Iris—Louisiana hybrids
3′   Zones 6–9

Louisiana iris is the name given to several naturally occurring iris species and some introduced hybrids of species that include *I. fulva*, *I. brevicaulis*, *I. nelsonii*, and *I. giganticaerulea*. They constitute the foundation for hundreds of selections. Stalks with four to eight flowers emerge from clumps of sword-shaped leaves two to four feet tall. The flowers may be rust red, blue, white, yellow, or purple, in many shades. Members of the group tend to "walk" in a bed and are difficult to confine. They grow in a wide range of soil, from wet, boggy, and clayey to moist and well drained. For best performance, they should receive direct sunlight for several hours a day.

Siberian iris

Yellow Flag
Iris pseudacorus
4′   Zones 5–8

One of the tallest-growing irises, the yellow flag forms heavy, massive clumps of evergreen sword-shaped leaves with thick midribs. In early spring it produces yellow flowers up to four inches across on stalks slightly taller than the leaves. It adapts readily to almost any soil, to full sunlight or shade. This iris is so aggressive and multiplies so rapidly that portions have to be removed to keep plants within bounds. It makes an excellent specimen in water gardens and in plantings at the edge of water.

Siberian Iris
Iris sibirica
2–3′ x 2′   Zones 3–8

The Siberian iris is an especially good, long-lived evergreen perennial. It produces relatively fine-textured leaves to only about a half inch wide. Heavy vase-shaped clumps of crisp, refined foliage provide a strong contrast to most other garden greenery. Large, prominent flowers in purple, blue, white, and violet appear in late spring. There are hundreds of cultivars available, with new introductions each year.

Yellow flag, easily grown and a rapid spreader

Drooping panicles of the Virginia willow.

Virginia Willow
Itea virginica
Saxifragaceae
4–8' x 4'   Zones 7–9

The Virginia willow is an open, airy native deciduous shrub widely present in the southeastern United States in lowland swamps and floodplains and along streams. Multistemmed and upright in form, it produces white flowers in compact, four-inch drooping to upright racemes in late spring. Not normally attractive by itself, the shrub can contribute to larger plantings during its fairly long flowering period. The Virginia willow is more floriferous in full sunlight but will tolerate some shade. It grows in soils from wet to relatively dry.

Ixora
Ixora coccinea
Rubiaceae
2–5' x 3'   Zone 10

An everblooming tropical, the ixora has dense flat clusters of tubular flowers in brilliant shades of red, orange, yellow, yellow orange, and white. In warm, frost-free climates, the upright-growing evergreen shrub is favored for hedge plantings and as an accent plant in a container. Flowering is nearly continuous year round, but the heaviest flowering is in summer. The shrub grows and blooms best in sandy, well-drained soils in full sunlight. Because it is tolerant of salt spray, it can be placed close to coastal waters.

Ixora, which flowers year-round in subtropical climates

Florida Jasmine
Jasminum floridum
Oleaceae
3–4' x 5'   Zones 8–9

The Florida jasmine is a very dependable medium-sized evergreen shrub. Unlike many shrubs promoted as medium-sized, which eventually grow large and require special pruning, this one stays relatively low-mounding for many years. In spring, fragrant golden yellow star-shaped flowers appear on long arching stems with leaves of three to five leaflets. Despite being called an evergreen, the plant will drop most of its foliage in harsh winters. It performs best in a well-drained soil and full sunlight. Its attractions are most visible when it is planted in a raised bed or atop a retaining wall, where the stems can drape.

Florida jasmine's small yellow flowers, lasting for an extended period in spring.

Primrose Jasmine
Jasminum mesnyi
8–15' x 15'   Zones 7–9

Primrose jasmine flowers

The primrose jasmine, a rapid-growing evergreen shrub of rigid, very dense mounding habit, has long arching stems with dull green compound leaves. Starting in early spring and continuing into early summer, bright yellow flowers to nearly two inches across bloom along the four-angled branches. This jasmine is fine for growing on slopes and embankments to provide soil stabilization where mainte-

Primrose jasmine cascading over a rock formation (right

Fragrant pink windmill jasmine flowers

nance is difficult. The shrub is also attractive where the pendulous branches can spill over a wall. *J. nudiflorum,* the winter jasmine, is similar but deciduous. It grows to ten feet or more, and yellow flowers appear before the foliage.

Windmill Jasmine
Jasminum nitidum
6′   Zones 9–10

A handsome semitropical evergreen vine or shrub, the windmill jasmine comes from the South Pacific. Its fragrant white starlike flowers can have a blush on the underside of the petals and the tubular base. Wiry stems support thick, leathery leaves to three inches long. The greatest show of flowers is in spring, but the plant blooms intermittently throughout the year.

Black Walnut
Juglans nigra
Juglandaceae
40–50′ x 35′   Zones 4–9

A large, bold enduring deciduous tree with an oval to rounded canopy, the black walnut is widely adapted in the United States. Large leaves of up to twenty dull green leaflets turn yellow in autumn. The deeply furrowed bark is dark charcoal-colored and is particularly interesting in winter, when the tree is bare. Large furrowed nuts, sometimes more than two inches in diameter, contain delicious edible kernels within a thick husk. The walnut's natural habitat combines deep fertile, well-drained slightly alkaline to neutral soil and full sunlight.

Black walnut foliage

THE JUNIPERS

Cupressaceae

Although there is considerable diversity of form, foliage, and color within the large and complex genus of the junipers, its species and cultivars share several qualities. The nicely aromatic foliage is of one of two types—either flared and needlelike or overlapping and scalelike. The bark on most junipers shreds into thin pieces, usually revealing an orange underbark. But the foliage can range from somewhat lustrous green to dull silvery gray, and several selections have variegated foliage. There is also a broad range in growth habit, from sprawling and prostrate to narrow and columnar. Junipers perform best in relatively dry, well-drained sandy soil and full sunlight, although they tolerate other conditions. They perform poorly in constantly wet soil and in full shade. Twig blight, cedar rust (apple rust), bagworms, and spider mites are the most troublesome pests for the junipers.

Foliage and fruit of the white cedar

Simpson

White Cedar, Ashe Cedar

Juniperus ashei
15–20′ x 12′   Zones 7–9

The white cedar, a juniper with dull green foliage, can grow under adverse conditions, especially in very dry thin, infertile limestone soil and in hot sun. The female plant produces glaucous blue quarter-inch fruit that a large variety of birds consume in its native western habitat. This juniper grows relatively fast under the harshest of conditions. It will eventually form evergreen thickets.

Chinese Junipers

Juniperus chinensis **cultivars**
Sizes dependent on cultivars
Approximately zones 5/6–9

The Chinese junipers cannot tolerate very cold temperatures nor extremely hot, humid conditions. Nor do they do well in wet soil.

Common Pfitzer juniper

Blue-vase juniper, successful in hot, dry landscapes

116

J. chinensis 'Glauca', the blue-vase juniper, with a broad vase form, reaches a height of eight or ten feet and has blue green scalelike foliage.

J. chinensis 'Hetzii', the Hetzii juniper, is a large cultivar that grows quickly to nearly twenty feet and possesses dull green to silvery-colored scalelike leaves.

J. chinensis 'Pfitzerana', the Pfitzer juniper, is likely the most popular juniper for ornamental use and the one that has been put to such use the longest. It has a wide-spreading form with strong horizontal branches. The shrub can span fifteen feet or more while rising no more than five feet. It is long-lived and develops a picturesque, bonsailike form after twenty or so years of growth. Because of its strong horizontal growth pattern, this juniper is difficult to keep in bounds by pruning.

J. chinensis 'Mint Julep' is similar to the Pfitzer juniper, with a fountainlike form and mint green leaves.

J. chinensis 'Sea Spray', is an excellent spreading ground cover attaining a height no greater than a foot. It is reported to be one of the best junipers for large ground-cover plantings.

Shore juniper spilling from wall planter

Shore Juniper
Juniperus conferta
18″ x 4′   Zones 5–9

The spiny-looking foliage of the shore juniper is deceiving, the needlelike protrusions being surprisingly soft to the touch. The plant is one of the most popular ground covers for environments that are stressful because they are hot, dry, and sunny. The low, creeping form, with many nearly vertical soft stems, is ideal for slopes, planters, and other raised settings. The cultivar 'Blue Pacific' is extremely compact and has blue green foliage. 'Emerald Green' also has blue green leaves but grows only about a foot tall.

'Bar Harbor' creeping juniper

Creeping Junipers
Juniperus horizontalis cultivars
Sizes dependent on cultivars
Approximately zones 4–8

The creeping junipers are quite hardy, growing reasonably well as far north as zone 4 and as far south as zone 8. Heights seldom exceed two feet, but spreads may extend beyond ten feet. There are a number of proven selections.

J. horizontalis 'Bar Harbor' is a low, spreading plant only about a foot tall but spreading to over six feet. It has silvery blue foliage that turns a beautiful purple in winter.

J. horizontalis 'Douglasii', the Waukegan juniper, has steel blue foliage that turns purplish in cold climates. It grows to approximately fifteen inches, with a spread of six feet.

J. horizontalis 'Plumosa' has a dense, spreading habit. It grows about eighteen inches tall, with a spread of up to eight feet. The blue green foliage turns purplish in cold weather.

J. horizontalis 'Procumbens' has a blue green color, grows approximately six inches tall, and has a spread of more than ten feet, but it is somewhat slow-growing.

J. horizontalis 'Wiltoni', the blue rug juniper, has silvery blue foliage that becomes purple green in winter. It too grows only to about six inches, with a spread of over six feet.

Blue rug juniper, adaptable to a wide range of climates

In a related species, *J. procumbens* 'Nana' forms a compact mat with branches on top of one another. It may spread to ten or twelve feet in time.

Dwarf Japanese garden juniper

Cedars
Juniperus virginiana
Sizes dependent on cultivars
Zones 3–9

Chosen for their dense upright growth, cedars are some of the most preferred long-lived conifers. They grow widely throughout the United States, from the very cold Northeast to zone 9 in the South. Most are relatively slow-growing. The foliage can be needlelike on young growth and predominantly scalelike on older specimens. Cedars produce bluish berrylike fruit on female plants in fall and winter. They will tolerate a wide range of soils, from moderately

Red cedar on the Natchez Trace near Jackson, Mississippi

acid to very alkaline, even limestone. As they grow older, their youthful conical forms become more irregular and open, with picturesque silhouettes.

Juniperus virginiana, the eastern red cedar, is a favorite among the cedars. Native to a huge area of the country, the heavy conical tree grows to a height of thirty to forty feet and a spread of twenty feet. The dense dull green foliage makes it handsome as an accent "Christmas tree" specimen and equally beautiful in mass plantings. As a pioneer species, it is quick to enter cutover lands, appear in fencerows and hedgerows, and grow wherever there is

Canaert juniper as a specimen tree

open land with relatively dry alkaline to slightly acid soil. This grand cedar has given rise to several extremely popular cultivars. 'Canaertii', the canaert juniper, is a picturesque conical tree with strong upward-pointed sections of emerald green foliage; 'Glauca', the silver red cedar, is a dense pyramidal to

Silver red cedar with its distinctive silver gray foliage

conical tree that becomes more open and irregular with age. Its silvery gray foliage creates a strong contrast with most other foliage. 'Burkii' is a fast-growing cedar to thirty feet tall with soft blue green foliage. 'Cupressifolia', with yellow green foliage, is a dense-branching pyramidal tree growing to thirty feet.

Shrimp plant, which blooms for six or more months each year.

Shrimp Plant
Justicia brandegeana
Acanthaceae
3' x 3'   Zones 9–10

A perennial adapted to outdoor culture in the Lower South, the shrimp plant is a Mexican native. It provides nectar for hummingbirds, which feed from one-inch or larger white tubular flowers appearing from late spring into autumn. The bracts around the flowers are three-quarters of an inch long and are borne on dense two- to three-inch spikes resembling a shrimp in shape. Grow this plant where it receives several hours of sunlight, preferably in the morning. Moist, well-drained soils are required for best performance. Mulch during winter, and cut plants back to within a few inches of the ground each spring, just as growth begins.

Brazilian plume, a plant flowering well in sun or shade

Brazilian Plume
Justicia carnea
3' x 3'   Zones 9–10

Although the Brazilian plume is hardy only where temperatures seldom drop below freezing, the evergreen perennial is a summer bedding plant in many parts of the country. It has showy pink flowers during the warm months of spring, summer, and early fall. The funnel-shaped flowers are arranged in short, dense pineapple-shaped terminal clusters. For best performance, provide the plant with a moist, well-drained soil and full sunlight or partial shade. It does surprisingly well when in light shade for most of the day. The plant has large heavily veined medium green leaves that are up to three inches long and half as wide.

Mountain Laurel
Kalmia latifolia
Ericaceae
5' x 10'   Zones 4–9

Native from the Gulf of Mexico to Canada, the mountain laurel is one of the most beautiful and long-lived of flowering evergreen shrubs. The state flower of Connecticut and Pennsylvania, it is highly valued for its masses of dark pink buds opening to off-white to pink crinkle-edged flowers. The six-inch flower clusters bring color and elegance to the

Flowers of the mountain laurel

garden some time between March to June, depending on location. The flower color of cultivars varies from pure white to rose red. The leathery foliage is a lustrous dark green with red petioles. To grow this plant successfully, a well-drained acid soil and partial shade are required. Properly sited and with good cultural practices, the mountain laurel can enhance a garden for a lifetime.

Japanese Rose
Kerria japonica 'Pleniflora'
Rosaceae
3–6' x 5–9'   Zones 5–8

The Japanese rose performs well in shade and even better in full sunlight. It grows in most garden soils that are well drained. Mounding to broad-spreading clumps with upright-arching stems remain green all year. Flowering is most profuse in colder climates, but it will bloom fairly well in warmer areas. Bright yellow carnation-like double flowers to two inches across on long, gangly stems are a strong garden accent in midspring. Flowering is sporadic in summer, but a moderately heavy bloom is not uncommon in fall in some locations. After the spring bloom, remove a third of the old canes at or near ground level to maintain a long-lived specimen with high vigor. 'Shannon' is a recent introduction with large bright yellow single flowers.

Red-Hot Pokers
Kniphofia hybrids
Liliaceae
2–4' x 3'   Zones 6–8

A grasslike perennial, the red-hot poker is best adapted to sunny sites with well-drained soil. The keeled silvery gray leaves nearly three feet long and an inch wide form a rosette from which stiff, erect pokerlike flowering stems rise. Dense clusters of tubular florets appear in summer and fall. The plant cannot tolerate wet soil or a humid climate. It draws attention because of its exotic flowers, which in

Mammoth mass of the Japanese rose

the cultivars come in a wide assortment of colors, including yellow, apricot, orange, and orange red, as well as bicolors.

Clump of red-hot pokers in a herbaceous border

Goldenrain Tree
Koelreuteria bipinnata
Sapindaceae
30' x 25'   Zones 9–10

The autumn-flowering goldenrain tree, from China and Korea, grows well in a wide variety of loose, well-drained soils, provided that winter temperatures are mild. The form of the tree runs from broad oval to nearly flat topped. Large branched terminal panicles of intense yellow flowers are borne above the foliage in September and early October. The flowers drop like rain, as the name suggests. Papery oval sacs, which are seedpods, appear soon after flowering and persist through the winter, at first pink, then salmon, and finally brown. The deciduous tree is relatively short-lived because of its susceptibility to cold damage and insect pests such as scale and borers. This species is sometimes listed as *K. elegans* 'Formosana'.

Fruit of a goldenrain tree growing in the Deep South

Panicled Goldenrain Tree
Koelreuteria paniculata
30' x 25'   Zones 5–9

The most hardy rain tree, the panicled goldenrain tree, can be grown over most of the United States. It is differentiated from *K. bipinnata* in that the leaves are pinnately compound instead of bipinnately compound. Flower color is the same in both species, but flowering occurs in the panicled goldenrain tree some time from May to July, depending on location. The oval seedpods on this species are initially green, turning brown as they mature. Soil requirements are similar for both species, and they grow best in full sun.

Beauty Bush
Kolkwitzia amabilis
Caprifoliaceae
6–15' x 8'
Zones 5/6–9

Beauty bush flowers

One of the most reliable spring-flowering shrubs for cold climates is the beauty bush. A native of China, this deciduous plant is adapted to a wide range of soils, even those that are fairly dry. The upright to vase-shaped shrub has ascending branches that may bend to the ground. In early summer, cascades of light pink bell-shaped flowers blanket

Flowers of the panicled goldenrain tree, well adapted to cold climates.

the plant. The gray brown exfoliating bark on older plants gives the shrub a special appeal in winter. Older stems should be cut to the ground as soon as blooming is over, to encourage new growth and plant rejuvenation.

Golden Chain Tree
Laburnum × *watereri*
Fabaceae (Leguminosae)
12–15′ x 9–12′   Zones 5–7

Rich yellow flowers borne on racemes a foot and a half to two feet long cascade beneath the canopy of the golden chain tree in late spring, inviting the surmise that it might be a yellow tree wisteria. Smooth bright green bark and cloverlike compound leaves contribute seasonal

Large mass of beauty bush in Hershey, Pennsylvania

interest. The tree's small size makes it a good choice for gardens with limited space, so long as it is not crowded by other plants. Select a sheltered growing position that affords afternoon shade and has well-drained soil. There are a number of cultivars, of which 'Vossii' is the most popular.

Crape Myrtle
Lagerstroemia indica
Lythraceae
15–25′ x 12′   Zones 7–9

One of the truly great, all-time favorite small flowering trees of the South is the crape myrtle. Besides having marvelous flowering qualities, it possesses a handsome sculptural, muscular trunk, smooth, satin-textured buff-colored bark, and striking autumn foliage. Prominent terminal panicles of fringed or crinkled crepelike flowers appear throughout the summer months in white, pink, purple, red, or bicolors. The tree is tolerant of a wide range of soils, from moderately moist to dry. To flower well, it must have full sunlight for most of the day. Because of insensitive pruning, many never achieve their full aesthetic potential. A few popular cultivars from the scores offered today are 'Near East', with clear flesh pink flowers; 'Dallas Red', with deep red flowers; 'Natchez', with white flowers; 'Basham's Party Pink', with delicate

Specimen golden chain tree

Golden chain tree growing on an arbor

Mature crape myrtle trees in winter

Same planting in summer

Interesting bark on 'Natchez' crape myrtle.

lavender pink flowers; 'Watermelon Red', with rosy red flowers; 'Potomac', with clear pink flowers; 'Peppermint Lace', with red-and-white flowers; 'Mardi Gras', with purple flowers; 'Pink Lace', with clear pink flowers; 'Tuscarora', with dark coral pink flowers; and 'Muskogee', with light orchid flowers. *L. fauriei* is a tall, fast-growing

Kleiner

Crape myrtle flowers. Center: *'William Toovey' (15–20' tall), the most common of the 'Watermelon Red' selections. Clockwise, beginning with white flowers at lower left: 'Natchez' (20'), 'Griffin' (12'), 'Basham's Party Pink' (18'), 'Byers Red' (25'), 'Near East' (15'), 'Tuscarora' (18'), 'Apalachee' (15'), 'Miami' (18'), 'Acoma' (small, weeping), 'Regal Red' (18'), 'Cotton Candy' (12'), 'Carolina Beauty' (20'), 'Lipan' (12'), 'Peppermint Lace' (15'), 'Cordon Bleu' (dwarf).*

multiple-trunked white-flowering crape myrtle with large leaves and beautiful reddish brown to cinnamon-colored exfoliating bark.

'Watermelon Red' crape myrtle

Lamium, Beacon Silver
Lamium maculatum
Lamiaceae
6–8″   Zones 3–9

The silvery white leaves, edged in green, of the lamium, an increasingly favored ground cover, stand out particularly in dark, shady places. Opposite leaves are borne on square stems. Mauve pink hooded flowers appear from spring through summer. The plant is a vigorous grower that can be used to cover relatively large areas, but it is equally effective in small plantings. Its cascading

'Beacon Silver' lamium as a ground cover

growth habit suits it to hanging baskets and planters. Provide a moist, well-drained soil. 'Beacon Silver' is probably the most widely grown cultivar.

Lantana
Lantana camara
Verbenaceae
2–3' x 6'   Zones 8–10

A popular flowering, somewhat woody perennial, the lantana and its many new cultivars can be seen throughout its zones of adaptation during the hot summer months. Verbena-like flowers appear when small plants are set in early spring, and they do not cease flowering until cold weather arrives, though there are cycles when flowering is lighter. The plant can tolerate extremely harsh growing conditions in full sunlight and relatively dry soil, but it will not perform well in heavy, wet soil and shade. Low-mounding cultivars include 'New Gold', with bright yellow flowers; 'Lemon Drop', with yellow flowers; and 'Silver Mound', with white flowers. Upright-mounding cultivars include 'Irene', with magenta-and-yellow flowers; 'Dallas Red', with rich red flowers; and 'Christine', with pink flow-

'New Gold' lantana

Container of 'Dallas Red' lantana

ers. Flowers of a few of the new selections are sterile. Because these selections do not produce berries, they stay in flower continuously during the summer months, especially with light pruning.

Trailing Lantana
Lantana montevidensis
3' x 6'   Zones 8–10

The trailing lantana is an old garden favorite. The lilac to light lavender verbena-like flowers and aromatic foliage are produced on long trailing, vinelike stems that eventually form a broad, mounding shrub if not pruned. Flowering is cyclical during summer. Frequent tip pruning can induce more continuous flowering from early summer until frost. The plant grows in thin, dry soil and should have full sunlight for best performance, but it will tolerate a wide range of growing conditions. Late winter grooming is necessary in areas where the plant is not killed by freezes. Otherwise it becomes very untidy.

European Larch
Larix decidua
Pinaceae
50–75' x 25'   Zones 2–7

The European larch is one of few deciduous conifers. The large and imposing tree, which thrives in colder regions, has broad-spreading branches and needle-shaped leaves clustered on spurs of the previous season's growth. The upright conical form of the young tree becomes more irregular with time. This tree grows best in well-drained soil where there is full sunlight, though it is tolerant of a fairly wide range of soils and growing conditions. The cultivar 'Pendulum' has strong draping branches; 'Fastigiata' is upright-growing with a columnar form somewhat similar to the lombardy

Trailing lantana overflowing a retaining wall

European larch planted around 1816 by Thomas Jefferson when chinaberry trees died on the west lawn at Monticello.

125

Eastern larch in Duluth

poplar's. *L. laricina,* the eastern larch, which grows in zones 1–4, has light blue green foliage and an eighty-foot height and thirty-foot spread.

Laurel, Bay, Sweet Bay
Laurus nobilis
Lauraceae
10–30′ x 15′   Zones 7–9

The laurel, a dense upright-growing evergreen shrub to small tree with thick, brittle olive green leaves, has a rich history. The foliage was used to make crowns for the conquering heroes of ancient Greece and Rome. Today it is the bay leaf used in cooking. The plant also yields an oil for medicines and perfumes. This species is slow-growing. Because of its bold, crisp foliage, it is a popular choice for a small topiary tree in a container. Tub specimens grace the entrances of posh clubs, hotels, and office buildings. The plant grows in partial shade or full sunlight and in a porous, well-drained soil.

Laurel, the leaf of which is the bay leaf of cooking.

English Lavender
Lavandula angustifolia
Labiatae
3′ x 4′   Zones 5–9

English lavender, the true lavender, has dusky blue violet flowers borne on eight-inch spikes in

English lavender

summer. The plant grows into a rounded mound and has silvery gray foliage. It is grown for its fragrance, and sachets filled with it are put among linens and such to give them a delightful smell. It likes a well-drained soil and performs best in a raised bed. Plant lavender in full sunlight, and in masses or as perennial background hedging.

Old-fashioned Shasta daisies, a popular spring-flowering perennial

Shasta Daisy
Leucanthemum × superbum (Chrysanthemum × superbum)
Asteraceae (Compositae)
3′   Zones 5–9

The Shasta daisy is an excellent perennial for the sunny, well-drained garden. White two- to four-inch daisylike flowers with yellow centers appear from midspring through early summer. The permanent foliage is a dense low mass. Floral stalks extend fifteen to eighteen inches above the coarsely toothed foliage. This daisy is fine in a single clump or in a mass, ground-cover planting. Dig and divide the clump each fall or every second fall. Root rots, caused by fungi, can be a serious problem when the plant is in a poorly drained soil. Double-flowering types do best in light shade. 'Polaris' grows to about twenty-eight inches and has large flowers up to seven inches across. Other large-flowering cultivars include 'Giant Single' and 'Alaska'. Popular among the double-flowering types are 'Marconi' and 'White Swan'. 'Little Miss Muffet' is a dwarf cultivar with semi-double flowers.

Snowflake, Snowdrop
Leucojum aestivum (vernum)
Amaryllidaceae
12″ x 12″   Zones 4–9

The snowflake is one of the nice surprises among early-spring-flowering bulbs. Stalks of nodding white bell-shaped flowers with green splotches rise from clumps of narrow, strap-shaped glossy emerald green leaves. This bulb can stay put for fifty years or more. In many restoration projects, snowdrops have helped disclose garden paths and layout many years after the garden has been abandoned. This is one of the best bulbs for naturalizing. Very tolerant of a wide range of growing conditions, it grows best in a well-drained soil and full sunlight or partial shade. If you want to dig and divide old clumps of bulbs, wait until the foliage begins to die in summer.

Texas Sage
Leucophyllum frutescens
Scrophulariaceae
5–10′ x 6′   Zones 8–9

Texas sage in a Houston garden

A plant of hot, dry western landscapes, the Texas sage has its feltlike silver foliage and an abundance of small rosy lavender flowers. Sometimes referred to as the barometer plant, the large, irregular shrub times its flowering close to a period of rain. The shrub thrives in very dry, sandy soils and full sunlight. It is intolerant of the wet, humid conditions of the South, though it performs reasonably well in coastal plantings where the soil is predominantly sand. It is an excellent choice for xeriscapes.

Snowflakes, a spring-flowering bulb reliable nationwide

Leucothoe species known also as fetterbush

Foliage on the drooping leucothoe

form, it has tall, erect multiple stems that form a tight cluster before they flare out at the top into an umbrella-like canopy. Thick, leathery yellow green leaves cover the arching branches. In spring the stems bear white flowers similar to lilies of the valley. The shrub combines well with natives in naturalistic settings but is also effective as a large specimen in other planting schemes. It grows and flowers amazingly well in shade as well as in full sunlight. Its soil should be well drained. Periodic pruning is needed to remove old, nonproductive stems from within the center of the plant and to keep an untidy appearance from developing over the years.

Leucothoe, Fetterbush
Leucothoe axillaris
Ericaceae
2–4′ x 5′   Zones 5–9

This leucothoe, a low-mounding, spreading evergreen shrub native to the Southeast, has graceful arching, recurved branches. Young copper-colored spring leaves turn leathery with slightly rolled margins at maturity. Small white nodding flowers with constricted midsections resemble lilies of the valley and appear in late spring on one side of the zigzag stems under the foliage. A relatively slow-growing native, the plant has many attractions and should be used at close range so the seasonal changes and fine details can be appreciated. *L. fontanesiana (catesbaei),* the drooping leucothoe, is similar but grows to five feet with arching branches and a fountain-like form. Its white flowers are produced under pointed leaves in three-inch axillary racemes in late spring.

Leucothoe
Leucothoe populifolia (Agarista populifolia)
8–12′ x 6′   Zones 8–9

This leucothoe is a relatively new introduction among large evergreen shrubs. Unusual in

Gayfeather's blooms of summer and autumn

Fragrant white flowers resembling lilies of the valley, borne on the underside of the arching branches of this leucothoe.

Gayfeather, Blazing Star
Liatris spicata
Asteraceae (Compositae)
2–3′ x 2′   Zones 3–9

The gayfeather is a popular perennial for the herbaceous flower garden because of its tall, spiky stems of violet, lavender, lavender pink, and white flowers that appear from summer into autumn. The plant is best adapted to a relatively dry, well-drained soil and full sunlight. Because of the heavy flower heads, especially among some of the new cultivars, staking may be necessary.

Unusual rounded leaves of the ligularia

Ligularia, Kaempfer Goldenray
Ligularia tussilaginea
Asteraceae (Compositae)
15″ x 18″   Zones 8–10

A not especially well known perennial but always an impressive one in the shade garden, ligularia produces a mounding mass of large long-stemmed, nearly round leaves. Grown primarily for its distinctive bold foliage, it mounts a surprise in late autumn: clusters of attractive bright yellow asterlike flowers on tall stalks extending

well above the basal foliage. Handsome as a garden detail, it grows best in moist, well-drained soil that has been heavily fortified with organic matter. It tolerates morning sun but should be in partial shade during the heat of the day or the foliage will wilt badly. The cultivar 'Aureomaculata', the leopard plant, has green leaves with prominent yellow splotches; 'Argentea-Flacous' produces green leaves with creamy white spots. Both are well adapted to the South. 'The Rocket', a selection better adapted to the North, produces mounds of beautiful purplish leaves to eight inches across and flower spikes to three feet tall.

Wax-Leaf Ligustrum
Ligustrum japonicum
Oleaceae
10–20′ x 15′   Zones 7–9

The wax-leaf ligustrum, a large, dense upright-growing evergreen shrub or small tree produces leathery glossy green leaves. There is no hedge planting that provides privacy faster. It is adapted to most soils, provided that they are well drained, but is susceptible to root rot when grown

Wax-leaf ligustrum clipped as a hedge, with a specimen sago palm.

Wax-leaf ligustrum, scattering pollen that excites allergies

in wet, poorly drained soil. As a hedge, the plant is effective clipped or unclipped. It is sold as multiple-trunked "standards." Some people are very allergic to the pollen the terminal panicles of heavily scented white flowers produce in spring, when the plant is in bloom. 'Rotundifolium', the curly-leaf ligustrum, is a selection with twisted leaves. The cultivars 'Howard' and 'Frazieri' produce golden yellow variegated foliage. 'Jack Frost' has glossy green leaves with creamy white margins.

Fruit of the tree ligustrum

Tree Ligustrum
Ligustrum lucidum
20–30' x 20'   Zones 8–10

The tree ligustrum, with flat dull green leaves, is a prolific self-seeder and will grow six feet or more in a single season. It volunteers wherever birds leave droppings containing seeds. It is often a nuisance, because as a pioneer species, it is quick to appear in open fields, abandoned lots, and other places where maintenance lags. The plant is tolerant of most growing conditions, from wet to very dry soil, and from full sunlight to fairly heavy shade. The mature specimen produces grapelike clusters of dark blue berries at the end of its branches. An old plant with heavy berry set will have a weeping form in late autumn. Because of the tree's shallow, competitive root system, few plants will grow beneath its canopy.

Chinese Privet
Ligustrum sinense
10–20' x 20'   Zones 6–10

The Chinese privet, a fast-growing introduction from China many years ago, has escaped cultivation to become one of the most common invasive, volunteer plants in the United States, especially in the South. Land left untended for as little as a year can become engulfed with thickets of this privet. There is virtually no landscape safe from invasion, because birds drop seeds everywhere. Although

Clipped privet hedge in a Louisiana Creole garden, with a pineapple prominently displayed as a sign of hospitality

Variegated Chinese privet, commonly planted for accent and contrast

in the morning. Under ideal conditions, the bulbs multiply and clumps can be divided for propagation. There are scores of hybrids available for sale. Plant bulbs in the autumn. Most should go behind other plants, since they grow tall and may need staking when their heavy flower heads form.

Spicebush in fruit

volunteer plantings make good habitats and food sources for birds and other wildlife, their growth is a nuisance in most places. There are few soils and exposures in which the plant will not grow. This semievergreen ligustrum produces a mass of white flowers in spring and a huge crop of black berries every fall. The selection 'Variegatum', the variegated Chinese privet, is similar but has creamy white foliage, does not grow as large or as rapidly, and generally does not produce berries. It is a popular and highly visible plant in southern gardens.

Spicebush
Lindera benzoin
Lauraceae
6–12′ x 6′   Zones 4–8

The spicebush is a loose, broad-spreading irregular-growing native deciduous shrub with horizontal branches. Although found over a wide area, it is not abundant. Often it grows at moist woodland edges. Small yellow green spring flowers of the moderately slow-growing shrub are produced in the axils of leaves on female plants and are followed by brilliant scarlet oval berries in late summer and early autumn. Although normally part of naturalistic settings, the shrub, with its picturesque form, beautiful berries, and yellow autumn foliage, should be used more frequently elsewhere in the landscape. Its seeds are an excellent high-fat food source for migratory birds.

Garden Lilies
Lilium species
Liliaceae
2–5′   Zones 5–9

The hardy perennial garden lilies are favorites among summer-flowering bulbs. Tall-stalked with crowded leaves along erect stems, they produce beautiful bell-shaped flowers in many colors, including red, rosy pink, yellow, white, and orange. Many have extremely colorful markings. They do best in cooler regions and must have well-drained soil and full sunlight for most of the day, or at least

Royal lily in the Chicago Botanic Garden

American Sweet Gum
Liquidambar styraciflua
Hamamelidaceae
50–100′ x 30′   Zones 5–9

The American sweet gum is a native deciduous tree present over much of the United States. It possesses a narrow pyramidal form when young, but this becomes more irregular as the tree ages. Not particular about where it grows, it tolerates soils from dry and infertile to heavy and moist. It is a pioneer species, appearing in open fields and clearcut land as well as being a ready volunteer in carefully maintained landscapes. The tree grows fast. It produce maplelike leaves that turn brilliant shades of reddish purple to reddish yellow in fall. The seed-bearing structures, which are hard, prickly balls that drop in autumn and winter, are a nuisance in the landscape. The tree is one of few that will return to a desirable form after being topped. The cultivar 'Rotundiloba' is a fruitless selection with outstanding autumn color. *L. formosana*, the Formosan gum, is upright-growing with three-lobed maplelike leaves and brilliant autumn color; it does not produce gum balls.

American sweet gums as lawn specimens.

American sweet gum's foliage in autumn.

Tulip Tree, Yellow Poplar
Liriodendron tulipifera
Magnoliaceae
60–75′ x 35′   Zones 4/5–9

A highly popular large long-lived deciduous tree occurring over a wide area of the United States, the tulip tree has an erect narrow oval to pyramidal form. The large, broad coarse-textured leaves are

Tulip tree flower

Tulip tree foliage

in the shape of a tulip. They are bright green during the summer and turn yellow in autumn. The tree performs best in a fertile, moist slightly acid soil, but it cannot tolerate a high water table. When roots hit the water, the tree dies. Reserve the tree for a space that can handle its large size and the enormous quantity of leaves it drops. As with most fast-growing trees, the wood is somewhat brittle and subject to wind damage. Aphids attack the leaves, causing a sticky substance to fall on objects below the canopy. Leaf drop occurs when infestations are heavy.

Liriope
Liriope muscari
Liliaceae
12–18″   Zones 6–9

Liriope is one of the most popular and durable border and ground-cover plants in the southern United States. Adapted to a wide range of growing condi-

Mass planting of liriope at the Hermitage, an antebellum house in Ascension Parish, Louisiana.

tions, it grows best in a moist, well-drained slightly acid soil. Although it will survive in full sunlight, the quality of the foliage is much better if plants are shaded during the middle of the summer day. The long strap-shaped leaves form thick tufted clumps with purple or white spiked flowers emerging from the center from mid- through late summer. For evenness, clumps of only four to six plants should be set on eight-inch centers. If larger clumps are planted, they take a long time to spread uniformly. Foliage in full sunlight should be cut late every winter. Annual clipping is not as critical in the shade. The enlarged, onion-like sections on the roots store water and add to drought tolerance. *L. spicata*, creeping lilyturf, has narrow leaves and is fast-growing, often invasive, and more cold hardy—to zone 4—than the regular liriope. The many popular cultivars of the regular liriope, with variations in flowers and foliage, include 'Aztec' and 'Summer Showers', with bluish green foliage and creamy white variegation; 'Majestic', with

Ground cover of liriope in summer flower

leaves to two feet; 'Big Blue', with leaves to twenty inches; 'Christmas Tree', with large tapering flower spikes; 'Variegata', with creamy white variegated leaves; 'Silvery Sunproof', with white variegated leaves; and 'Monroe's White', with white flowers.

Cardinal Flower
Lobelia cardinalis
Lobeliaceae
2–4′   Zones 3–8

Clump of cardinal flowers at the Dawes Arboretum.

A striking red-flowered native perennial, the cardinal flower grows in much of the United States, but it is nowhere abundant. Colonies occur in fertile, moist acid to slightly alkaline soils in partial shade. The showy scarlet tubular flowers up to two inches long are produced in summer on tall spikes above the sparsely spaced narrow, pointed leaves. This very popular wild flower provides nectar for hummingbirds and butterflies. Because of environmental adversity, cardinal flowers are decreasing in number outside cultivation. Two new hybrids, 'Queen Victoria' and 'St. Elmo's Fire', produce very large plants with prominent beautiful flowers.

Mature specimen of the winter honeysuckle

Belle Honeysuckle
Lonicera × *bella*
Caprifoliaceae
8′ x 10′   Zones 4–6

The belle honeysuckle is a deciduous shrub that has become naturalized over wide areas of its range of adaptation, probably from seed spread by migrant birds. It grows well in part shade or full sunlight and does well in a wide range of soils. The shrub has blue green foliage and a dense, rounded habit with spreading, arching branches. In spring it has white to pink flowers that yellow as they age. Fruit a quarter inch in diameter turns red in late June or in July and often stays on the bush into early November. Ripened fruit is a favorite of American robins and other birds. Cultivars give a wider choice of flower color, with 'Atrorosea' having dark rose blooms with a lighter edge, 'Candida' pure white blooms, and 'Rosea' deep pink.

Belle honeysuckle, easily grown and with berries well liked by birds.

Winter Honeysuckle
Lonicera fragrantissima
6–8′ x 8′   Zones 4–8

The winter honeysuckle grows as a shrub and is among the earliest-blooming, from late winter into spring. The mounding deciduous to semievergreen plant with buff-colored multiple stems and exfoliating bark produces very sweet-scented creamy white paired flowers. The fragrance can become intense in tight spaces, especially during mild, humid weather. The oval to rounded yellow green leaves are sparsely distributed along the tall arching stems, so that the flowers are visible. Red berries a quarter inch in diameter are sometimes present in spring, but the foliage can obscure them. This honeysuckle is tolerant of a wide range of conditions, from moist to dry soil, and from full sunlight to moderate shade. The plant becomes more open and airy in partial shade. It is a good specimen shrub but can also make a dense hedge.

The very low-maintenance, long-lived shrub can be cut for indoor arrangements during a time of year when little is in bloom.

Japanese Honeysuckle
Lonicera japonica
20–30′ vine   Zones 4–10

Deciduous to semievergreen, the Japanese honeysuckle is a fast-growing vine that sometimes seems a friend, at other times a foe. A volunteer and pioneer species, it can aggressively engulf plantings along fences and in hedgerows if careful maintenance is lacking. But under control, it can be a delightful spring- and summer-flowering vine on garden structures or in ground covers. The sweet-scented tubular white flowers change to yellow the second day. This honeysuckle will grow under the most adverse conditions, from heavy, wet soil to very dry soil, in full sunlight or partial shade. The cultivar 'Halliana', Hall's honeysuckle, is less vigorous and is well adapted to dry landscapes. 'Purpurea' produces a rich purple-tinted foliage. *L. korolkowii*, the blueleaf honeysuckle, with rose-colored flowers and gray green foliage, is hardy in zones 4–7. *L. maackii*, the Amur honeysuckle, has white flowers that change to yellow, and its quarter-inch fruit turns red in autumn. It may, however, become a noxious weed. All honeysuckles require frequent pruning to control growth.

Japanese honeysuckle, an invasive vine with white flowers that turn yellow as they age.

Blueleaf honeysuckle

Tree form of the Amur honeysuckle, here in the National Arboretum

Coral honeysuckle, an easily managed vine

Coral Honeysuckle
Lonicera sempervirens
15–20′ vine   Zones 4–8

An easily managed honeysuckle vine, the coral honeysuckle produces clusters of orange red trumpet-shaped flowers with yellow centers, alone among honeysuckle blossoms in being without fragrance. The heaviest bloom is in spring, with scattered flowering into summer and autumn. Flowers are produced in the axils of paired leaves on terminal shoots. Under ideal conditions, the orange to scarlet berries can be showy. The semievergreen vine can be especially attractive on garden structures, such as arbors, fences, walls, and trellises. Among its selections are 'Sulphurea', with yellow flowers, and 'Superba', with bright scarlet flowers. *L. heckrottii*, the gold-flame honeysuckle, is a handsome shrubby vine yielding a profusion of peach pink flowers with yellow centers.

Yellow-flowering honeysuckle, a relatively recent introduction

Eight-foot specimen of the Chinese witch hazel

Chinese Witch Hazel
Loropetalum chinense
Hamamelidaceae
6–15′ x 8′   Zones 8–9

The Chinese witch hazel, the only species of its genus, is a tall-growing multiple-stemmed shrub. Small oval leathery dark green leaves are a contrast to the mass of thin strap-shaped petals of creamy white flowers that appear in spring on the slender branches. The shrub performs best in a fertile moist, well-drained slightly acid soil and in full sunlight. It will grow and flower reasonably well in considerable shade under larger trees. The mostly evergreen shrub is not well known but deserves much greater use when the desire is for a tall vertical shrub. Prune out old, non-

Ruby red flowers and foliage of a Chinese witch hazel cultivar at Disney World.

productive center stems to encourage new growth and rejuvenation. *L. chinensis rubrum* 'Burgundy' is a cultivar with burgundy-colored flowers, and the new foliage and flowers of 'Plum Delight' are a rich plum color.

Red surprise lily

Surprise Lily, Spider Lily, Lycoris
Lycoris radiata
Amaryllidaceae
10–12″ Zones 7–9

Appropriately named, the surprise lily pops up in late autumn when most other plants are going into dormancy. Coral red spider-shaped umbels form at the tips of bare stems in September and early October. Tufts of grasslike, or liriope-like, foliage springs up after the flowering and lasts for the winter. Each strap-shaped leaf has a light gray streak down the center. The autumn-flowering bulb must have well-drained soil, and its blooms are best when in full sunlight, although foliage may thrive in shade. The cultivar 'Alba' is white-flowering. *L. africana*, the golden surprise lily, produces golden yellow spider-shaped flowers and wide yellow green leaves. *L. squamigera* produces clusters of lavender rose flowers in July and August.

Turkey Ivy, Creeping Jenny
Lysimachia nummularia
Primulaceae
4″ Zones 3–8/9

Turkey ivy is a prostrate rapid-growing perennial herbaceous ground cover that forms a thick mat of soft creeping stems with nearly round yellow green leaves. Solitary showy yellow flowers are produced in the axils of the leaves in the spring and early summer. The ground-hugging plant performs best in partial shade in a moist porous, well drained soil. Its growth is somewhat unpredictable and not very competitive in large plantings. It can be most effective in pocket plantings in rock gardens and as a detail in groupings of various plants, where a position at close range ensures that its nice features are fully appreciated. 'Aurea' is a cultivar that has yellow foliage. *L. congestiflora* has clusters of red-throated yellow cup-shaped flowers. It forms a low mat of foliage and is an especially good ground cover for shady areas.

Turkey ivy, a noninvasive yellow green carpetlike ground cover

Flowers of the cat's claw.

Cat's-claw, an aggressive climbing vine

Cat's-Claw
Macfadyena unguis-cati
Bignoniaceae
Vine to 100′   Zones 8–10

Cat's-claw, with its hooked, clawlike tendrils, is a clinging vine often found growing on walls and in trees where winters are mild. The evergreen foliage is yellow green with one to three three-inch leaflets. Dense clusters of bright yellow trumpet-shaped flowers two to four inches across appear in spring. Flowering does not take place until the plant is several years old. Spread is rapid because of the many seeds that are borne in brown seedpods twelve to fifteen inches long. Many consider the rampant grower a pest, and when it is removed from a building, the points at which the tendrils were attached remain very evident. The vine's underground bulblike structures makes it suitable for dry places but also difficult to eradicate.

Osage Orange, Bois d'Arc
Maclura pomifera
Moraceae
30′ x 40′   Zones 4–9

Often seen growing in relatively infertile alkaline soil, the Osage orange is a native deciduous tree that thrives in fer-

tile, moist soil with a sunny exposure. Five-inch-long leaves are glossy green on top, pale underneath, and they turn yellow in autumn. Flowers are inconspicuous, but fruit is large and showy. Grapefruit-sized and green turning yellow, it is not edible. Squirrels open the fruit for the seeds embedded in the core, and goldfinches and other birds eat the seeds. The canopy is a mass of

Fruit and foliage of the osage orange.

twiggy branches, thorny when young, with an arching habit. The bark is orange-colored and deeply furrowed. Drought tolerant, this messy tree has been used through the years in windbreaks and hedgerows.

THE MAGNOLIAS

Magnoliaceae

The magnolias are a large and complex group of prized ornamental plants. While the anatomical and morphological characteristics of their flowers and reproductive structures place them in the same genus, the similarities just about end there. There is no simple formula holding for the growth and optimum performance of all. Magnolias vary in size from relatively small and shrublike plants to giant trees. There are both evergreen and deciduous types. The ecological conditions that affect growth and distribution are extremely diverse. Magnolias grow from the tropics to very cold regions of the temperate zone. Some fare well in relatively heavy, wet soil and others only in the mostly dry, well-drained soil of bluffs and rolling topography at higher altitudes. But all are marvelous for the landscape, both hybrids and cultivars being introduced every year.

Cucumber Magnolia
Magnolia acuminata
40–80′ x 30′   Zones 3–8

The cucumber magnolia has a strong upright pyramidal form as a young tree but becomes somewhat irregular, with wide branches, at maturity. This magnolia is prevalent in the Upper South and the more northerly parts of the nation. The relatively large coarse-textured leaves to seven inches long have wavy margins and are lightly pubescent on the undersides. Greenish yellow cup-shaped flowers with twisted outer petals to five inches long bloom in spring but are often concealed by the foliage. Because of the tree's vigor, it is used as understock on which other

Flower of the cucumber magnolia

Cucumber magnolia

species are grafted. It grows best in a fertile moist, well-drained soil and in full sunlight. Provide ample space for this giant native tree.

Delicate flowers of the white saucer magnolia

White Saucer Magnolia
Magnolia denudata (heptapeta)
15–25′ x 12′   Zones 5–9

One of the most beautiful of the magnolias, the white saucer magnolia is a small upright-growing deciduous tree. In late winter or early spring it produces six-inch cup-shaped ivory white flowers, which, similar in shape to the Oriental types, are subject to freeze damage. The tree is somewhat temperamental about growing conditions. Always provide a fertile, well-drained soil and a position in full sunlight, preferably on the south side of a building.

Fraser's magnolia at the Gloster Arboretum

Specimen tree of the southern magnolia

Southern magnolia flower

period. That problem can be less severe if the lower limbs are left on the tree, allowing the dense foliage to conceal many of the falling leaves. Some popular cultivars of this magnolia are 'Majestic Beauty', with very large flowers and a pyramidal form; 'Samuel Sommer', with large leaves and large flowers; 'Russet', with compact russet brown foliage and a pubescent surface on the lower side of the leaves; and 'Little Gem', petite in form, flower, and foliage.

Tulip Magnolia
Magnolia liliiflora (quinquepeta)
10–12' x 12'   Zones 4–8

Beginning as a multiple-stemmed upright-growing shrub, the tulip magnolia eventually grows into a small broad-spreading tree with an umbrella-like canopy. The delightfully scented early-spring flowers look like dark purple tulips with a lighter purple center. The plant performs best in a fertile moist, well-drained soil in full sunlight or moderate shade. The cultivar 'Nigra' produces even darker purple flowers, has a more treelike form, and is perhaps a better choice than the species.

Southern Magnolia
Magnolia grandiflora
40–75' x 35'   Zones 7–9

A stately, enduring popular evergreen tree, the southern magnolia is found throughout the southeastern United States. The upright pyramidal form and very dense foliage make the tree a dominant specimen in plantings. Large stiff, leathery dark blue green leaves up to eight inches long form a contrasting background for the fragrant large white flowers up to twelve inches across. The summer flowers are followed by cylindrical cones that split to reveal shiny bright red seeds that hang from filament-like threads in autumn. The tree will grow in a wide range of soils, from moderately wet and heavy to well-drained. It prefers full sunlight. This magnolia can cause a considerable maintenance problem because of its leaf fall over an extended

Tulip magnolia

Bigleaf Magnolia
Magnolia macrophylla
30–50' x 25'   Zones 6–8

Considered by some to be the most glorious and spectacular of all the magnolias, the bigleaf magnolia produces, as

Gigantic foliage and striking flower of the bigleaf magnolia

Pyramidal magnolia, a rare native

The pyramidal magnolia is a slender upright deciduous tree with a distinctive pyramidal form. A cluster or whorl of leaves occurs at the end of stout ascending branches. Each leaf, about eight inches long and four inches wide, has conspicuous lobes at its base. Fragrant creamy white flowers three to five inches across with loose strap-shaped petals tapering toward the base appear in early spring. The cones, to about four inches long, are rose-colored in autumn. The tree is common in woodlands as understory growth in sandy, fertile soil near streams. *M. fraseri*, the Fraseri or ear-leafed magnolia, is somewhat similar, but its spatula-shaped leaves are larger, to fifteen inches long. It too has lobes, or "ears," at the base of each leaf. The white to pale yellow flowers are ten inches in diameter and have clawlike basal appendages.

Oriental Magnolia, Japanese Magnolia, Saucer Magnolia
Magnolia × soulangiana
25–35′ x 20′   Zones 5–9

With very fine parents, *M. liliiflora* and *M. denudata*,

Oriental magnolia

the name implies, very large leaves, to thirty inches long and twelve inches wide. These are paper-thin and fragile. The flower bud stands upright to twelve inches tall before opening into full late-spring bloom as surely the most exotic of all magnolia flowers, with a span of twelve to fifteen inches. The large deciduous tree of upright oval form has an open canopy and strong, thick coarse-textured branches. It can be understory growth where there is porous, well-drained soil. Its native habitat includes bluffs along sandy streams in upland, hilly country. Although the tree will grow in full sunlight, high winds often riddle the leaves of an exposed specimen. This magnolia is effective on a woodland edge where the bold foliage contrasts with the foliage of other plants. *M. ashei*, the Ashe magnolia, produces six-inch white flowers in spring. Hardy in zones 6 to 9, it has leaves similar to but smaller than those of the bigleaf magnolia, and the plant is more shrublike.

Flower and foliage of the Ashe magnolia

Grove of Oriental magnolias on the LSU campus

the oriental magnolia is a popular small- to medium-sized flowering deciduous tree. Because the prominent saucer-shaped flowers, four to six inches across, appear before the foliage, when most other plants are still dormant, the tree makes a powerful impact in the late-winter to early-spring landscape. The bare tree, with its silvery gray bark and huge silver-colored flower buds, is striking during the winter. This magnolia is fairly particular about where it grows. It performs best in a fertile, well-drained soil in full sunlight or partial shade. Among popular related cultivars are 'Rustica Rubra', with rose red flowers; 'Alexandrina', with large dark rosy purple later-blooming flowers; and 'Lennei', with large rounded deep purple flowers that have light purple centers.

popular cultivars are 'Rubra', with purplish rose flowers; 'Royal Star', with white double flowers; 'Waterlily', with pink buds opening to nearly white flowers; and 'Centennial', with pinkish white flowers having many petals.

Umbrella Magnolia
Magnolia tripetala
15–35' x 20'   Zones 5–8

The umbrella magnolia is a relatively small deciduous magnolia and sometimes has a shrubby form with multiple stems. Heavy branches with umbrella-like clusters of leaves at the end of terminal shoots form an open, irregular canopy. The leaves are large, often to two feet long and nearly ten inches wide, with a broad oval shape abruptly

Star magnolia

Star Magnolia
Magnolia stellata
6–12' x 8'   Zones 4–9

The star magnolia, a wide-spreading shrubby plant that eventually grows into a tree, produces multiple stems with closely arranged leaves. Fragrant creamy white flowers with ten to fifteen strap-shaped petals, each about three inches long, bloom in late winter and early spring. This magnolia performs best in a fertile moist, well-drained soil in full sunlight or partial shade. In shade, it grows open and airy with fewer flowers. The plant is very effective as a specimen shrub or as a small tree in a small space. Some

Seedpod of an umbrella magnolia at Monticello.

Flowering umbrella magnolia tree

tapering at both ends. The creamy white cup-shaped flowers to ten inches in diameter with thin six-inch petals are less symmetrical than the flowers of most magnolias and have an unpleasant odor. This magnolia is often found in moist, wooded hills and is especially prevalent in the mountains of the eastern states. It grows well as a cultivated species with partial shade and in a fertile, well-drained acid soil.

Sweet-Bay Magnolia
Magnolia virginiana
20–35′ x 20′   Zones 5–9

A semievergreen tree in most areas, the sweet-bay magnolia occurs over a wide area of the United States in relatively wet acid soil near ponds and sandy streams. The leaves, three to five inches long, are dull silvery green on top with silvery white undersides. When the leaves flutter in the wind and the undersides of the leaves show, the shifting colors make an arresting sight. White cup-shaped lemon-scented flowers to three inches in diameter occur in late spring and early summer. The tree is sometimes single

Oregon hollygrape in flower

Oregon Hollygrape
Mahonia aquifolium
Berberidaceae
3′ x 5′   Zones 5–8

The Oregon hollygrape, an evergreen shrub native to the northwestern United States, grows best in partial shade where the soil is moist, fertile, and slightly alkaline. Like other mahonias, it is intolerant of heavy, compacted soil. Spiny, hollylike leaves comprise five to nine leaflets. The foliage has a leathery texture, is dark green on its upper surface, and turns reddish purple in winter. This mahonia is a many-stemmed plant that forms dense low, broad clumps with an irregular spread. Clusters of flowers hug the main stem in late winter or in spring, depending on the zone. Grapelike clusters of blue black fruit covered with a silvery bloom mature in summer. The shrub is useful in mass plantings, planters, and naturalistic settings, and as a ground cover. Cultivars exist with distinctive growth habits and leaf variations.

Flower and foliage of the sweet-bay magnolia

trunked but can also be seen in its native habitat as a multiple-trunked mass of many root suckers around the main trunk. It is particularly handsome on a woodland edge, where the silvery leaves and smooth gray bark contrast with other foliage.

Leatherleaf Mahonia
Mahonia bealei
6′ x 3′   Zones 6–8

Grapelike fruiting cluster of the leatherleaf mahonia.

Coarse-textured foliage growing in horizontal tiers is a mark of the leatherleaf mahonia, an evergreen introduction from China. The shrub has a stiff, erect growth habit and is clump-forming. It performs best in partial shade and soil that is moist, well drained, and slightly acid. The nine- to fifteen-inch dark blue green compound leaves are leathery and hollylike. Yellow racemes three to six inches long appear above the foliage from late winter through early spring. Clusters of blue black grapelike berries covered with a whitish bloom mature in summer. Mockingbirds love the berries and vigorously defend their food source. An annual spring pruning that removes a third of the older growth to near ground level is essential for maintaining a dense low mass.

Chinese mahonia in flower

Chinese Mahonia
Mahonia fortunei
4′ x 3′   Zones 8–10

Dark blue green fernlike compound foliage and a dense low growth habit make the Chinese mahonia one of the loveliest plants for shady locations with porous, well-drained soils. The shrub is a slow grower with several basal shoots forming an upright, irregular pattern. In time, the plant may become sprawling to mounding with flexible stems. Lemon yellow flowers are borne in racemes to six inches long in early spring. Fruiting is erratic and is of little ornamental value. Remove some of the tallest canes periodically to maintain a dense low mass. This mahonia is effective in naturalistic settings. It is attacked by powdery mildew but has few other problems.

Burmese Mahonia
Mahonia lomariifolia
6′ x 4′   Zones 8–10

Long, spiny leaves with twenty or more leaflets up to four inches long give the Burmese mahonia a very coarse texture. The medium green foliage is in horizontal tiers on top of tall canes. Terminal whorls of yellow flowers, each four

Burmese mahonia

to seven inches long, are present in spring. The young plant has few stems, but as it ages, new stems appear at the base, producing an upright, multiple-stemmed layered top. The shrub has some drought tolerance but grows best in a fertile, well-drained soil and is tolerant of more sunlight than other mahonias. Like all members of the barberry family, it has a yellow inner bark.

THE FLOWERING CRABAPPLES

Rosaceae

There are over six hundred types of crabapples, representing at least thirty species of European, Asian, and North American origin. Books, pamphlets, and other publications devoted to a description of the multitude of species and cultivars are available in libraries, and the Cooperative Extension Service at land-grant universities can furnish additional information. An experienced nurseryman can give advice on what is best suited to a particular locality.

Few flowering ornamental plants have the beauty of a crabapple in full bloom. Together, the many species are among the most widely grown of small flowering trees in American landscapes, with at least one of them adaptable to every climate from zone 3 to zone 9. The trees offer variety to the discriminating gardener in that they have flowers from white to reddish purple, some of them, notably those of *Malus angustifolia*, possessing a wonderful fragrance besides. Fruit may be green, yellow, or red in sizes varying from a quarter inch to two inches. It is used in jellies and preserved as spiced fruit. It is also an important food for migrating and resident birds. The trees' leaf shape may be serrated, lobed, or with cut margins. Leaf color varies from light to dark green and sometimes includes purple. Plants vary in size, growth habit, and growth rate. All are deciduous. Some are shrublike, but most are trees growing to a height between fifteen and twenty-five feet. By planting several species or cultivars, gardeners can have crabapples flowering for a number of weeks. In zones 8 and 9, flowering is in March and April; in zone 4, it is in May

Delightfully fragrant flowers of a southern crabapple.

and June. Very few crabapples grow and blossom well in the Deep South, probably because of the trees' chilling requirement and the region's abundance of insects and diseases. For that region, *M. angustifolia, M. floribunda, M.* 'Callaway', and *M. sieboldii* var. zumi are among the better ones. In the North, there are hundreds of selections from which to choose.

Crabapples are very

Flowering crabapples as specimen trees in Birmingham, Michigan.

'Selkirk' crabapples in the Midwest

hardy and will grow in a wide range of soils, though they perform best in a well-drained soil that has a pH of 5.5 to 6.5. They should receive full sunlight, in order to maintain vigor and maximize flower production. Fire blight, apple scab, and cedar rust (apple rust) all afflict crabapples. Asian varieties are resistant to cedar rust, but the Asian types are like the American in being highly susceptible to apple scab. San Jose, oyster, and Putnam scale attacks crabapples,

Sargent' crabapples, seldom more than eight feet tall

Zumi crabapple in flower

but all three are easily controlled by applying oil sprays just as the plant starts growth in spring. Aphids are a nuisance, but a number of insecticides are available that will control them when applied properly. Borers can cause problems but generally do not attack healthy, vigorous plants.

Apples, *Malus sylvestris,* are very closely related to crabapples. If fruit is over two inches in diameter, it is classified as an apple. There are

Fruit of the crabapple, by definition under two inches in diameter.

Zumi crabapple with its autumn show of red fruit

Espaliered apple trees, which can be confined to a small space in the landscape

146

Orange-fruited crabapple

Yellow-fruited crabapple

hundreds of apple cultivars, and they have the same growing requirements and are subject to the same insect and disease pests as crabapples.

Giant Turk's Cap
Malvaviscus arboreus
Malvaceae
8' x 8'   Zones 8–10

Giant turk's cap

Native to Mexico, giant Turk's cap is a widely grown subtropical plant in the southern United States. It will tolerate a wide range of growing conditions but does best in full sunlight in a fertile, well-drained soil. It produces multiple ascending stems and has a sprawling form. Leaves are heavily veined and have a heart-shaped base. Their size varies with the plant's location but is sometimes longer than four inches. Flowers are bright scarlet, drooping, and up to three inches long. Blooming in summer and more heavily in autumn, the plant can carry some blossoms in winter if there is not a frost to destroy them. The plant is well adapted to the stresses of inner-city gardens and is often seen growing along the south side of walls. Hummingbirds feed on the nectar of the red flowers.

Large specimen of the smaller-flowering turk's cap

Turk's Cap
***Malvaviscus arboreus* var. drummondii**
5' x 4'   Zones 8–9

Growing well in a variety of soils, including those that are alkaline, this turk's cap does best in sandy, rocky soil in full sunlight. The heart-shaped foliage is two to three inches long and is a dull yellow green with conspicuous veins on the underside. Solitary bright red twisted flowers to an inch and a half long have prominent stamens. The plant blooms throughout summer but most heavily in fall. Scattered blossoms continue until there is a killing frost. Flattened, berrylike fruit is most copious in autumn.

Mandevilla vine on trellis in New Orleans

Mandevilla
Mandevilla × amabilis
Apocynaceae
Vine to 15′   Zones 9–10

The mandevilla is a tropical woody, twining vine that produces prominent tubular flowers to three inches across. The blossoms are pale pink on opening and change to a deep rose. Dark green leaves are up to three inches long and half as wide. In cooler climates, the summer color of the vines can be enjoyed by planting in containers, but these must be moved to a greenhouse over winter. The plant requires a loamy, peaty soil with good drainage, and it flowers well only in a sunny exposure. In tropical and subtropical areas, the profusion of flowers is continuous. 'Alice du Pont' is a very popular cultivar that is probably a hybrid of *Mandevilla × amabilis* and *M. splendens*.

Firecracker Vine, Manettia
Manettia cordifolia
Rubiaceae
Vine to 15′   Zones 8–10

A perennial with light, lacy foliage, the firecracker vine produces an abundance of tubular red flowers an inch and a half long from late spring until frost. The heaviest flowering occurs in autumn, before light freezes kill the plant to the ground. After the foliage has turned brown, cut the vine off at ground level and cover the roots with mulch. The vine grows best in a moderately fertile, well-drained soil and in full sunlight. It is readily propagated from root cuttings, by inserting a spade into the ground about a foot from the crown and waiting for severed roots to sprout. The vine can adorn arbors, trellises, and fences. Its flowers attract hummingbirds.

Chinaberry
Melia azedarach
Meliaceae
30′ x 20′   Zones 7–9

Chinaberry foliage

Introduced from Asia and Australia, the chinaberry was one of the most widely planted deciduous trees in the South prior to 1950. Its immature berries were ammunition for many a child's popgun. It will grow almost anywhere but thrives in rich soil and full sunlight. It has a broad, umbrella-like crown with a dense, twiggy mass. Fast-growing and drought-tolerant, the tree is relatively short-lived, often dying because of San Jose scale. Glossy dark green compound leaves are to twenty inches long and twelve inches wide. Lilac-colored flowers are borne in five- to eight-inch panicles in early spring. Some people find their sweet scent objectionable. The marble-sized fruit turns from green to sandy yellow in autumn and hangs on the tree into winter.

Firecracker vine flowers, profuse from late spring through autumn

Dawn Redwood
Metasequoia glyptostroboides
Taxodiaceae
80' x 30'   Zones 5–8

The dawn redwood, from China, once thought to have been extinct for millions of years, now graces American gardens. It grows best in full sunlight where soils are moist, fertile, slightly acid, and high in organic content. A deciduous tree with soft, flattened foliage that is about six inches long and of a feathery texture, this ancient species has brown shredded bark, similar to that of the cypress. Autumn leaf color is apricot gold to bronze. Upright and conical in form, with strong horizontal branches that become irregular with advancing age, the tree has a place in parks and playgrounds, or massed in a screen.

Deciduous dawn redwoods with a Colorado blue spruce.

Le Duc

Dawn redwood foliage

Grouping of dawn redwoods in the Missouri Botanic Garden

Banana Shrub
Michelia figo
Magnoliaceae
20′ x 15′   Zones 8–10

On a still, warm spring day, the banana-like fragrance of the banana shrub's flowers carries more than a hundred feet. The inch-and-a-half creamy yellow flowers are edged in maroon. The medium-textured leaves are a lustrous dark green and up to three inches in length. Velvety brown buds are prominent in late autumn and winter. The plant has an upright oval form with a dense mass. It grows best in a fertile moist, well-drained acid soil (pH 5.5–6.5) and prefers full sunlight or partial shade. It is a long-lived shrub or small tree suitable as an evergreen accent. Two cultivars of the hybrid *Michelia × foggii* that do well in zone 9 are 'Allspice', a vigorous grower with lustrous dark green foliage and very fragrant white flowers, and 'Jack Fogg', a plant of

upright habit with glossy dark green leaves and white flowers that have a pinkish purple edging on the petals. 'Maudii', a cultivar of the hybrid of *M. doltsopa* and *M. figo*, has large leaves and large, intensely fragrant creamy white flowers. *M. doltsopa* is a very large evergreen tree to ninety feet that is harvested for timber in the Himalayas. In early spring, it produces fragrant large white magnolia-like flowers with twelve to sixteen petals up to three inches long. It makes a handsome ornamental tree in zones 9 and 10.

Bee balm flowers

Bee Balm
Monarda didyma
Labiatae
2–3.5′   Zones 4–8

Bee balm is a herbaceous perennial with flowers that add brilliant color to the garden from late spring into summer. Bees and butterflies are attracted to the blossoms with tubular petals in globe-shaped heads because of their high nectar content. The foliage, which is spicy scented and medium green, is borne on four-sided stems and can be up to four inches long. Growing well in urban gardens and adapted to a wide variety of soils, the plant may be invasive. Divide and replant every third year. This perennial can be considered for borders, naturalized gardens, and bold groupings where there is sunlight for much of the day. Cultivars are available with hooded flowers in white, pink, scarlet, wine red, and violet purple. Three new, mildew-resistant cultivars are 'Gardenview Scarlet', with bright scarlet flowers; 'Marshall's Delight', with pink flowers; and 'Prairie Night', with royal purple flowers. *M. citriodora*, lemon mint, which has white to pink flowers, is better adapted to warmer climates and will grow in calcareous soil.

Old specimen of the banana shrub.

Flowers of the 'Allspice' banana shrub, which, like those of other hybrid cultivars, are two to four times as large as the regular banana shrub's blooms.

Weeping white mulberry

White Mulberry
Morus alba
Moraceae
40' x 30'   Zones 4–9

The white mulberry has fruit that is white, pink, or purplish violet. The tree was imported from China many years ago, with the intention of feeding its leaves to silkworms and developing a silk industry in the United States. The industry did not thrive. Like the red mulberry, the white mulberry withstands drought and tolerates urban and seaside environments, but it has limited use in the landscape. A number of cultivars are superior to the species. Some are fruitless, some have a distinctive leaf shape or unusual fall color, some are pyramidal, some are weeping. 'Pendula' and 'Urbana', weeping mulberries, are long-lived and are often grown as prominent accent plants.

Fruit and foliage of the red mulberry.

Red Mulberry
Morus rubra
50' x 40'   Zones 4–8

Fast growth, coarse texture, and a broad-spreading canopy are characteristics of the red mulberry. Its fruit, to an inch and a half long, resembles blackberries and is consumed by several species of birds. As fruit falls or is dislodged from the tree, it can create a mess. Dark green leaves, three to nine inches long, vary considerably from tree to tree. Yellow autumn color occurs on this deciduous tree when it grows in the open. The tree thrives in fertile, moist alkaline to acid soil and prefers full sunlight. The cultivar 'Fruitless' is reported to bear no fruit.

Rose Banana, Dwarf Banana
Musa ornata
Musaceae
10' x 6'   Zones 8/9–10

A tropical perennial native to India, the rose banana is planted in the Deep South for its lush, exotic foliage and fast rate of growth. It can be massed or grown as a single clump in the ground or in a container. Like all bananas, it is propagated by division of clumps in spring. Grow it in full sunlight and in fertile moist, well-drained soil. Leaves run as long as four feet and as wide as a foot, and they have a pinkish purple midrib. The plant is upright-growing and multiple stemmed. Blue pink bracts up to eight inches long cover yellow flowers that bloom in summer and cease with killing frost. Inedible fruit to three inches in length is

Rose banana

yellowish green. Cut back freeze-damaged parts of the plant to about fifteen inches of the ground after the first killing frost. 'Nana' is a dwarf cultivar for small areas.

Common Banana
Musa × paradisiaca
Size: 20′ x 8′   Zones 8/9–10

Grown for its large, bold-textured tropical foliage, the common banana is a treelike perennial that grows well in full sunlight or partial shade and in a moist, well-drained soil. It has an umbrella-like form with large leaves and a thick trunk comprising the sheathing bases of the leaves. The bright green leaves are up to nine feet long and eighteen inches wide. Flowers are in heavy pendulous structures with foot-long maroon bracts and yellow centers. Flowering continues for several weeks during summer but only for

Common banana, with fruit

plants more than eighteen months old. On plants that have reached that age, a few yellow green bananas from eight to fourteen inches long are produced on long stalks. They are edible, but the quality is questionable.

Grape Hyacinth
Muscari neglectum
Liliaceae
Less than 1′   Zones 5–9

A colony of grape hyacinths

One of the pleasant surprises of spring is the grape hyacinth, a native of the Mediterranean region that can be a particularly good plant for naturalizing. Although its bulb does not perform well in the hot, humid South, it does exceptionally well farther north. Very fragrant purplish lilac funnel-shaped flowers appear on stalks rising six to eight inches above the clustered strap-shaped leaves. A porous, well-drained soil is absolutely essential for all spring-flowering bulbs.

Southern Wax Myrtle
Myrica cerifera
Myricaceae
20′ x 20′   Zones 7–9

Southern wax myrtle

The southern wax myrtle is a large, fast-growing native evergreen shrub or small tree that grows in thickets and woodlands, near swamps, and on clear-cut fields. A good choice for poorly drained sites, it prefers moist acid soil but tolerates a wide range of growing conditions. It can thrive in either full sunlight or partial shade. The aromatic olive green leaves are up to three inches long. Blue gray nutlets to an eighth of an inch in diameter are covered with a waxy substance that since colonial times has been used to make scented candles. This evergreen makes an excellent specimen tree and is also good for screening in clipped or unclipped hedges. *M. pennsylvanica*, the northern bayberry, is similar and is hardy in zones 2–6.

Mature nandina in fruit

Nandina
Nandina domestica
Berberidaceae
5′ x 3′   Zones 6–9

Adapted to a wide variety of growing conditions, the nandina performs best in fertile, well-drained soil and in full sunlight or partial shade. It is a fine-textured upright oval evergreen that forms clumps, with foliage borne on stiff canes. The very large leaves are composed of many dark green two-inch leaflets. Young growth is tinged with red, and old foliage turns wine red in winter. In spring, white flowers are borne in terminal panicles. Bright red berries a quarter inch in diameter are produced in prominent grapelike clusters in autumn and winter. Established plants must be pruned annually to keep them from becoming leggy and unfruitful. Prune out a third of the older, taller canes each spring. Among compact cultivars are 'Compacta', to three feet tall; 'Pygmaea', to fifteen inches; 'Nana', between twelve and eighteen inches; and 'Harbour Dwarf', low-growing and spreading by underground stolons. 'Alba' is a white-fruited selection.

Dwarf nandina, with red foliage year-round

THE DAFFODILS, JONQUILS, AND NARCISSUS

Amaryllidaceae

The narcissus group is divided into eleven major divisions on the basis of the plants' flower parts, number of flowers on each stem, and foliage types. The spring-flowering bulbs of all eleven divisions, however, are similar in their cultural requirements. Best performance is in a porous, well-drained soil. When planted in overfertile soil, plants tend to grow foliage at the expense of their flowers. They do well in full sunlight or partial shade. In areas where the soil freezes, bulbs should be planted to a depth of five or six inches. In the South, the appropriate depth is three to four inches. Many spring-flowering bulbs can remain in place for many years, repeating and flowering annually. They do not perform as well when crowded, however, and may be lifted, separated, and replanted in summer as the foliage turns brown and dies. If foliage is removed while still green, little or no flowering will occur the following year. Each area has its cultivars of proven performance out of the thousands available, with many new ones being added each year.

Jonquil
Narcissus jonquilla
12–15″   Zones 3–9

The jonquil has thin, narrow dark green leaves that are rolled and reedlike. Each hollow flowering stem may bear two to six sweet-scented golden yellow flowers. Of clump-forming spring-flowering bulbs, this narcissus is one of the most enduring.

Old clump of jonquils

Naturalized planting of old-fashioned jonquils, common at old homesites

Daffodil

Narcissus pseudonarcissus

12–15″ Zones 3–9

Daffodils are known by
everyone for their large
trumpet-shaped flowers. The
flowers, singles or doubles,
may have petals that are
white, yellow, pink, or orange red. The cup may be
the same color as the petals

'Fortune' daffodils

or a different color. The leaf is flat and relatively wide and
is covered with a silvery bloom.

Narcissus

Narcissus tazetta

6–24″ Zones 3–9

The division of narcissus with plants that are most often
popularly called by that name includes those the stems of
which support multiple flowers. The single or double flow-

*'Silver Chimes'
narcissus.*

Daffodil planting in Washington inspired by Lady Bird Johnson

Old 'Seventeen Sisters' narcissus at Monticello

ers are generally white or yellow, and the fragrance is strong. Two cultivars, 'Pearl' and 'Paper White', are favorites for indoor forcing in pebble or dish gardens. Two recent introductions that are reported to be superior to the old narcissus for indoor forcing are 'Ziva' and 'Galilee'.

Walking iris

Walking Iris
Neomarica gracilis
Iridaceae
18–24″   Zones 8–10

Yellow green fan-shaped leaves that are thick at the base are the distinctive foliage of the walking iris. The plant spreads by proliferations, that is, small plants, formed on the end of flowering scapes when they touch the ground. Flowers about two inches across are white with blue markings and

appear in clusters in spring. The plant is excellent for growing in containers, or as a ground cover where freezes are infrequent. A protected location in full sunlight or partial shade and a fertile, well-drained soil are best for this iris.

Oleander
Nerium oleander
Apocynaceae
12′ x 10′   Zones 8–10

The oleander is a large multiple-stemmed evergreen that is well adapted to the coastal South. It endures wind and heat, along with soil that is poor, dry, and sandy. The shrub must have full sunlight for profuse flowering. Its narrow leaves are dull dark green and oblong to eight inches, and they have a prominent midrib. The plant has a rounded form, with its canelike stems arising from a tight crown. Flow-

Oleander

155

Rosy pink and white oleanders at the Los Angeles Arboretum

Fire Spike
Odontonema strictum
Acanthaceae
6′ x 2′   Zones 9–10

A tropical perennial, the fire spike produces terminal spikes of bright red flowers in autumn. It will grow in any well-drained garden soil and in full sunlight or partial shade. Where freezes do not occur, it will flower for an extended period in autumn and early winter. It is likely to die back to the ground in winter toward the upper limits of its range of adaptation. The dark green leaves, borne on opposite sides of the stem, are up to six

ers up to three inches across are produced from April to June in white, pink, salmon, red, or purple. The plant is excellent for massing and screening, and dwarf cultivars are fine in containers. All parts of the shrub are poisonous, but that should not deter its use, since many ornamental plants are similar in this respect.

Black Gum
Nyssa sylvatica
Nyssaceae
50′ x 25′   Zones 4–9

The black gum has lustrous dark green leaves to five inches long and two and a half inches wide that turn red to purple in early autumn. It is one of the most dependable native trees for autumn color, which it often exhibits by late summer. The mature tree has horizontal, spreading branches and a rounded to flat canopy. The tree grows in a wide variety of soils but prefers one that is well-drained, with a pH of 5.5 to 6.5. The fruit of the female tree is an oblong drupe to a half inch long that is bluish black in early autumn. A number of birds eat the fruit. Leaf spot disease, which causes leaf drop, is a problem, particularly in the Deep South. Frequently planted as a shade tree, this species is, however, very sensitive to air pollution.

Black gum and Siberian dogwood in Boston

ire spike

inches long and have wavy margins. Hummingbirds sip the nectar of the flowers during their fall migration.

Mondo, Monkey Grass

Ophiopogon japonicus
Liliaceae
6–12″   Zones 5–10

Mondo, native to Asia, is probably the most satisfactory ground cover in the South. Adapted to various soil conditions, the tufted perennial grows best in a fertile, moist soil. The thin, narrow erect dark blue green leaves are up to a foot long. In full sunlight the foliage may bleach, but the plant will grow there. It does best, though, in partial shade and survives surprisingly well in deep shade. Fall is the preferred time for planting, but successful planting can occur at any time provided that there is enough moisture. Established, the plant can be trimmed in early spring by raising the lawn mower blade to the highest cutting position. Selections of the plant include 'Variegatus', with green-and-white striped leaves; and 'Nana', with leaves under four inches tall. *O. planiscapus* 'Arabicus' has narrow purple black foliage.

Dwarf mondo

Mondo ground cover at Live Oak Gardens

Prickly-Pear Cactus
Opuntia humifusa
Cactaceae
2′ x 3′   Zones 7–10

Native to the southwestern United States, the prickly-pear cactus is a spined succulent with an upright to prostrate spreading form that becomes shrublike with age. It grows in a wide range of soils, including those that are alkaline and have a high salt content, provided that they are well drained. The plant has green spiny, leaflike modified stems that are flat, oval, or rounded and three to six inches across. In late spring and in summer, prominent bright yellow tulip-shaped flowers appear. Seeds are in edible pods, two to three inches in diameter, that mature to a shade of purple. This cactus is pest-free and has a place in xeriscapes, rock gardens, and other plantings where the soil is dry and relatively infertile.

Prickly-pear cactus in New Mexico

Sweet Olive
Osmanthus fragrans
Oleaceae
15′ x 10′   Zones 8–9

Cool fall temperatures are heralded by the elusive but strong fragrance of the sweet olive's blossoms. Tiny white

Foliage and flowers of the sweet olive

Hollylike leaves of the fortune osmanthus

flowers in drooping clusters appear in several cycles from October through spring. Their sweet perfume spreads several hundred feet on a warm day. Leaves begin coppercolored, but when they are mature, having reached a length of two inches and a width of three-quarters of an inch, they become a lustrous dark green. An evergreen shrub from Asia, the dense and compact plant is upright to oval in form. Long-lived and slow-growing, it performs best in moist, well-drained soil that is fertile and slightly acid and in full sunlight or partial shade. *O. aurantiacus* produces coppery yellow flowers.

Native devilwood in flower

Variegated osmanthus

tumn color, not outstanding, is yellow to red. The flowers are not noteworthy either, but the fruit, a nutlet a third of an inch long, is enclosed in an inflated, bladderlike structure resembling the fruit of hops. The tree is graceful, with broad horizontal branches. It does well in urban landscapes and deserves wider acceptance.

Wood Sorrel, Oxalis
Oxalis crassipes
Oxalidaceae
8″ x 10″   Zones 4–9

Native to Argentina, the wood sorrel is a fast-growing perennial that thrives in fertile, moist soil and in full sunlight or partial shade. It has cloverlike leaves and forms mounding clumps with a medium-fine texture. Foliage arises stemless from a starchy rootstock on potato-like bulblets, or swellings. The plant can be extremely invasive and should be planted where it can be confined. Rose-colored flowers with darker veins and centers appear in

Osmanthus × *fortunei* is similar but has leaves that are more hollylike and only one cycle of flowers in autumn. *O. americanus*, the devilwood, is a native, but not common, species with fragrant white flowers in spring and beautiful dark green foliage. *O. heterophyllus* 'Variegatus' has a similar growth habit and variegated foliage.

Flowers and cloverlike foliage of the wood sorrel

American Hop Hornbeam
Ostrya virginiana
Betulaceae
30′ x 20′   Zones 4–9

The American hop hornbeam is a small native understory tree growing best in moist sandy, loamy soil that is slightly acid. It thrives in full or partial shade. The elmlike leaves to five inches long and two and a half inches across are rough and sandpaper-like on the upper surface. Au-

Foliage and flowers of the American hop hornbeam

loose clusters from early spring through summer and fall, and sometimes even in a mild winter. 'Alba' is a lovely white-flowering form. Several other selections are available with white, pink, yellow, or red flowers, and some with maroon foliage.

Autumn color and fruit of the sourwood in Georgia.

Sourwood
Oxydendrum arboreum
Ericaceae
40' x 15'   Zones 4–9

A slow-growing native tree of upright pyramidal to oval form with slightly drooping branches, the sourwood grows well in full sunlight and partial shade. It prefers a deep fertile, well-drained soil that is slightly acid and is seen especially in landscapes at high elevations. In early summer this tree produces fragrant creamy white flowers in drooping racemes at the tip of the branches. The glossy dark green leaves turn scarlet to scarlet purple in autumn and are a good contrast to other foliage. The tree is sensitive to environmental stress, particularly in urban settings.

Pachysandra
Pachysandra terminalis
Buxaceae
8–10″   Zones 4–7/8

Pachysandra, because of its range of adaptation, ease of growth, and resistance to pests, may be the most widely grown ground cover in the eastern United States. An evergreen perennial, it grows best in fertile, well-drained acid soil (pH 5.5–6.5) and in filtered sunlight to shade. The lustrous olive green spoon-shaped foliage is two to four inches long on six- to eight-inch stems. Small creamy white flowers on spikes three to five inches tall are present in late spring. The plant is intolerant of full sunlight, foot traffic, dry soil, or exposure to high winds. Several cultivars are available with variegated or deeply serrated foliage or a compact growth habit. 'Silveredge' has narrow silvery white margins around green leaves, 'Green Carpet' is low and compact, and 'Cutleaf' has deeply serrated leaves.

Summer-flowering sourwood in Kentucky

'Cutleaf' pachysandra

Ground cover of pachysandra, with hostas in flower

Peonies in Columbus, Indiana

Peonies
Paeonia **hybrids**
Paeoniaceae
1.5–3′   Zones 3–8

Peonies have long been held in high esteem as flowering garden plants, with bloom occurring in May or June, depending on latitude. They thrive in most garden soils, but a fertile, well-drained slightly alkaline loam is best. The sweet fragrant two- to six-inch flowers may be exquisite singles or large doubles and come in colors from pure white to deep red. They are excellent cut flowers and often last a week when cut in full bud. The mounding plants, with their deep green foliage, are attractive before, during, and after flowering. Grow them in full sun in a border or in mass plantings. They are very hardy herbaceous perennials and apart from *Botrytis* rot of the buds have few serious pests. Hybrids and cultivars vary in flower size, fragrance, and color. *P. suffruticosa,* the tree peony, is a deciduous shrub that grows five to seven feet high and blooms in late May. Its flowers can be white, pink, red, lavender, or yellow. The dark green foliage is deeply serrated.

THE PALMS

Palmae

Palms are highly decorative subtropical to tropical evergreens that are a prominent part of the landscape in zone 10. A few of the more hardy grow in zones 8 and 9. There are about two hundred genera and more than 2,700 species in the palm family, varying from large, majestic trees to small shrubs. Most have single trunks, but multiple-trunked species add interest to the landscape. Palms are used as ornamental specimens, container plants, and patio trees, as well as in seaside, street, and mass plantings. A moist, well-drained soil and a sunny location are best for most, although some are highly adaptable to soil conditions. Two sorts of leaves are seen in palms: palmate or fan shaped, and pinnate, or feather shaped. Leaf size varies, with some feather-shaped fronds achieving twenty feet in length and some of the fan-shaped reaching five feet in width. Fairchild Tropical Gardens, in Coral Gables, Florida, has one of the most extensive palm collections in the United States.

Queen Palm
Arecastrum romanzoffianum
25–30′   Zone 10

A beautiful, fast-growing palm with a wide adaptability to soils, the queen palm has feather-shaped arching or drooping leaves that may exceed fifteen feet in length. It has a moderate tolerance of salt but is not a good choice as a seashore tree.

Queen palms at Epcot Center

Butia palm and cabbage palms growing at Hilton Head Island, South Carolina.

Butia Palm, Pindo Palm
Butia capitata
10–20′   Zones 8–10

The butia palm has bluish gray feather-shaped leaves that are up to five feet in length. It is one of the five cold hardi-

European fan palm

est palms and sometimes lives for several years in the lower part of zone 8. It produces very tart fruit in large clusters, which is used in jellies and enjoyed by birds. It has a stout trunk, grows well in a wide variety of soils, and is a good seaside specimen.

Chinese fan palm

European Fan Palm
Chamaerops humilis
2–5′ x 6–12′   Zones 9–10

A clump-growing, multiple-crowned species that grows slowly to a dwarf height, the European fan palm tolerates many kinds of soil and is a good palm for the small garden. One of the best types for the seaside, it has a high tolerance to salt. It may be killed to the ground by severe freezes but will return in most of zone 9. *Livistona chinensis,* the Chinese fan palm, is similar but has larger, softer yellow green leaves and is not as hardy.

Canary Island Date Palm
Phoenix canariensis
30–60′   Zones 8–10

The Canary Island date palm is a grand, stately palm that grows to a great height. Its feather-shaped leaves in a dense crown may attain twenty feet in length. The trunk of an old tree can be up to three feet in diameter. One of the hardiest of the highly ornamental palms, this species is good as a specimen and in seaside plantings.

Pygmy date palm, often a palm for containers in colder regions

Canary Island date palms in City Park, New Orleans

Pygmy Date Palm
Phoenix roebelenii
6′ x 4′   Zone 10

The pygmy date palm is a small palm with graceful arching to slightly drooping feathery leaves up to five feet in length and gray green in color. Old petioles linger for lengthy periods and should be removed as they turn yellow. The plant makes an excellent indoor specimen if it can be given light of a high intensity.

Senegal Date Palm
Phoenix reclinata
25′ clump   Zones 9–10

The Senegal date palm is a multiple-trunked species with feather-shaped leaves that grows best in a well-drained soil. Suckers at ground level eventually produce a clump that is too large for small properties. Severe leaf burn occurs in hard freezes.

Senegal date palm

Needle Palm
Rhapidophyllum hystrix
3–5′   Zones 7–10

The needle palm is slow-growing and very hardy. Its fan-shaped leaves are borne on trunks that may be single or clumped. This native species does best in shade. The needles on the trunk are hazardous to children and anyone else unaware of their presence.

Needle palm, the hardiest of the palms

Broadleaf lady palm, an excellent container specimen

Dwarf Palmetto
Sabal minor
3–6′   Zones 6–10

Leaves of the dwarf palmetto, a stemless, native species, are fan-shaped and five to eight feet long with a width of one to three feet. The plant thrives in wet, swampy areas, where it reaches its maximum size. It is not easily eradicated but is difficult to transplant, especially when large. It has a sparse canopy and a mounding form with stiff upright leaves in several planes. Outstanding in the understory of a deciduous forest, it has blue green leaves that are darker there than when it is grown in full sunlight.

An old dwarf palmetto specimen in the Atchafalaya Basin.

Broadleaf Lady Palm
Rhapis excelsa
8–10′   Zones 9–10

Semishaded areas are best for the low-growing, clump-producing broadleaf lady palm, which has dark green leaves and a growth habit recommending it as an indoor or outdoor container plant. It should be planted where protection from the cold is possible.

Royal Palm
Roystonea regia
50–75′   Zone 10

A highly ornamental fast-growing palm, the royal palm is fine as a specimen and for street and mass plantings. Green leaf sheaths three feet or more in length form a crownshaft around the upper trunk and add to the impressive effect. The large tree has a high tolerance of salt spray and withstands hurricane-force winds better than other palms.

Royal palms in Naples, Florida

Cabbage Palm
Sabal palmetto
30–60′   Zones 8–10

One of the hardiest and most adaptable of palms, the cabbage palm will grow in soil from wet to dry. It has gray green fan-shaped leaves up to eight feet across. Leaf bases persist after the leaves are lost, but the lower part of the heavy trunk is smooth. The tree has a high tolerance of salt and is extensively used as a seaside specimen and in street plantings. *S. texana (mexicana)* and *S. blackburniana* are similar to the cabbage palm, but the trunks are almost bare, with few leaf bases attached.

aw palmetto

Saw Palmetto
Serenoa repens
3–4′   Zones 8/9–10

An excellent native palm in Florida and other coastal areas, the saw palmetto is shrublike and generally has a twisted recumbent trunk. The dark green leaves are fan-shaped. The plant has a high tolerance for salt and is successful in an exposed area along the shoreline, in a border, or as a container specimen. It makes an excellent coarse-textured ground cover in sandy soil near the coast.

Windmill Palm
Trachycarpus fortunei
20–40′   Zones 8–10

The windmill palm is a slender-trunked tree with large, deeply divided dark green fan-shaped leaves up to three feet across. The trunk is covered with persistent brown burlaplike fibers. This tree is easy to transplant and grow and is the most widely planted palm in the colder part of its region of adaptation. It is most effective in clumps where the individual trees vary in height.

Christmas Palm
Veitchia merrillii
15–25′   Zone 10

The Christmas palm produces clusters of striking crimson fruit an inch and a quarter long in winter, when vacationers who go south find the plant radiating a yuletide welcome. It has stiff green ascending leaves that can be six feet long. The tree grows only in the lower part of zone 10.

Christmas palm, grown for its showy red fruit.

Windmill palms, relatively cold hardy

165

Indoor planting of the Washington palm, a very tall-growing, slender palm

Jerusalem Thorn, Parkinsonia
Parkinsonia aculeata
Leguminosae
25' x 20'   Zones 8/9–10

A small fast-growing tree that can survive only in areas where winters are mild, the Jerusalem thorn likes fertile, well-drained soil and full sunlight. The fine, delicate compound yellow green leaves are eight to sixteen inches long with their numerous leaflets less than three-quarters of an inch wide. A profusion of fragrant yellow pealike flowers are borne on long, slender pedicels in late spring, and again cyclically during summer. The prominent thorns on twigs, branches, and trunk can be dangerous to the unsuspecting. The tree is salt-tolerant and does well in hot, dry locations. It is short-lived and is highly sensitive to freezes, compacted soil, excessive rainfall, and poor drainage.

Jerusalem thorn in flower

Washington Palm
Washingtonia robusta
60–100'   Zones 9–10

The Washington palm is a slender fast-growing, robust tree with bright green fan-shaped leaves. The older leaves persist and clothe the trunk. Adaptable to various soil conditions, this palm is picturesque as a street tree. Sometimes grown as a specimen, it is best in groups. It is not as hardy as *W. filifera,* the petticoat palm, which has large fan-shaped leaves on long stems that form a broad, dense canopy and the trunk of which is clothed in a dense thatched petticoat of old leaves. The petticoat palm makes a stiff, erect specimen and is planted primarily as a street tree.

Parrotia
Parrotia persica
Hamamelidaceae
40' x 30'   Zones 4–8

The lustrous medium to dark green leaves of the parrotia turn a beautiful, rich red, yellow, and orange in autumn. Red flowers with conspicuous crimson stamens appear in early spring before leaves, which are five inches long and two and a half inches wide. The plant grows best in well-drained slightly acid loam and in full sunlight, except in the Deep South, where partial shade

Leaves of the parrotia in autumn which can range from yellow through orange to scarlet.

is needed to prevent sunburn. It can become a multi-stemmed shrub or a small single-stemmed tree with ascending branches and a rounded head. The exfoliating bark of older branches has colors of silvery white, green, and brown that punctuate the winter garden. Because of the gorgeous fall color, interesting bark, unusual flowers, and freedom from insect and disease pests, the plant should be allotted a larger role in gardens.

Virginia Creeper
Parthenocissus quinquefolia
Vitaceae
25–100′ vine   Zones 3–9

The Virginia creeper, a native deciduous vine, thrives in a moist soil in full sunlight or partial shade. So fast-growing that it can be invasive, it climbs trees and walls of buildings and covers trellises, arbors, and fences. The palmate leaves have five leaflets and are dark green on the upper surface and pale underneath. The rosy red leaves of autumn can be spectacular. Seeds, a quarter inch in diameter and developing in long clusters, are dark blue in autumn. They are a food for native and migratory birds. A freedom from pests, drought resistance, and a tolerance of urban environments are assets of this rampant vine.

Boston ivy on wall

Boston Ivy
Parthenocissus tricuspidata
25–75′ vine   Zones 4–8

Boston ivy produces glossy dark green three-lobed leaves up to eight inches wide that turn crimson red in autumn. It is a high-climbing deciduous vine similar in all respects to the Virginia creeper except for leaf shape, which is here more ivylike.

Virginia creeper in autumn color at the University of Colorado.

Virginia creeper in its namesake state

Red passionflower

Red Passionflower
Passiflora coccinea
Passifloraceae
Vine to 40′
Zones 8/9–10

A fast-growing tropical vine, the red passionflower produces scarlet flowers three to five inches across that last but a day. The vine blooms best during the short days of spring and fall. Its dark green leaves are up to five inches in length and half as wide. Full sunlight is best, but the plant will grow and flower well in partial shade. It needs plenty of water to support its large leaf mass, but it is not fussy about soil, though its vigor is greatest where there is high fertility and good drainage. It generally dies back to the ground in the upper part of zone 9.

Le Duc

Fruit, flower buds, and foliage of the royal paulownia

Flowers of the royal paulownia

Royal Paulownia, Empress Tree
Paulownia tomentosa
Bignoniaceae
30–40′ x 30′   Zones 5–9

The royal paulownia is a fast-growing deciduous tree native to China. It has dark green heart-shaped leaves up to ten inches in length and width. Fragrant purple blue foxglovelike flowers in panicles a foot long appear in summer. A many-seeded fruit, resembling a cotton boll, matures in autumn.

Normally messy, the tree may have little value in the residential landscape, though it may be a handsome park tree. Lumber from the tree is shipped to Japan in large quantities, where it is prized for inlays on the hope chests of prospective brides.

Window box of geraniums

Geranium
Pelargonium × hortorum
Geraniaceae
2′   Zones 9–10

The geranium is grown throughout the United States as an annual bedding, container, and window-box plant. In areas that seldom receive a killing frost, it can be grown as a perennial. It requires a fertile, well-drained soil and full sunlight. Leaves are dark green and sometimes highly scented. Flowers are in umbels of white, pink, scarlet, red, or a bicolor. Blooms continue from spring into fall and in warm climates may be year-round. Large numbers of cultivars are available at garden centers.

Pentas
Pentas lanceolata
Rubiaceae
3′ x 1′   Zones 9–10

The pentas is a tall-growing perennial with showy two- to three-inch flower heads composed of closely positioned tubular flowers an inch in length. Cultivars are available

Pentas, perennials with a long flowering period.

with white, pink, or red blooms, and plants are in continuous flower from spring until frost. The plant grows best in full sunlight and in a fertile, well-drained soil, but it also performs well in relatively infertile soil, provided that it is not wet.

Red Bay
Persea borbonia
Lauraceae
40′ x 20′   Zones 8–9

Red bay

Native from North Carolina to Florida and west to Texas, the red bay is a small evergreen tree that grows in sandy soil and needs full sunlight. The tree has an upright form and a dense canopy and is usually multiple stemmed. The thick dark green leaves can be as long as five inches. They are aromatic and used to flavor food. Inconspicuous small flowers appear in May. Dark blue drupes about half an inch long are prominently borne on hairy red stems in autumn and winter. This evergreen's primary ornamental value is on wet sites in naturalistic settings.

Amur Cork Tree
Phellodendron amurense
Rutaceae
30–45′ x 30–45′   Zones 3–7

A beautiful broad-spreading tree with a rounded, open crown, the Amur cork tree has only a few horizontal branches. Compound leaves to fifteen inches long and about four inches wide are a shiny dark green in summer and change to a yellow or bronze yellow in autumn. The yellowish flowers on the female tree in late spring are subdued and are followed by black fruit in autumn. Of interest year-round is the ridged, furrowed gray brown corklike bark on the older tree. Good growth is possible in soils running from acid to alkaline, and there is drought resistance, as well as an insusceptibility to serious pests. Reportedly, the tree is tolerant of air pollution. It is a good shade tree

for extensive residential landscapes or in parks, golf courses, or other large public areas.

Mock Orange
Philadelphus coronarius
Saxifragaceae
10′ x 10′   Zones 5–8

One of the most reliable of spring-flowering deciduous shrubs, the mock orange thrives in full sunlight where the soil is moist, fertile, and

Mock orange flowers

well drained. It will also grow in partial shade and in less fertile soil. It has an upright oval to mounding form with

Foliage of the Amur cork tree.

Contorted trunk of a mature Amur cork tree in the Brooklyn Botanic Garden.

Specimen mock orange in a landscape.

high arching branches. Medium green oval leaves are one to four inches long. Fragrant white dogwoodlike flowers an inch and a half across with showy yellow stamens bloom in midspring. The shrub is easy to grow, and few insects and diseases afflict it. More compact cultivars

Mock orange, native to the Pacific Northwest.

'Argentine' mock orange at the Washington Park Arboretum, in Seattle.

with either yellow or variegated foliage are available. Among hybrids worthy of notice are *Philadelphus × lemoinei*, *Philadelphus × virginalis*, and their cultivars. *P. lewisii* is a shrub to ten feet native to western North America.

Split-Leaf Philodendron
Philodendron selloum
Araceae
10' x 10'   Zones 8/9–10

Native to tropical America, the split-leaf philodendron is usually grown in a container but can thrive outdoors in a warm climate. It is a shrublike evergreen that eventually develops a short trunk and grows to ten feet or more. Dark green lobed leaves three feet by three feet create a bold tropical effect in the landscape. Philodendrons are not especially soil specific but require one that is moist and fertile. They are an excellent choice for shady areas or areas receiving only morning sun. In full sunlight, this philodendron's leaves may burn, be stunted, or turn yellow green. The plant may die back to the ground after subfreezing temperature but, if mulched heavily, will return to tropical splendor in spring.

Split-leaf philodendron

Blue Phlox, Spring Phlox
Phlox divaricata
Polemoniaceae
12–15"   Zones 5–9

A native perennial, blue phlox is evergreen to semi-evergreen in the Deep South but is of little interest when not in flower. Fine, sticky hairs line the edges of its leaves,

Blue phlox at Afton Villa

Blue phlox

Summer phlox in Rhode Island

which are light green in spring and turn darker in warm weather. In March and April, clusters of five-petaled flowers an inch across decorate the plant on erect stems above the foliage. The original flower color is lavender blue, although selections having white and light pink blossoms are available. A moist, well drained soil and partial afternoon shade are ideal for the plant. Divide clumps in late autumn. Excellent for rock gardens, this phlox can also serve as a ground cover or a seasonal bedding plant.

Summer Phlox, Garden Phlox
Phlox paniculata
2–3′ x 1′   Zones 3–9

Few plants need as little attention, grow as well, and provide as much color in the garden over as extended a period as the summer phlox. A fertile moist, well-drained soil and full sunlight are needed for the fast-growing, heavy-feeding perennial. Flowering is most profuse in summer, but some blossoms may appear in autumn. Flowers range from white to purple, with pink, orange, lilac, lavender, and red among the gardener's choices. Individual flowers are an inch across and each large, round panicle borne atop a sturdy stem includes many flowers. After the first frost, cut stalks back to within six or eight inches of the ground, divide established clumps, and mulch heavily.

Moss Pink, Thrift

Phlox subulata
12–15″ x 6–10″
Zones 3–8

Moss pink

Moss pink is an evergreen plant of compact form and creeping growth habit that excels in rock gardens and as edging. The medium green foliage is fine textured and has a mossy appearance. Hot pink star-shaped flowers about three-quarters of an inch in diameter burst into bloom during the first warm days of spring. Cultivars with flowers in white and shades of pink are available, but they are not as vigorous as the plant with hot pink flowers. Full sunlight and a dry, well-drained soil are essential for this phlox.

New Zealand Flax

Phormium tenax
Agavaceae
4′ x 4′   Zones 8–10

New Zealand flax, an introduction from the country for which it is named, is tolerant of wide temperature fluctua-

Clipped hedge of the Fraser's photinia

tions and salt spray and grows well in almost any well-drained soil. Its sword-shaped leaves are tough and leathery, reaching a length of six feet and a width of four inches. The leaves, with shredded tips, are stiff in dry climates and arching where humidity is high, and their margins have an orange to red line. Numerous dull red flowers two inches long are borne on zigzag scapes that may be ten feet in height. The plant flowers best in dry soil and a very warm environment. Its strong tropical character, distinctive color, unusual foliage, and rosette form make it a standout in rock gardens, planters, or seaside plantings. The cultivar 'Sundowner' is an excellent selection for container culture.

Fraser's Photinia

Photinia × fraseri
Rosaceae
10–12′ x 8′   Zones 7–9

Upright-growing with an oval form, Fraser's photinia can do well in full sunlight or partial shade. A loose, well-drained soil is required; wet soil leads to root rot. This evergreen has leaves up to five inches in length. The coppery red color of the young leaves, lasting for several weeks, draws attention, as does the red of the buds and young shoots. White flowers in flat clusters four to six inches across appear in spring and have a fetid odor. Round red fruit about a quarter inch in diameter is sometimes present in late summer through winter. The shrub is used extensively in screens, hedges, and espaliers. Large-

New Zealand flax, surrounded by a cotoneaster ground cover in San Francisco

scale planting is not advisable in the Lower South because of the danger of root rot and leaf spot.

Red-Tip Photinia
Photinia glabra
10' x 8'   Zones 8–9

Red-tip photinia, a native of Japan, is a large evergreen shrub resplendent each spring in its brilliant red new

triking foliage of the red-tip photinia

growth. The red leaves, two to three inches long and an inch wide, change to green after several weeks. Throughout the growing season, new foliage is red, but it is never as lush as in spring. Panicles of white flowers three to five inches in diameter are prominent in spring and may be followed by round, berrylike fruit in summer. The shrub must have near-perfect drainage, a loose soil, and good air circulation, and it must receive full sunlight. Its

upright oval form suits it for hedges, screens, and both mass and accent plantings. Fire blight may kill new growth, as well as some older branches, on this or any other photinia. This photinia is not tolerant of *Entomosporium* leaf spot, which in some years causes severe defoliation.

Chinese Photinia
Photinia serrulata
20' x 10'   Zones 7–9

The Chinese photinia, a popular introduction from China, has a dense, pyramidal to broadly oval form with several stems branching near the ground. The thick oblong glossy dark green foliage of the large evergreen shrub is up to eight inches long and half as wide. Clusters of white flowers four to six inches across are showy in spring. The prominent orange red berries from late summer into winter are more abundant in the upper zones of the plant's range of adaptation. Good drainage and full sunlight are necessary for best growth. The shrub can be considered for screens and hedges. Larger specimens of this photinia and others may be reclaimed by selective pruning to produce a

Chinese photinia flowers

Autumn fruit of the Chinese photinia

small tree. The Chinese photinia is the most cold hardy of the species, and it has some tolerance of leaf spot.

Dwarf Alberta Spruce
Picea glauca 'Conica'
8–10′ x 2–3′   Zones 2–6

The dwarf Alberta spruce is slow-growing and widely used as a novelty plant, both in the landscape and in containers. White spruce, of which this shrub is a cultivar, grows to sixty feet and is not widely employed in landscaping. The conical dwarf has very dense light green needles that rarely exceed a half inch in length. Its ease of propagation and compact growth make it probably the most common dwarf conifer.

Dwarf Alberta spruce

Norway spruce

Norway Spruce
Picea abies
Pinaceae
60′ x 30′   Zones 2–7

The Norway spruce, like other spruces, performs best in moist, well-drained soil that is acid and sandy. It can do fairly well under less than ideal growing conditions provided that there is adequate moisture. All spruces have needles that are square in cross-section, whereas firs have needles that tend toward the flat. The stiff needles on this evergreen last for several years and are straight or curved, ending in a blunt or horny point. Up to an inch in length, they are light or dark green. Often planted as a specimen but better adapted to use in windbreaks and shelter belts, the tree is very cold hardy and needs full sunlight for best growth.

White spruce in the Rocky Mountain National Park, Colorado

Colorado spruce at Newport, Rhode Island

Colorado Spruce
Picea pungens
30–60' x 10–15'   Zones 3–7/8

A distinctive narrow to broadly pyramidal form and dull green, bluish, or silvery white leaves make the Colorado spruce an interesting accent in landscapes. The evergreen needles, to an inch and a quarter long, are stout, rigid, and very prickly. A rich, moist soil and full sunlight are ideal for this drought-tolerant species. Selections varying in foliage color and plant form include 'Fat Albert', 'Glauca Pendula', 'Hoopsii', 'Koster', 'Moerheimii', and 'Thompsenii'.

at Albert' Colorado spruce

Japanese Pieris
Pieris japonica
Ericaceae
5–6'   Zones 5–8

Pendulous pearl-like creamy white flowers erupt in early spring on the Japanese pieris from buds that are prominent from late summer through winter. Lustrous dark green leaves are arranged around the stem, rosettelike. The leaves are up to three inches long and an inch wide. This evergreen shrub grows best in morning sun and in a soil

Japanese pieris with autumn fruit

that is cool, moist, well drained, and slightly acid. It has a relatively dense mass and an upright oval form. Green fruit turns brown in late summer and looks like beads on a string. Over thirty cultivars have been introduced, varying in characteristics like size and form and the color of leaf and flower.

Temple Bells Pieris
Pieris ryukyuensis 'Temple Bells'
4' x 3'   Zones 6–9

The species to which the temple bells pieris belongs is believed to have originated in the Ryukyu Retto Islands, at the southern tip of Japan. Some, however, maintain that the plant is a cultivar of *P. japonica*. The growth

Temple bells pieris

habit of the plant is erect, with branches and foliage in horizontal, pagoda-like tiers that result in a rounded shrub. This pieris is a slow grower. New leaf growth is a lustrous light green flushed with apricot bronze. The color deepens to reddish bronze, then, in summer, to emerald green. In early spring, rounded ivory white bell-shaped flowers, large for this genus, appear in sizable clusters. The plant should gain popularity as it becomes better known.

THE PINES

Pinaceae

The pines include over ninety species in the Northern Hemisphere that yield lumber, rosin, turpentine, pulp for paper manufacturing, and food for wildlife. Valued as needled evergreen ornamentals, they grow at rates varying from slow to rapid. The slash pine and longleaf pine can attain heights in excess of eighty feet. Cultivars of other species can be under four feet. Needlelike adult foliage is borne in bundles of two, three, or five, depending on the species. When young, most species have a pyramidal form. At maturity the form becomes open, with a rounded canopy. Most pines will grow in a wide variety of soils but do best in well-drained soil that is slightly acid. Full sun is the preferred light, but the plants will grow in partial shade. In the landscape, they can play a role in screens, windbreaks, mass plantings, and backgrounds, and as specimens and lawn trees.

Shortleaf pine

Multiple-stemmed specimen of 'Umbraculifera' Japanese red pine

Japanese Red Pine
Pinus densiflora
50′ x 40′   Zones 3–7

The Japanese red pine has lustrous bright green leaves with fine-toothed margins. Growing to five inches long the leaves are in bundles of two. The tree has a broad-spreading flat crown. Its horizontal branches are frequently on trunks that lean. Orange red bark and an interesting form add to its value as a specimen tree. The cultivar 'Umbraculifera' grows to only fifteen feet and is a strong structural landscape plant.

Shortleaf Pine
Pinus echinata
80′ x 50′   Zones 6–9

The shortleaf pine's dark bluish green needles, two to five inches long, usually occur in pairs. Cones, which are an inch and a half to two inches long, take two years to mature and remain on the tree for several years. The tree has irregular whorled, spreading branches and a broad upright oval form. The bark is always rough.

Lawn planting of slash pines

Slash Pine
Pinus elliottii
100′ x 60′   Zones 8–9

The slash pine has glossy dark green needles up to a foot long in bundles of two or three. When it is old, its gray to reddish brown bark has heavy ridges of long, thin scales. Early purple pollen cones and large seed cones connected to the branches by short stems are also distinguishing characteristics of this fast-growing upright species.

Spruce Pine
Pinus glabra
75′ x 40′   Zones 8–9

The young spruce pine has a broad oval form and retains its branches to ground level; the older tree has an open, irregular form. There are two yellow green needles to each bundle, and they are twisted and three inches long. The oaklike bark has narrow ridges and shallow furrows. The tree tolerates heavier and wetter soils than most pines and is free of the fusiform rust that attacks many of them. The numerous cones are small.

Young spruce pines, showing their low branching habit

Slash pine pollen cones in spring

Mugo Pine
Pinus mugo
15–20′ x 30–80′   Zones 2–7

Only selected cultivars of the mugo pine, a species that is not native to the United States, are widely grown in landscapes. These are clipped to keep them under five feet in height and of equal spread. Needles are two to a bundle, of medium to dark green, and they last for five years or more. Three compact, low-growing round cultivars are 'Compacta', 'Gnom', and 'Mops'.

Mugo pine in Seymour, Indiana

Longleaf pine, very long needled, with white terminal buds.

Longleaf Pine
Pinus palustris
100' x 60'   Zones 7–9

The longleaf pine is a long-lived species that prefers a sandy soil and has an open canopy with an oval to upright form and horizontal branching. The needles, three to a bundle and up to eighteen inches long, give a coarse texture to this pine. The tree has prominent silvery white terminal buds in winter.

Cones are six to twelve inches long, and scales are tipped with spines.

Eastern white pine

Eastern White Pine
Pinus strobus
50–80' x 20–40'   Zones 3–7

Bluish to silver green needles mark the widely planted eastern white pine. The needles, in bundles of five, are five inches long. The mature tree has ascending horizontal branches that are more graceful than those of other pines. The slender six- to eight-inch cones hang like pendants on the branches. This fast-growing pine does not tolerate air pollution, strong wind, an alkaline soil, or a high salt concentration in the soil. Several cultivars differing in growth habit are available.

Distinctive cones of the eastern white pine.

Scotch pine

Scotch Pine
Pinus sylvestris
30–60' x 30–40'   Zones 2–7

The Scotch pine's stiff, twisted needles, in bundles of two, are about three inches and blue green. The tree must have well-drained acid soil for best performance. Individual specimens may become picturesquely distorted. This pine has been grown as a Christmas tree under managed conditions. Cultivars are available with variations in form and leaf color.

Loblolly Pine
Pinus taeda
100' x 60'   Zones 7–9

The loblolly pine is a popular timber tree in the South. Its dull green needles, six to nine inches long, grow in bundles of three. Each scale of the six-

Loblolly pine pollen cones in spring

inch cones is spined and thickened at the end. The tree grows fast for the first twenty years and provides excellent high shade for camellias and azaleas. The trunk has broad, thickened ridges divided by shallow furrows. Lower branches droop slightly. Pollen cones are yellow, and the pinecones are attached directly to the branches without stalks.

apanese black pine on the University of Georgia campus

Japanese Black Pine
Pinus thunbergiana
75′ x 35′   Zones 4–8

The Japanese black pine has stiff, sharp-pointed bright green needles four and a half inches long in bundles of two. This pine is broad-spreading, with horizontal branching and no well defined central leader for several years. It is usually grown as an accent to impart an Oriental character to the garden. It is reported to be the most salt-tolerant of the pines.

Chinese Pistache, Pistachio
Pistacia chinensis
Anacardiaceae
30–35′ x 35′   Zones 6–9

The Chinese pistache is one of the most trouble-free and desirable trees for lawns, parks, and street plantings. Free from insect and disease pests and drought tolerant, the deciduous tree has compound leaves ten to twelve inches long that are a lustrous medium green. Flowers on both the male and the female plant are insignificant, but the cherry red fruit on the female tree is showy after leaves drop in late fall. The tree grows well in a wide variety of soils, including the relatively dry. It has the most spectacular fall color of any tree in the Deep South, turning brilliant yel-

Chinese pistache in autumn color

low, orange, or red in November. When the thin leaves drop, they become very brittle, and a single mowing usually reduces them to a fine mulch.

Pittosporum
Pittosporum tobira
Pittosporaceae
10′ x 15′   Zones 8–10

Native to Japan and China, the pittosporum is an evergreen shrub with a dense broad-spreading to mounding form and strong, irregular branches. It grows well in sun or part shade in a soil that is moist, well drained, and loose. The thick, leathery leaves are dark green and up to four inches long and two inches wide. The flowers, creamy white to pale yellow, are borne in terminal clusters in

Variegated pittosporum

spring and possess a fragrance somewhat like that of citrus. Seedpods open in autumn to expose red seed. Tolerant of salt spray, the shrub makes an excellent screen, hedge, or accent plant. The selection 'Variegata' has pale green-and-cream leaves and is not as vigorous as the species. 'Wheelers Dwarf', only three to four feet high and wide, and not as cold hardy as the standard shrub, makes an excellent container and ground-cover plant. 'Shima' is a dwarf cultivar with variegated foliage.

Dwarf pittosporum

London Plane Tree
Platanus × acerifolia
Platanaceae
70–100' x 60'   Zones 5–8

Medium to dark green leaves seven inches long and eight to ten inches wide make the London plane tree a high-profile, coarse-textured part of the landscape. The exfoliating bark, olive green to cream, is eye-catching. The tree is well adapted to city conditions and is planted in parks and along streets, but sometimes its large size, huge spreading branches, and big leaves are a liability. Ball-shaped fruit matures in fall and is generally borne in pairs. The tree grows in full sunlight and in a wide range of soils, even those which are alkaline. Canker and lace bug are serious pests.

Sycamore, American Plane Tree
Platanus occidentalis
75–100' x 60'   Zones 4–9

The sycamore is a huge native tree with coarse-textured leaves and white winter bark. As the bark peels, white inner layers are revealed that add interest to the landscape, particularly in winter. Pointed, lobed medium to dark green leaves are four to nine inches in length and somewhat wider. A huge trunk supports large crooked branches that make up the open,

Sycamore foliage

Winter bark of a sycamore in Arkansas

Pleached London plane trees at the University of California at Berkeley.

spreading canopy. The flowers are unimpressive, and the fruit that matures in autumn is single and ball-like. Not for small areas or street plantings, this plane tree is good for open spaces where meticulous maintenance is not important. The large leaves decompose slowly and can clog storm sewers. Anthracnose often causes defoliation, the death of young shoots in early spring, and even the death of mature trees.

Plumbago, the cultivars of which may have blue or white flowers.

Oriental Arborvitae
Platycladus orientalis
Cupressasceae
10–25′ x 15′   Zones 6–9

The leaves of the oriental arborvitae grow in flat, closely spaced vertical planes. This bold, heavy conical evergreen performs best in full sunlight and in well-drained soil. Very dense and compact when young, it is looser and more open when mature. Bagworms may defoliate and even kill it. There are numerous cultivars, with differing forms and some with variegated foliage.

Plumbago
Plumbago auriculata
Plumbaginaceae
2–3′ x 5′   Zones 8/9–10

Plumbago has an oval to mounding form and is semi-climbing where there is a supporting structure. The soft, arching branches turn downward, and the plant is dense. Sometimes dying back to the ground in winter, it will normally return in spring. It grows fast and likes a hot, sunny area and a moist, well-drained soil. Terminal clusters of phloxlike sky blue flowers are present from May until the cool weather of fall. Even during cold weather there can be sporadic blooming. An annual spring pruning is needed for a neat plant and maximum flowering. A white cultivar, 'Alba', is available.

Fernlike foliage of the African fern pine

African Fern Pine
Podocarpus gracilior
Podocarpaceae
8–20′ x 8′   Zone 10

Although the African fern pine will grow quite large with age, the pendulous tropical tree is often pruned to maintain a height under six feet. Its dark blue green fernlike leaves, four inches long and a quarter inch wide, have a fine texture. This evergreen grows in full sunlight or partial shade and performs well in any good garden soil. It can be a container plant, part of a screen or hedge, or a specimen plant. Flowers and fruit are of no ornamental value.

Arborvitae on the grounds of the Louisiana State Capitol

Podocarpus

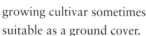

Leaves and fruit of the podocarpus.

Podocarpus, Japanese Yew
Podocarpus macrophyllus
10–20′ x 10′   Zones 8–10

The podocarpus is a slow-growing evergreen from Japan in wide use in the Lower South, where *Taxus*, or the true yew, is not adapted. Its most distinguishing characteristic is its narrow, upright form, which makes it a favorite large shrub or small tree for screens and clipped hedges. Leaves up to four inches long and a third of an inch wide are a lustrous dark green on top and paler underneath. The plant grows well in full sunlight or partial shade and likes a well-drained soil. Fruit on the female plant is borne atop an accessory part known as an aril, which is blue black when the seeds mature in summer. Though not especially palatable, the ripened arils are edible, and some birds consume them. 'Maki' is the most popular cultivar. 'Prostrata' is a low-growing cultivar sometimes suitable as a ground cover.

Broadleaf Podocarpus
Podocarpus nagi
15–25′ x 10′   Zones 8/9–10

The thick blue green foliage of the broadleaf podocarpus is leathery. The lance-shaped evergreen leaves, up to three inches long and an inch and a quarter wide, have numerous lengthwise veins. Full sunlight or partial shade and a well-

Broadleaf podocarpus foliage

drained soil are necessary for good growth. The tree form is narrow and upright, and lower branches tend to be pendulous. The plant is slow-growing, like other members of the genus. Bluish fruit about a half inch in diameter matures in summer. This podocarpus makes an excellent container or specimen plant.

Mayapple
Podophyllum peltatum
Berberidaceae
10–18″   Zones 3–9

A loose moist, well-drained organic soil is required for the mayapple. The herbaceous perennial normally occurs in colonies. Drooping foliage that emerges in late winter becomes flat and umbrella-like. Light green leaves may be a foot across and are palmately divided into five to nine segments. The creamy white saucer-shaped flowers have six to nine waxy petals with many prominent stamens. The flowers, which bloom in March and April, are up to two inches wide. The plant combines well with ferns and violets in naturalistic settings where there is a heavy layer of leaf mulch.

Colony of mayapples in a humus-rich woodland setting

Solomon's Seal
Polygonatum biflorum
Liliaceae
2–3′ x 2′   Zones 3–9

Graceful, arching branches with richly veined leaves to four and a half inches in length make the Solomon's seal a val-

Solomon's seal

ued surprise perennial in early spring. Pendulous clusters of white bell-shaped flowers with a hint of green are present in summer. The plant thrives in shade in a deep, rich soil with a bountiful supply of leaf mold. It is an excellent choice for the perennial border and wild garden. *P. commutatum*, great Solomon's seal, grows to six feet, about twice the size of the common species. Its fragrant white flowers are followed, in autumn, by black berries. Leaves turn a rich yellow at that time of year.

Silver-Lace Vine
Polygonum aubertii
Polygonaceae
Vine to 30′   Zones 4–8

Requiring a sunny exposure and a well-drained, sandy soil, the silver-lace vine is one of the fastest-growing vines. Foamy sprays of white flowers in slender panicles to six inches long cover it in summer. Leaves are dark green and have a coarse texture. The plant is relatively easy to grow and has no major pests. It does not appear to like hot, humid weather and therefore is not widely cultivated in the Deep South. It clings to any support and quickly covers fences and walls.

Magic carpet polygonum

Magic Carpet Polygonum, Trailing Knotweed
Polygonum capitatum
2–3″ trailer   Zones 9–10

Pink flowers in dense heads to three-quarters of an inch across blanket the magic carpet polygonum in summer. Reddish leaves to an inch and a half long are one of the ground cover's added attractions. The plant is easily grown in most garden soils if there is full sunlight. It is grown as an annual farther north but is a perennial in the Deep South. It roots easily from cuttings.

Wild Orange, Trifoliate Orange
Poncirus trifoliata
Rutaceae
8′ x 10′   Zones 6–10

A deciduous native of China, this hardiest of citrus, the wild orange, thrives in fertile moist, sandy loam in full sunlight or partial shade. It grows on wet and infertile sites and in hot, dry places. Leaves have three leaflets, and often occur in clusters. The plant's form is open and indefinite, with multiple stems and angular, thorny branches. White flowers an inch across perfume the spring air with the heavy

Silver-lace vine on garden arbor in Columbia, South Carolina

Flowers of the wild orange

Eastern Cottonwood
Populus deltoides
70–100′ x 50–70′   Zones 3–9

The eastern cottonwood is a native deciduous tree commercially important for its lumber. It is fast-growing and thrives in moist, fertile soil in full sunlight at woodland edges. It is fairly long-lived in drier regions. The yellow green foliage is up to five inches long and wide and makes a quaking sound in a good breeze. Male flowers (catkins) appear in early spring before the foliage, and female flowers are not prominent. The tree has an upright oval form of medium density and texture. It is weak wooded, its seeds are a nuisance, and it has a shallow, highly competitive root system.

sweet fragrance associated with orange blossoms. Very seedy inedible fruit matures in fall and is a dull lemon color. The shrub can be grown as an espalier or in an impenetrable hedge. It can be used as grafting stock for edible citrus, or it can be planted as a specimen for its picturesque winter form.

White poplar foliage

White Poplar
Populus alba
Salicaceae
30–50′ x 25′
Zones 3–8

Though not native, the white poplar is widespread in the United States, probably because of its adaptability to soils from poor to fertile and from dry to moist. The three-pointed, lobed maplelike leaves are dark green on top and chalk white underneath. This deciduous tree is fast-growing, with an irregular to broad-spreading oval canopy and a relatively short trunk. With the slightest breeze, the leaves move to reveal their light undersides. In addition to the tree's other assets, it tolerates pollution and hot urban landscapes. It is short-lived, however, and has brittle wood and a shallow root system that suckers freely.

Picturesque configuration of old cottonwoods, often found along dry riverbeds, here at the Fort Davis National Historical Site, Texas.

Lombardy Poplar
Populus nigra 'Italica'
50' x 15'   Zones 3–9

Fast growth and a narrow columnar form are trademarks of the Lombardy poplar, which is frequently seen in screens and windbreaks. A favorite on midwestern farmsteads, it is a dominating plant in the landscape because of its highly visible form. Canker is a serious disease, and it is difficult to maintain a regular, unbroken planting because parts of trees and entire trees die. The tree is fast-growing and tolerant of dry soil, and it can be used in tight spaces.

Lombardy poplars

Wild plum

Chickasaw plum in the south orchard of Monticello

Bush Cinquefoil
Potentilla fruticosa
Rosaceae
1–4' x 4'   Zones 2–7

A shrubby plant with slender upright stems and a low, rounded form, the bush cinquefoil is suited to extreme cold and gives satisfactory performance in poor, dry soil. It does best, however, in a fertile moist,

Ammen

Bush cinquefoil

well-drained soil. Flowers are profuse in full sunlight but satisfactory in partial shade. In early spring the leaves are gray green, but they change quickly to bright green and then to dark green. Flowers are buttercup yellow and up to an inch in diameter. Flowering is continuous from early summer until frost. The plant must be pruned annually to keep it looking neat. Numerous cultivars give a wide choice of leaf color, flower characteristics, and plant form. 'Abbotswood' and 'Gold Star' are two outstanding cultivars.

Wild Plum
Prunus americana
Rosaceae
10' x 15'   Zones 4–9

Dense colonies of the native wild plum arise from the numerous root suckers it produces. The small flowering tree has a short, crooked trunk and a broad-spreading crown with many branches. Umbels of two to five flowers on slender stalks bloom in late winter and very early spring. Flowers up to an inch and a half wide are white with some red pigmentation. The red fruit ripens in summer. *P. angustifolia*, the Chickasaw plum, is similar.

Taiwan flowering cherry

Flowers of the Taiwan flowering cherry

inch-long racemes of small creamy white flowers are prominent. The fruit, a quarter inch in diameter, turns black in autumn and may remain on the tree for months if birds like robins do not eat it. Many branches, some near the ground, blend into an upright oval form covered with dense lustrous green foliage. Broken or crushed stems exude a distinct maraschino cherry odor.

Purpleleaf plum in Colonial Williamsburg

Taiwan Flowering Cherry
Prunus campanulata
15–25' x 15'   Zones 7/8–9

The best flowering cherry for the Lower South, the Taiwan flowering cherry has a very short chilling requirement and will blossom the first week of warm weather in late winter. Along the Gulf Coast it has bloomed as early as January 10 and as late as mid-March. Drooping rosy pink bell-shaped flowers in clusters of two or more are about an inch in diameter. If cold does not damage the small cherrylike fruit, it turns red and then, when fully ripened, almost black. Fruit matures about two months after flowering. Volunteer seedlings are common under the mature tree. This species will tolerate high shade and heavy soil but will not live long in wet soil.

Fruit and foliage of the cherry laurel

Cherry Laurel
Prunus caroliniana
10–40' x 15'
Zones 7–10

Prized as a privacy screen, the cherry laurel is a non-native large evergreen shrub or small tree that grows in well-drained soil in sunlight or partial shade. Leaves to four inches are leathery and vary considerably in shape. In early spring,

Purpleleaf Plum, Myrobalan Plum
Prunus cerasifera
15' x 25'   Zones 5–8

Dark maroon purple foliage makes the purpleleaf plum a highly visible tree in the landscape. Fragrant light pink flowers appear before the leaves in early spring. Small plumlike fruit in late summer is not of major ornamental value. This plum has an upright to oval form with dense ascending branches. It is short-lived, because it hosts a number of insect and disease pests. 'Atropurpurea' and 'Newport' are two popular cultivars. *Prunus × cistena,* the purple sand cherry, is a related hybrid that is smaller, and some of its cultivars have intense leaf coloration. Full sunlight and well-drained soil are required for both the purple-leaf plum and the purple sand cherry.

lowering almond

Flowering Almond
Prunus glandulosa
3–5' x 4'   Zones 4–9

Double pink or white flowers cluster along the stems of the flowering almond in early spring. Blossoms a half inch in diameter appear before plants leaf out. The small red fruit of summer is of little value. Grow the small deciduous shrub in full sunlight in a soil that is porous and fertile. Normally with several upright stems, the plant has a form that is mounding, with an open density. Used for landscape enrichment and as a design detail, the shrub needs periodic pruning to rejuvenate it and to maintain an orderly appearance. Cultivars include 'Rosea Plena', with pink double flowers; 'Alba Plena', with white double flowers; and 'Rosea', with pink flowers.

English Laurel, Common Cherry Laurel
Prunus laurocerasus
10' x 25'   Zones 6–8

The English laurel is a large shrub with evergreen leaves six inches long and three inches wide. Two glands are present at the base of the dark green blades. The dense, widespreading shrub makes a bold statement in the landscape. White flowers with a slightly repugnant odor are borne in

racemes two to five inches long in spring. The purple to black fruit is difficult to see in the heavy foliage. Salt-tolerant, this laurel grows best in moist, well-drained soil that is amended with organic matter. Full sunlight or partial shade and a low level of fertility are preferred. Several cultivars, with differing growth and leaf characteristics, have been introduced, among them 'Magnoliifolia', 'Schipkaensis', and 'Zabeliana.'

Amur Cherry
Prunus maackii
35' x 20'   Zones 2–6

Exfoliating bark with a cinnamon brown metallic sheen is a feature of the Amur cherry. Two- to three-inch racemes of white flowers in late spring are followed in August by black berries. The young tree is pyramidal, but the older specimen becomes rounded and dense headed. Best suited for cold climates, the deciduous tree requires a well-drained soil.

Bark of the Amur cherry

Mexican plum fruit and foliage

Mexican Plum
Prunus mexicana
15–20' x 20'   Zones 7–9

A small native deciduous tree that occurs at woodland edges and as weak understory growth, the Mexican plum likes fertile moist, well-drained soil. It has a highly irregular form

English laurel in the Blue Ridge Mountains

but tends to be upright to mounding. Veins are prominent on the yellow green leaves, which are up to four inches long and two inches wide. White flowers with a pinkish cast are three-quarters of an inch in diameter and have a tacolike fragrance when they open in early spring. In August, fruit an inch and three-quarters across and of questionable palatability ripen to purplish red. This plum has good drought tolerance.

Japanese Apricot
Prunus mume
20′ x 10′   Zones 6–9

Flowers of the Japanese apricot

The flowering Japanese apricot is highly prized in its native land for its spectacular show of early spring blossoms. Fragrant double or single flowers are to an inch and a quarter in diameter, and on the cultivar 'Peggy Clarke' are a deep rose color. Depending on the cultivar, of which there are over 250 in Japan, the flowers may be white, pink, rose, or red. This is a fast-growing tree that should be pruned in spring as soon as flowering is completed to ensure flowering the following year. Some recommend that only half the branches be cut back in spring, since those not pruned will have a heavy flower-bud set in summer.

Okame Flowering Cherry
Prunus 'Okame' (*Prunus × incamp* 'Okame')
10–20′ x 15′   Zones 5–9

Developed at the National Arboretum, the Okame flowering cherry is an early bloomer with light pink flowers. It grows rapidly and will generally have a significant number of flowers when only three years old. It does not produce fruit when isolated, but when pollinated by other cherries it will produce half-inch berries that ripen to a purple black. Oak root rot can kill the tree in a few weeks, and San Jose scale can also be devas-

tating. This cherry is not fussy about soil as long as it is well drained. Its lavish display of flowers, medium-textured leaves, and fast rate of growth make it worth considering for the landscape as a specimen or in a mass planting.

Ornamental flowering peach

Peach
Prunus persica
10–25′ x 15′   Zones 5–9

The peach is the queen of summer fruit trees. It requires frequent spraying to control curculios and bacterial rot in the fruit, borers in the trunk, and fungal disease in the leaves. A fer-

Okame flowering cherry

Double-flowered red ornamental peach

tile, well-drained soil and a sunny location are a must for success. In landscapes, the flowering peaches that are usually grown require less maintenance than fruiting cultivars. The trees are deciduous and flowering occurs before leaves. Flowers, single or double, are most often pink but may be white, red, or a bicolor. Among the all time favorites is 'Peppermint Stick', which has red, white, and red-and-white striped flowers on the same branch or plant, and 'Alba Plena', which has large white double flowers.

Black cherry fruit and foliage

Black Cherry
Prunus serotina
15–40′ x 40′   Zones 3–9

The black cherry is a native deciduous tree with lustrous dark green leaves that turn coppery yellow to red in autumn. In

Mockingbird feeding on fruit of the black cherry.

spring, there are pendulous six-inch clusters of white flowers. Green fruit changes to red and then black as it ripens. Ripening occurs in midsummer in zone 9 and into late summer farther north. The fruit is used in jellies, and it is steeped in alcohol to make cherry bounce, a popular liqueur in French Louisiana. This cherry thrives in most soils except the very wet and very dry. The leaves, resembling those of the peach, are up to three inches long. Like others of its genus, the tree is short-lived.

Kwanzan Flowering Cherry
Prunus serrulata 'Kwanzan'
10–30′ x 15–30′
Zones 4–8

Of the dozen or more cultivars of the *serrulata* group, the Kwanzan flowering cherry

Carnation-like blossoms of the Kwanzan flowering cherry.

is the hardiest and the most widely planted. In the Deep South, leaves are present in late spring, when flowering occurs, but elsewhere the flowers are borne on bare branches. Rich pink carnation-like double flowers are up to three inches in diameter. The dark green leaves are up to five inches long and half as wide. Leaves are bronze when young and turn an orange bronze in autumn. This cherry is the last one to flower in the southern part of its range of adaptation. Plant in a well-drained soil in full sunlight or partial shade. The tree is highly susceptible to borers and virus infections and is generally short-lived.

Weeping Higan Cherry
Prunus subhirtella 'Pendula'
10–15′ x 15′   Zones 4/5–8

The graceful, pendulous branches of the weeping Higan cherry are laden with almond-scented semidouble flowers. Bloom is in early spring, when pink buds open into three-quarter-inch white blossoms. The rounded red fruit turns black when ripened. Seeds will germinate and produce trees

Weeping Higan cherry in Washington, D.C.

that are very similar to the parent. This is an extremely fast-growing species, and if it stays free of virus diseases, it can live longer than the ten to fifteen years that are typical. Spectacular in form and flower, the tree gives a strong accent to the landscape. This cherry grows in well-drained soil in a sunny location.

Pomegranate flowers and buds

Cox

Yoshino cherries from Japan growing in Washington, D.C.

Close-up of flowers of the Yoshino cherry

Yoshino Cherry
Prunus × yedoensis
30′ x 25′   Zones 5–8

Slightly fragrant white to light pink flowers with a deeper pink throat, four or more to a cluster, adorn the Yoshino cherry in March and April. Clouds of flowers make the plant a thing of unusual beauty. The glossy bright green foliage appears after the flowers and turns yellow in autumn. This cherry grows in a moderately well drained soil and flowers best in full sunlight, although it is satisfactory in partial shade. It blooms rather sporadically in the Deep South, probably because chilling requirements are not satisfied. Thousands of people travel to Washington, D.C., each year to see the spectacular display of blossoms by this species around the Tidal Basin.

Pomegranate
Punica granatum
Punicaceae
8–10′ x 6′   Zones 8–10

One of the oldest cultivated fruiting plants, the pomegranate is an Asian native that has become a popular flowering and fruit-bearing plant in southern gardens. The multi-stemmed deciduous shrub of upright oval form is medium

dense when in leaf but rather open when bare. Shiny new coppery-colored foliage becomes leathery and turns yellow in autumn. Orange red double flowers about three inches in diameter bloom in late spring. There are cultivars with white, yellow, or variegated flowers, single or double. An edible brownish yellow to red fruit, three to four inches in diameter, ripens in late summer and in fall. Not every pomegranate sets fruit, but 'Wonderful' and 'Sweet' are two cultivars that flower and fruit well. 'Pleniflora' has double flowers of scarlet red; 'Multiplex' has white double flowers.

Scarlet Fire Thorn, Pyracantha
Pyracantha coccinea
Rosaceae
6–18′ x 6–18′   Zones 6–9

The scarlet fire thorn is a large semievergreen to evergreen shrub with broad, rambling branches. Judicious pruning is necessary to keep it in bounds. It has stiff, thorny branches that are open and spreading. Lustrous dark green leaves are an inch or two long and up to three-quarters of an inch wide. An abundance of white flowers with a fetid odor are

Orange-fruiting 'Lalandei' scarlet fire thorn in Pittsburgh

Variegated scarlet fire thorn

Pyracantha in flower

borne in three-inch clusters on the previous year's growth. In September, the small orange applelike fruit is at its showiest. It lasts into winter. The shrub grows in sunlight to partial shade in soil that is moderately acid to slightly alkaline. Fruiting is best in full sunlight. This species is an excellent barrier plant and an outstanding espalier specimen. Some cultivars are suitable for low, clipped hedges. 'Lalandei' is a widely planted cultivar that is extremely hardy. Other cultivars of different parentage include 'Lowboy', which is wide-spreading and low-growing; 'Harlequin', which has variegated foliage; and 'Cherri Berri', which has red fruit. The many cultivars differ in hardiness, fruit color, and form. *P. angustifolia* is a hardy low-growing species that has yellow orange fruit.

Pyracantha
Pyracantha koidzumii
8–15′ x 12′   Zones 8–10

Evergreen leaves to two inches long and three-quarters of an inch wide are produced on the pyracantha, a large upright shrub that appears unkempt unless properly pruned. Clusters of white flowers are attractive in spring, but the quarter-inch rounded red fruit present from early fall into winter is the distinction of the plant. Drought-tolerant, it prefers a well-drained soil and plenty of sunlight. Lace bug, spider mites, and fire blight may be problems. Prune the plant when it is

Mass planting of pyracanthas at Hodges Gardens, Many, Louisiana

Fruit of the pyracantha

191

in flower so fruiting wood is left. Maintenance pruning during the growing season is recommended. Cultivars varying in growth habit and cold hardiness are available. 'Low-Dense', 'Red Elf', and 'Ruby Mound' grow to less than six feet in height and have a mounding habit. 'Santa Ana' and 'Victory' are two large-growing cultivars.

Bradford Flowering Pear

Bradford pear in autumn color

***Pyrus calleryana* 'Bradford'**
Rosaceae
20–30′ x 25′   Zones 4–8

Selected from the Callery pear, introduced from China, the Bradford flowering pear is a cultivar with dense upright growth and heavy flowering. It is very tolerant of fire blight but is subject to damage from wind and ice. It grows in soil from dry to moderately moist. Clouds of white flowers appear with the new foliage of early spring. A fast-growing tree, this pear has outstanding autumn color of red to purple. Clusters of russet-colored fruit up to a half inch in diameter hang from the branches in autumn and winter. 'Aristocrat' is a cultivar with large, glossy leaves and more horizontal branching. 'Autumn Blaze', 'Capitol', 'Chanticleer', 'Redspire', and 'Whitehouse' have a pyramidal form and outstanding flowering qualities.

Callery pear in flower

Bradford pears at the Concordia Parish Courthouse, in Vidalia, Louisiana

Common Pear

Pyrus communis

15′ x 25′   Zones 4–9

There are many, many cultivars of the common pear, differing in fruiting characteristics, resistance to fire blight, and regional adaptability. The tree has lustrous dark green leaves up to four inches long and two inches wide. The white flowers of early spring are followed by large fleshy fruit ranging from green to yellow. Most ripen in late summer or early fall.

Fruit and foliage of the common pear

THE OAKS

Fagaceae

One of the most widely grown genera in America, the oaks comprise a large number of native and nonindigenous mostly deciduous species. A few evergreen species are found in warmer climates. Oaks are grown extensively for ornamental purposes and as a source of timber. The primary demarcation in the genus is between white oaks, the acorns of which mature in one season and the leaves of which are without bristle tips, and red oaks, the acorns of which take two years to mature and the leaves of which normally have bristle tips on the lobes. Oaks will grow in a wide variety of soils but thrive in those that are deep, rich, and moist. A few species do well under stressful moisture and soil conditions. Great diversity exists among oaks regarding their size, form, and acorns. The trees are long-lived and durable. One or another will meet almost any situation in which a medium or large tree is desired.

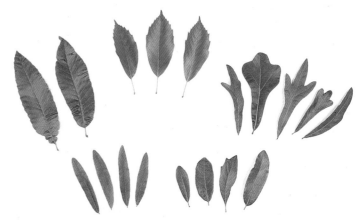

Leaves. Top row, left to right: *sawtooth oak (two leaves), Japanese evergreen oak (three leaves), water oak (five leaves, showing variation).* Bottom row: *willow oak (four leaves), live oak (four leaves, showing variation).*

Sawtooth Oak

Quercus acutissima

30–50′ x 30′   Zones 6–9

The sawtooth, bristle-tipped chestnutlike leaves of the sawtooth oak are up to eight inches long and of a glossy dark green. For an oak, this deciduous tree is fast-growing. It has broad-spreading branches and makes an excellent shade tree. It produces acorns at an early age, and its autumn color is yellow to brown.

White Oak

Quercus alba

50–75′ x 60′   Zones 5–9

The broad, coarse-textured blue green foliage of this white oak turns a brilliant red to burgundy in late autumn. Typical of white oaks, it has leaves with five to seven smooth-edged lobes. The striking ash gray bark peels into irregular plates. Pyramidal when young, the tree becomes an upright, broad-spreading tree when mature.

Southern Red Oak
Quercus falcata
75–120' x 60'   Zones 7–9

Leaves of the southern red oak are large, coarse textured, asymmetrically lobed, and bristle-tipped. The tree has comparatively good autumn color for a southern species. Its foliage persists into winter. *Q. falcata* var. pagodifolia, the cherry-bark oak, is similar but has more uniformly lobed leaves and a reddish bark. *Q. rubra* is similar to the southern red oak but is adapted to zones 4–8.

Japanese Evergreen Oak
Quercus glauca
20–30' x 20'   Zones 8–9

One of few evergreen oaks, the Japanese evergreen oak is a small, dense tree of an upright oval form similar to the American holly's. It makes an outstanding lawn specimen and can be used for privacy screening when planted in mass. Leaves are a lustrous dark green, leathery, and five inches long with prominent toothed margins on the upper half. *Q. acuta*, also commonly called a Japanese evergreen oak, is similar but has smooth, wavy leaf margins.

Laurel Oak
Quercus laurifolia (hemisphaerica)
50' x 30'   Zones 6–9

The laurel oak is semievergreen, with thick, leathery lustrous dark green leaves to four inches long and two inches wide. It has a pyramidal to rounded form, grows rapidly, may attain a height of sixty feet, and makes an excellent street tree.

Bur Oak, Mossy-Cup Oak
Quercus macrocarpa
50–80' x 50'   Zones 3–8

The bur oak is a slow grower, upright in form, that produces large coarse-textured leaves to a foot long and half as wide, with five to seven lobes on the upper portion, two to three on the lower. The upper leaf surface is a shiny dark green, and the lower surface is grayish and fuzzy. The tree

Leaves. Left to right: *white oak, southern red oak, bur oak, cow oak, Nuttall oak, Shumard oak.*

is known for its unusually large acorns borne in cups with fringed edges.

Blackjack Oak
Quercus marilandica
20' x 15'   Zones 6–9

The blackjack oak is a scrubby oak that grows in barren, sometimes quite sandy soil. Leaves with three ill-defined lobes are up to seven inches long. Thick and leathery, the leaves have brown undersides.

Blackjack oak, a small tree with coarse-textured leaves

Cow Oak, Basket Oak
Quercus michauxii
50–70' x 40'   Zones 7–9

Large and coarse textured, with scalloped edges, the leaves of the cow oak change to coppery yellow in autumn. The tree is upright oval in form and quite dense. The ash gray exfoliating bark is prominent during winter. *Q. prinus*, the chestnut oak, is similar but is found over a larger area, from zone 4 to zone 8.

Water Oak
Quercus nigra
50–100' x 50'   Zones 5–9

One of the fastest-growing oaks, the water oak has upright-arching branches that make it a not implausible substitute for the American elm. Dark green spatula-shaped leaves drop off the tree from fall into spring. As the tree ages, it experiences extensive dieback and continually drops debris, requiring frequent clearing. The tree will grow, however, where many oaks will not.

Nuttall Oak
Quercus nuttallii
30–50' x 35'   Zones 7–9

The Nuttall oak has an oval to rounded canopy with the upper branches ascending and the lower branches horizontal. Bristle-tipped leaves are five to nine inches long, with five to nine lobes, and have outstanding yellow autumn color. This oak grows in soils ranging from wet to dry.

in oak in autumn color at Kansas State University

Pin Oak
Quercus palustris
50–75' x 40'   Zones 4–8

The pin oak has been widely grown as a street tree because of its brilliant red autumn color. In recent years, however, it has lost some favor because of insect and disease problems and the yellowing caused by the iron deficiency associated with a high pH. This robust-growing oak has a strong pyramidal form and an interesting branching habit. *Q. coccinea*, the scarlet oak, is similar to the pin oak, producing shiny dark leaves to six inches, with seven lobes. The scarlet oak does not appear prone to the iron chlorosis affecting the pin oak.

Willow Oak
Quercus phellos
50–80' x 40'   Zones 5–8

Considered by many to be a superior oak in many landscape applications, the willow oak has a dense oval crown. The fine-textured light green willowlike leaves turn to a yellow or russet in autumn. Like the water oak, this oak holds its leaves into winter in the Lower South. It is a cleaner, neater tree than the water oak, however. It adapts to a wide range of soils.

English Oak
Quercus robur
40–90' x 50'   Zones 4–7/8

A beloved tree in England, where one of the species is estimated to be over a thousand years old, the English oak is less widely planted in the United States. Some cultivars are fairly popular through the upper region of the nation, in-

English oak of columnar form in Louisville, Kentucky

cluding 'Attention', 'Fastigiata', and 'Skymaster', which have columnar to pyramidal forms and are well adapted to a small space. The coarse-textured leaves of this oak are dark green on top and paler underneath.

Northern red oak, a very popular tree

Red Oak
Quercus rubra (borealis)
60' x 60'   Zones 4–8

Leaves of this red oak can be eight inches long and six inches wide, with seven to ten lobes. They are a lustrous dark green on top and grayish on the underside, with tufts of brownish hairs. A fast grower, the tree is symmetrical, with a rounded top, when mature. It suffers from no serious pests and is excellent as a shade, park, or street tree.

Shumard Oak
Quercus shumardii
50–75' x 40'   Zones 5–9

The Shumard oak possesses large shiny bright green leaves that are deeply and uniformly lobed. It is one of the most

dependable of shade trees and consistently displays an excellent red color in autumn. The mature tree has a rounded, wide-spreading canopy. It is one of the most durable oaks in the South.

Post Oak
Quercus stellata
25–40' x 30'
Zones 5–9

Typically the post oak grows naturally in dry, gravelly, or sandy soil with rock outcroppings. Seldom selected for the landscape, it may be desirable to keep it when fashioning a landscape from ground

Post oak, a small oak that was used for fence posts in early times.

that is its native habitat, provided that good conservation practices have left it sound. Its large glossy dark green leaves, which are leathery and coarse textured, can be attractive during the growing season. The leaves do not show much autumn color but stay on the tree well into the winter months.

Black Oak
Quercus velutina
40–50' x 40'   Zones 3–8

The black oak gets its name from the black furrowed bark on the mature tree. Deeply lobed leaves up to ten inches long are a shiny dark green. This oak grows in sandy to clay soil that is relatively infertile and dry.

Black oak, with large, coarse leaves

Allée of 175-year-old live oaks at Rosedown plantation

Live Oak
Quercus virginiana
30–50′ x 75′   Zones 8–10

The live oak is the most widely planted broadleaf evergreen tree in its range of adaptation. Glossy dark blue green leaves to three inches in length are leathery and have varied shapes. The tree has a short, thick trunk and deeply ridged black bark. Broad-spreading, mounding, and picturesque, the unpruned tree will have lower limbs that touch the ground. It is long-lived and tolerant of many different soils, even those with a high salt content.

Live oak on LSU campus

Indian Hawthorn
Raphiolepis indica
Rosaceae
2–3' x 4'   Zones 7–10

An intermediate-sized evergreen shrub from China, the Indian hawthorn is now widely planted in the southern United States. It likes sunlight and grows well in a fertile moist, well-drained soil. A low, dense mounding form is shared by most cultivars. The somewhat oblong dark green leaves are more dense near the branch tips. The heaviest flowering is in spring, when blossoms, varying by cultivar from white to deep pink, cover the plant. Half-inch flowers are borne in clusters, and black fruit stays on the plant for several months. The shrub is susceptible to cercospora leaf spot, and fire blight may kill parts of the plant. *R. umbellata* is a larger, more upright-growing species that has fragrant white flowers in spring.

'Clara' Indian hawthorn, of broad, mounding form

'Springtime' Indian hawthorn.

Carolina Buckthorn
Rhamnus caroliniana
Rhamnaceae
10–15' x 10'   Zones 6–9

The woodland edge, where the soil is moist, fertile, and slightly acid, is the perfect place for the Carolina buckthorn. The native deciduous tree's

Late summer berries of the Carolina buckthorn.

large, broad oblong leaves have pointed tips and prominent parallel veins. Leaves are dark green on their upper surface and can be six inches long and two inches wide. The flowers of late spring are of little consequence, but the quarter-inch fruit of late summer and into fall is emphatic as it turns red and then black. The tree is free of seriously damaging insects and diseases. *R. cathartica* is more hardy, and *R. frangula* 'Asplenifolia' has narrow, fernlike leaves.

THE AZALEAS AND RHODODENDRONS
Ericaceae

Approximately eight hundred species and thousands of cultivars are in the genus to which azaleas and rhododendrons belong. Early settlers in North America found both azaleas and rhododendrons growing over a wide area. The popular Indian azaleas were introduced only in 1848, however, and since then have been widely planted in southern gardens. Over the years, many other species and cultivars have become available.

Although closely related, there are some major differences between azaleas and rhododendrons. Most of the differences are taxonomic. Rhododendrons are characterized by large thick, leathery evergreen leaves that are scaly, although there are also a few deciduous types. Large clusters of bell-shaped flowers form at the end of sturdy stems. Rhododendrons normally are seen in cooler regions with rolling topography. Azaleas, on the other hand, have fairly small leaves, many of the types are deciduous, and their funnel-shaped flowers appear to be less clustered.

The most important requirement for growing either azaleas or rhododendrons is good drainage, in a peaty soil or one that is high in organic matter. Mulching helps keep the soil cool, retain moisture, reduce heaving in cold areas, and replenish organic matter. The plants are fairly exacting about soil acidity. The best pH range is between 5.0 and 6.0. Where the soil is more acid, they grow more slowly. With a high soil pH, leaves turn yellow—become chlorotic—and even die.

Size varies from the low, spreading satsuki and kurume azaleas to the mammoth, mounding evergreen rhododendrons. In sunlight the plants generally produce dense foliage, whereas in shade they have a more open and airy canopy.

The evergreen rhododendrons are the most cold-hardy, capable of tolerating temperatures well below 0 degrees Fahrenheit. The southern Indian azaleas may be damaged when the temperature falls below 20 degrees Fahrenheit. Injury is more pronounced when freezes occur early in the season, before the plants have been exposed to cooler temperatures that let them become dormant, or harden them off. But late freezes can be devastating to swollen flower buds and to partially open flowers.

Azaleas can be pruned severely to rejuvenate old and overgrown shrubs. Pruning should be done in spring as soon as flowering is over. Pruning later than that reduces or eliminates the next season's bloom.

Lace bugs, spider mites, and aphids are the most common insect pests; root rot, dieback, and petal blight are all fungal infections of azaleas.

Florida Azalea
Rhododendron austrinum
6–10′ x 8′   Zones 5–9

A native deciduous azalea of upright multiple-stemmed form, the Florida azalea produces clusters of golden yellow to orange tubular flowers. The flowers are highly fragrant, occur in early spring, and are produced in great numbers in full sunlight. This azalea often occurs along sandy streams and can become treelike as it ages.

Honeysuckle azalea

Honeysuckle Azalea
Rhododendron canescens
6–15′ x 8′   Zones 4–9

The honeysuckle azalea is an upright-growing native plant with multiple stems and, in early spring, clusters of fragrant tubular flowers in shades of pink to near-white. This azalea blooms best in full sunlight but will grow in shade, where it becomes sparse, open, and treelike. Other native deciduous azaleas include *R. alabamense*, with white flowers; *R. arborescens*, with white to light pink flowers; *R. bakeri*, with yellow to orange flowers; *R. calendulaceum*, with orange to scarlet flowers; and *R. prunifolium*, with red summer flowers.

Florida azalea

Catawba Rhododendron
Rhododendron catawbiense
6–12' x 8'   Zones 4–8

The Catawba rhododendron has beautiful flowers and luxuriant foliage. The dark green leaves of the large, hardy plant are up to six inches long and three inches wide. The lilac purple flowers appear in trusses five to six inches in diameter during spring, the exact timing dependent on location and cultivar. There are over a hundred cultivars varying in form, size, and flower color. These are native to areas with mild summers and moist to wet winters and do best with afternoon shade.

Mass planting of 'Fisher's Pink' Indian azaleas

Twelve-foot specimens of 'Cynthia' rhododendron

Indian Azalea, Southern Indian Azalea
Rhododendron indicum
6–10' x 8'   Zones 8–9

The most popular and widely planted flowering shrub in southern gardens, the Indian azalea has a broad, mounding form with a dense evergreen mass. In early spring, flowers two to three inches across in clusters of two to five appear in white, pink, salmon, orange, red, or a bicolor. 'Formosa', 'Pride of Mobile', 'George L. Tabor', 'Mrs. G. G. Gerbing', and 'Judge Solomon' are some of the all-time favorites among the many cultivars.

Satsuki, Macrantha Azaleas
Rhododendron eriocarpum
3–6' x 4'   Zones 7–9

Both the Satsuki and Macrantha azaleas flower late in the season—in May in the Deep South. Satsukis are mounding plants generally under three feet high that have large white, pink, or red flowers, sometimes blotched or flecked. The Gumpos are the best known of the Satsukis. Macranthas grow larger, and their blooms may be pink, coral, or red. There is a double-flowering form. The pink and coral Macranthas flower cyclically, with the heaviest bloom much later than on most other large azaleas.

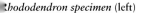

Rhododendron specimen (left)

'Gumpo Pink' Satsuki azalea

'Pride of Mobile' Indian azaleas at Stanton Hall, in Natchez

Kurume Azalea
Rhododendron obtusum
3–6' x 4'   Zones 7–9

Most people like the Kurume azalea best in mass plantings, where it is kept to a height of three feet or less. It has a

compact growth habit and small, dense evergreen leaves. In early spring the single or hose-in-hose flowers an inch and a half in diameter appear in clusters of two or three. Their colors are many, including white, pink, red, and orange red. 'Christmas Cheer' is a good red, 'Snow' is a fine white, and 'Coral Bells' is an excellent pink.

'Snow' (white), 'Christmas Cheer' (red), and 'Coral Bells' (pink) Kurume azaleas.

'Pride of Mobile' Indian azaleas at Afton Villa

Plumleaf azalea at Callaway Gardens, near Pine Mountain, Georgia

Plumleaf Azalea
Rhododendron prunifolium
10′ x 8′   Zones 5–9

The plumleaf azalea is a deciduous species that can be found growing along sandy ravines and stream banks. Its native habitat is southwestern Georgia and eastern Alabama, and it is a plant featured at Callaway Gardens, Pine Mountain, Georgia. The orange red to red flowers are a pleasant addition to the garden in July and August. The several cultivars include 'Coral Glow', 'Peach Glow', and 'Pine Prunifolium'.

Hybrid Azaleas
Rhododendron hybrids
Zones dependent on cultivars

Hybridizers have introduced an array of azaleas from which the gardener can choose.

Carla hybrids were developed jointly by North Carolina State University and Louisiana State University. Most are in an intermediate range of growth between Indian and Kurume types. They perform well in zones 7–8. Colors vary, but most are in shades of pink or red. They are free-flowering.

Exbury hybrids are upright-growing deciduous shrubs reaching heights of twelve feet and widths of nine feet. The foliage turns red in autumn. In late spring, beautiful two- to three-inch flowers in colors that include

Exbury hybrid azalea

near-white, cream, yellow, orange, rose, and red, sometimes as bicolors, are borne in trusses of eighteen or more flowers. The many Exbury hybrids withstand temperatures as low as −20 degrees Fahrenheit.

'Fashion' Glen Dale hybrid azalea

Glen Dale hybrids are hardy to 0 degrees Fahrenheit and have flowers as large as Indian azaleas but make smaller plants. Some leaf fall occurs in the upper zones of adaptation and during very cold winters in more southerly regions. Flowering in both early winter and early spring in the coastal South but only in early spring elsewhere, the plants have blossoms in white, pink, orange pink, red, and combinations of those colors. Two of these easily grown hybrids are 'Fashion', with orange red flowers, and 'Glacier', with white.

Girard hybrids have flower buds that are hardy from −5 to −15 degrees Fahrenheit. There are both evergreen and de-

'Sunglow' Carla hybrid azalea

'Fashion' azalea, a cultivar with several cycles of bloom

'Girard's Hot Shot' azalea

ciduous types, and some grow compactly. All have large flowers in white, pink, lavender, red, or a blend of several of those colors. The flowers may be single, double, or hose-in-hose.

Robin Hill hybrids are reported to be hardy to 0 degrees Fahrenheit. They are relatively low-growing evergreen

'Watchet', one of the best Robin Hill hybrid azaleas

plants that flower well. Flowers up to three inches across are ordinarily present in spring, but moderately heavy bloom also occurs in autumn and winter, and scattered bloom in late summer. The colors are from white to deep red. Favorites are 'Gillie', an orange, and 'Watchet', a clear pink.

Shining Sumac
Rhus copallina
Anacardiaceae
10′ x 15′   Zones 5–8

Shining sumac in autumn

The shining sumac produces dramatic color in the autumn landscape. It grows under a wide range of conditions but does best in a well-drained soil and in full sunlight. The plant is upright in form and sparely branched. It has a flat, spreading crown. Growing fast when young, the plant later multiplies freely from root suckers and seed. Compound dark green leaves are up to a foot and a half long, with each leaflet having a green wing along its stem. The bright red foliage of autumn is more pronounced when the plant is in full sunlight and in a dry soil. Clusters of compact, fuzzy crimson berries stand out in fall and last into winter.

Staghorn Sumac
Rhus typhina
8–15′ x 20′   Zones 3–9

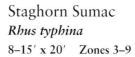

Staghorn sumac

Native to North America, the staghorn sumac suckers freely from its roots and spreads to form large colonies. Both leaves and fruit give exceptional color in fall and winter. Compound leaves a foot or two long are bright green in summer and yellow to scarlet in autumn. In June or July, there are greenish flowers in dense panicles up to eight inches long. Densely packed pyramidal panicles of fruit turn crimson in fall, a darker red in winter, and often hang on the plant until spring. The striking branches resemble deer antlers. This sumac grows in full sunlight and is adapted to many soils but prefers one that is well drained. It is especially effective in naturalized areas.

Roadside colony of shining sumac in summer

Smooth Sumac
Rhus glabra
8–15′ x 15′   Zones 5–8

Quickly forming colonies in open fields, rights-of-way, and such, the smooth sumac is a small native deciduous tree well adapted to most soils. The compound leaves reliably take on striking shades of red every autumn. Compound clusters of fuzzy crimson berries may remain all winter. This sumac is probably the only one to have its fruit consumed by many kinds of birds.

Fruiting clusters of the smooth sumac

Foliage of the black locust.

Black locust in flower

Black Locust
Robonia pseudoacacia
Fabaceae
25–50′ x 20–35′   Zones 3–8

Moist, well-drained alkaline or acid soil is suitable for the black locust, which grows in full sunlight or partial shade. The deciduous tree is fast-growing for the first three to five years, and root suckers are common as the tree matures. Compound foliage eight to fourteen inches long is medium green. The highly fragrant creamy white flowers are typical of the legumes. They occur in dense pyramidal racemes in spring before leaves appear. Dark orange brown seeds are borne in reddish brown pods. The fine-textured tree has an open, airy canopy and an upright form with broad-spreading branches. It can adjust to dry landscapes.

Lily-of-China, Nipponlily
Rohdea japonica
Liliaceae
2′ clump   Zones 7–10

The lily-of-China has been cultivated for more than five hundred years in Asia, where it is reported to bring good luck and a long life. Dark green leaves two feet long and three inches wide are borne in a basal rosette. The ever-green perennial is well adapted to moist soil and requires shade for most of the day, particularly after midday. The plant grows slowly and multiplies to form small colonies with arching leathery foliage. The insignificant pale yellow flowers on short spikes, typical of aroids, are concealed by the foliage. Clusters of bright red fruit follow. There are over fifteen hundred cultivars, many with stripes, variegation or other distinctive leaf characteristics. Among the cultivars are 'Marginata', 'Multiflora', and 'Variegata'.

Lily-of-China

THE ROSES

Rosaceae

Over a hundred species of prickly evergreen and deciduous shrubs and vines belong to the genus of roses. Most widely cultivated are the garden roses, which have been selected and hybridized to create the thousands of cultivars now available. These are grown in rose gardens, as landscape specimens, in mass displays, on fences, walls, and trellises, and in containers. As cut flowers, roses are unsurpassed for their many colors and sizes and their wonderful fragrance. Some of the plants also produce decorative fruit, the rose hips enjoyed by gardeners and wildlife alike. Garden roses fall into three categories: contemporary roses, including the hybrid teas, floribundas, grandifloras, miniatures, and climbers; classic or old garden roses, including hybrid, perpetual, tea, musk, polyantha, China, and damask types; and the species roses and their hybrids, including *Rosa banksiae, Rosa hugonis, Rosa laevigata, Rosa multiflora,* and *Rosa rugosa.* The plants should be set in beds of a size that enables easy cultivation. They require an open, sunny exposure, good drainage, and a fertile soil. Many of the hybrids are subject to insect and disease damage and require frequent spraying over the entire growing season and one or two prunings each year.

Lady Banks' Rose
Rosa banksiae
Climber to 20′   Zones 7–9

The Lady Banks' rose is a rampant climber that may outgrow its intended space. It produces an enormous number of yellow flowers, usually double, about an inch in diameter. The early spring blossoms have a slight fragrance, but one white cultivar, 'Alboplena', is the most fragrant. Prune after spring flowering. This rose forms a large, dense mass and requires a sturdy support.

Garden Roses
Rosa × hybrida
1′–10′   Zones 3–10

The garden roses include the most popular roses in American gardens:

Hybrid teas have beautiful large classic blooms of almost any color. They are esteemed the aristocrats of the rose world and usually bear individual blooms on long, sturdy stems. Hybrid teas generally grow to a height of about six feet and a spread of about four. They grow in most areas of the United States and bloom continuously in the warm months.

Floribundas have a place in the landscape where massed color is desired. Their blossoms are smaller than those of the hybrid teas, but they develop in much larger number.

'Amber Queen' hybrid tea rose, a recent introduction.

'Leprechaun' floribunda rose.

Lady Banks' rose

'Shreveport' grandiflora rose in a landscape planting at the American Rose Society's national headquarters, in Shreveport, Louisiana.

'Pride 'n' Joy', a miniature rose that seldom exceeds a height and spread of eighteen inches.

Bouquetlike clusters are in a diversity of colors. Plants are of low to medium height.

Grandifloras combine features of the hybrid teas and of the floribundas. Generally, they are more like the hybrid teas in height, and the floribundas in their clustering of flowers.

Climbers produce arching canes six feet and more in length. Some are freestanding, but most require the support of an arbor, trellis, or fence.

Climbing rose on a trellis at the Benjamin Franklin Museum, in Philadelphi

The color and form of the flowers vary greatly, and the plants may require two growing seasons to reach their full potential.

Miniatures are generally under a foot and a half in height and have tiny flowers and leaves. They are very hardy and can be grown as container specimens, even indoors.

'Carefree Wonder', one of the best of the shrub roses, a relatively new classification of garden roses.

Tree roses are grafts of a hybrid tea, floribunda, grandiflora, climber, or miniature on a long, sturdy stalk. They are appropriate as accent plants in the rose garden.

Shrub roses are different from any of these. They are usually compact plants that lend themselves to shaping as shrubs or hedges.

Classic or old roses are, according to some, those introduced before 1867 and, according to others, those available for more than seventy-five years.

Cherokee Rose
Rosa laevigata
Climber to 20′   Zones 7–9

From China, the Cherokee rose has gone on to be naturalized over much of the southeastern United States. After establishing itself, it grows rapidly, forming a thick mass of long, arching branches that need support. Numerous fragrant white five-petaled single flowers with yellow stamens appear in early spring, and there are a few through summer. In autumn and winter, large pear-shaped spiny red hips are on this plant. *R. bracteata*, the Macartney rose, is similar, with fragrant white flowers but orange hips.

Russell's Cottage' rose

Multiflora Rose
Rosa multiflora
3–10′ x 10′   Zones 5–8

A barrier planting can easily be created by the impenetrable growth of the multiflora rose, which is widely used in hedges. Of limited appeal in residential landscapes, however, it is hardy, and produces white flowers an inch across in spring. Small red fruit hangs on the branches in autumn and winter.

Canarybird Rose
Rosa xanthina
6′ x 6′   Zones 4–7

The canarybird rose bears yellow single flowers on arching branches and resembles *R. hugonis*, the Father Hugo rose. The hips of this rose turn reddish, and then purple black when fully mature. The seeds in the hips are a food for birds.

Canarybird rose with large fruit of late summer and into autumn.

Cherokee rose at Longue Vue Gardens

Rosemary in an herb garden

inches long and three to four inches wide have prominent veins. Orange yellow daisylike flowers with brown purple centers are three to four inches across. Flowering occurs from spring into early summer. The plant is appropriate in perennial gardens, in detail groupings, and in naturalistic settings. *R. maxima* is similar; its flowers are yellow with brown centers.

Fountain Plant, Coralbush
Russelia equisetiformis
Scrophulariaceae
2–4' x 4'   Zones 9–10

The fountain plant, with arching rushlike, almost leafless branches, can survive only in nearly frost-free areas. Most of the year it is covered with bright red tubular flowers half

Dwarf Rosemary
Rosmarinus officinalis
Labiatae
2–5' x 3'   Zones 7–9

Native to the Mediterranean region, the dwarf rosemary is an aromatic shrublike evergreen herb that was at one time widely planted in American gardens and is regaining popularity. It adjusts to most garden situations, but prefers a well-drained soil and full sunlight. The mature plant has an upright form with twisting, irregular, and curving branches. Small, fleshy needlelike leaves are an eighth of an inch long and bluish green. In late spring, clusters of light blue to lavender flowers about a half inch in diameter appear in the leaf axils. This perennial herb is grown in rock gardens and in detail plantings and has culinary uses. It is tolerant of salt spray.

Coneflower
Rudbeckia fulgida
Compositae
3'   Zones 6–8/9

The coneflower is a native perennial adapted to poor, dry soils but thriving under good growing conditions where there is plenty of sunlight. Large gray green leaves six to eight

Fountain plant in the New Orleans Botanic Garden

'Goldsturm' coneflower

an inch in length. It grows best in sunlight where the soil is relatively dry and well drained. As a pot plant protected from subfreezing temperatures, it will flower during the warm months. Keep it relatively dry during the cold months, and supply moderate water during spring and summer.

Silver gray foliage of the white willow in a public park

White Willow
Salix alba
Salicaceae
75' x 50'   Zones 2–7/8

One of the best upright willows for wet places where little else will grow is the white willow. Its leaves, up to four inches long and three-quarters of an inch wide, are bright green on their upper surface and whitish on their lower. The foliage is golden yellow in autumn. The large, low-branching tree forms an open broad, round canopy. It is somewhat messy, constantly dropping leaves, twigs, and branches, and is susceptible to a number of insects and diseases. A half dozen cultivars varying in hardiness and leaf and stem color have been introduced.

Babylon Weeping Willow
Salix babylonica
20–35' x 35'   Zones 6–8

Much confusion exists between the Babylon weeping willow and the possibly three or more clones that make up the species. Its leaves, up to six inches long and three-quarters of an inch broad, are light green on top and grayish underneath. The tree grows best in full sunlight and in soil that is

Weeping willow at Mt. Auburn Cemetery

moist and well drained. The somewhat flatly oval to rounded canopy and arching, pendulous branches make it a favorite among trees with a weeping form. Male and female flowers occur on the same plant in early spring, the male as yellow green catkins about two inches long. The fast-growing brittle, short-lived deciduous tree is subject to wind damage, but aesthetically it is superb as an accent near a body of water. Root rot is common in the Lower South.

Pussy Willow
Salix discolor (caprea)
12–20′ x 15′   Zones 3–9

A large native deciduous shrub or small tree, the pussy willow is grown for its catkins, which are used in ornamental indoor arrangements. Oblong leaves up to four inches long are wavy, toothed, and attractive. The soft-wooded plant is well adapted to moist soil but will succeed in soil of almost any kind. In full sunlight or partial shade, it is fast-growing but short-lived.

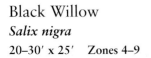

Pussy willow in spring

Flowering specimen of the elder-berry.

Black Willow
Salix nigra
20–30′ x 25′   Zones 4–9

In North America, the black willow is seen along rivers and streams and on open floodplains. Adaptable to most soils, from wet to fairly dry, the native deciduous tree holds appeal for its rapid growth, quick shade, and tolerance of alterations of grade in the land around it, but it is relatively short-lived. It is a medium-dense tree with an upright, leaning trunk and a highly irregular form. In early spring, bright yellow green leaves grow to a length of six inches and a width of three-quarters of an inch. The foliage turns yellow in fall. Capsules open in fall to release a multitude of small seeds with fluffy, cottonlike caps.

Elderberry
Sambucus canadensis
Caprifoliaceae
8–10′ x 10′   Zones 4–10

The elderberry is a widely distributed native deciduous shrub to small tree found growing at the edge of woodlands and in rights-of-way and unmanaged open spaces. It grows rapidly in soil from wet to fairly dry. Forming clumps, it is upright with an irregular broad-spreading canopy. White flower heads ten inches or more in diameter can be on view from spring until frost. The flowers develop into purplish black berries, harvestable from summer until a freeze occurs, that are the basis for wine and jelly and a food for birds.

Mockingbird eating elderberry fruit of late autumn.

Black willow on the bank of the Mississippi

Lavender Cotton
Santolina chamaecyparissus
Compositae
1–2′ x 2–4′   Zones 6–9

Lavender cotton forms a dense, broad-mounding shrubby mat with silvery gray green leaves that emit a strong aroma when bruised. Button-shaped yellow flowers up to three-quarters of an inch in diameter are borne on stalks rising four to six inches above the evergreen foliage. Blossoming can continue through the summer if the plant is not clipped. Nevertheless, the plant is as a rule clipped to keep it low and compact. A dry, well-drained soil and a sunny location are necessary for best growth. The plant is effective scattered in rock gardens, massed in borders, or employed as a ground cover in a small area, either alone or as an interplanting with other ground covers. Alkaline soil is acceptable. *S. virens* is similar but has greener leaves.

Chinese tallow tree, very dependable for autumn color in the Deep South

tiful display. The yellow green leaves are up to ten inches long, with four to eleven pairs of leaflets apiece.

Chinese Tallow Tree
Sapium sebiferum
Euphorbiaceae
20–35′ x 20′   Zones 7–9

Native to Asia, the Chinese tallow tree has heart-shaped leaves up to three inches long that come to an abrupt point. Yellow green catkinlike male flowers are up to four inches long, and there are separate small female flowers at the base of these. The fast-growing deciduous tree will do well in full sunlight or partial shade and in a wide variety of soils. It has beautiful autumn color with leaves running from yellow through orange to deep red, depending on the temperature. The change of color may not occur until December in the Deep South. Bees work the flowers for pollen and nectar, and some birds eat the seed. The tree can be messy, with a lot of dieback and falling debris. Its plentiful seeds, resembling popcorn, germinate by the score near the trees.

Silvery gray foliage and yellow flowers of lavender cotton.

Western Soapberry
Sapindus drummondii
Sapindaceae
30′ x 15′   Zones 6–9

One of the best trees for growing in dry or alkaline soil, the western soapberry makes a desirable medium-sized shade tree. In fall, it has outstanding yellow leaf color in addition to bright yellow globular berries. In May and early June, white flowers in panicles up to a foot long and eight inches wide put on a beau-

Western soapberry, the white May flowers of which are followed by golden yellow fruit in autumn.

Sweet Box
Sarcococca hookerana
Buxaceae
3–6′ x 4′   Zones 5–8

The sweet box, a low-growing evergreen with lustrous dark green medium-textured foliage, is not well known but is attractive, clear, clean, and crisp. Fragrant flowers, clustered in the

Close-up of the foliage of the sweet box

leaf axils in March and April, are small and white and mostly hidden by the foliage. Clusters of blue black berries follow in summer and autumn, and they too are visible only on close inspection. The hardy shrub deserves consideration for shady locations with slightly moist soil.

Sassafras in autumn, showing its three leaf shapes.

Sassafras
Sassafras albidum
Lauraceae
20–35′ x 20′
Zones 4–8

Native to the eastern United States, the sassafras appears in open fields, along fencerows and rights-of-way, and at the edge of woodlands. The deciduous tree thrives in relatively poor dry, sandy upland soil and in full sunlight. Its leaves are dark green and may be unlobed, mitten-shaped, or three-lobed. Early spring flowers are greenish yellow, and the fruit on the female plant turns blue black in midsummer. Coarse textured, the tree has a slender, upright oval form with short, strong horizontal branches in distinct tiers. Young branches are yellowish green, and the bark on the older tree is charcoal-colored and deeply furrowed. Autumn color—yellow, orange, and red—can be outstanding. Leaves are pulverized to make filé for gumbo, and the bark of the roots makes sassafras tea.

Strawberry Geranium
Saxifraga stolonifera
Saxifragaceae
4–6″   Zones 6–10

The strawberry geranium, a popular herbaceous perennial ground cover for small-scale planting, grows best in a loose fertile, moist soil and likes only morning sun. It forms a dense, low mass and spreads by reddish brown runners, or stolons. Fuzzy gray green succulent leaves have white marks along the veins on top and are reddish underneath. The foliage is rounded and can be three inches across. White flowers with two dominant petals are borne in delicate purple racemes as tall as ten inches. Plant in a cool, protected location in the Deep South, where the plant is nearly evergreen. It dies back to the ground farther north but will return in spring. 'Tricolor' is a cultivar that has attractive green-and-white variegated foliage with pink edges.

Strawberry geranium in spring flower.

Stonecrop, Gold Moss
Sedum acre
Crassulaceae
4–6″   Zones 4–9

A well-drained soil and a sunny location are ideal for stonecrop. The fine-textured chartreuse foliage that spreads

Stonecrop planting at John F. Kennedy grave in Arlington National Cemetery

Stonecrop in spring flower

to form a dense mat can be a ground cover for small patches or a specimen in rock gardens. In March and April, heads of small bright yellow star-shaped flowers sparkle above the foliage. The plant is easily propagated by laying stem cuttings on a tilled bed and lightly covering with sandy soil.

Autumn joy sedum

Autumn Joy Sedum
Sedum spectabile 'Autumn Joy'
12–18″ x 12″   Zones 3–10

Large, flat clusters of rosy pink flowers turn the autumn joy sedum into a spectacle in late summer and on into autumn. Use it as an accent or a ground cover. The roundish blue green foliage dies back in winter but returns in spring. The plant prefers full sunlight and a soil that is relatively dry and well drained.

Dusty Miller
Senecio cineraria
Compositae
1–2′   Zones 4–10

In the Deep South, dusty miller is a perennial, but farther north it has

Dusty miller

to be handled like an annual bedding plant. The woolly white leaves are thick and have interesting cut margins. Full sun and well-drained soil are essential for good growth. Under conditions of high humidity, or in a situation of less than ideal drainage, the plant performs poorly and may die from rot. Yellow daisylike flowers appear in spring, but the foliage is what commands attention. Where the plant overwinters, it should be cut almost to the ground in spring to make way for new, more attractive growth.

Giant Redwood
Sequoiadendron giganteum
Taxodiaceae
50–60′ x 30′   Zones 6–8

Native to the West Coast, the giant redwood is one of the largest and longest-lived trees in existence. Unlike the ordinary redwood, this evergreen tree will grow in the East. In the wild it can reach a height of over 250 feet. Its needles, up to a half inch in length, are blue green and fall only after two or three years. Cones, to three inches long, are upright in the first year but hang down as they mature in

Young giant redwoods in Massachusetts

the second year. The young tree is pyramidal to oval, whereas at maturity the tree loses the lower branches and has a narrow pyramidal crown. The thick, spongy bark is a rich cinnamon brown. This redwood prefers deep moist, well-drained acid soil, though it tolerates dry soil.

Setcreasea, Purpleheart
Setcreasea pallida
Commelinaceae
10–15″ x 18″   Zones 8/9–10

A herbaceous perennial that grows in almost any soil, setcreasea does best where the soil is porous, moist, and well-drained and the plant can be in full sunlight or partial shade. It is appreciated primarily for its violet purple foliage, but small white to pinkish purple flowers are also a feature for most of the growing season. The sprawling, irregular habit makes this species useful as a bedding plant, in hanging baskets, and as a ground cover in a protected location. For best foliage color, place so that it receives only morning sun, since hot afternoon sun causes leaf burn. Some winter protection is necessary in the northern part of zone 9.

Southern Smilax, Small's Brier
*Smilax smallii
(lanceolata)*
Liliaceae
Vine to 40′
Zones 7–10

Fruit and foliage of the southern smilax

A stout, vigorous native evergreen vine, the southern smilax grows in fertile soil in thickets and fields and along the edge of ditches and streams. It is often found climbing into the top of deciduous trees, where it is most evident in winter. The leaves of the vine are a lustrous dark green on top, with the lower surface paler. They can be two to five inches long and up to two inches wide. The small greenish summer flowers are insignificant, and the small red fall fruit is dull. The distinctive foliage is shown to its best on trellises and arbors. It is sometimes cut for flower arrangements. The vine can become a pest, because it reseeds freely.

Mass planting of setcreasea in Natchez that has escaped winter freezes

Texas sophora in flower

Texas Sophora
Sophora affinis
Fabaceae (Leguminosae)
15–25' x 15'   Zones 7–9

A native deciduous tree, the Texas sophora grows in small groves along streams in the limestone soil of Texas and Oklahoma. It has dark green leaves up to ten inches long that are composed of nine to nineteen leaflets. Pink-tinged white flowers of a bonnet shape hang during late spring in racemes two to six inches long. This understory tree is of upright form, with spreading branches and a rounded canopy. It performs well in dry locations.

Japanese Pagoda Tree
Sophora japonica
40–50' x 40'   Zones 4–8

One of the best large ornamentals to have come from Asia, the Japanese pagoda tree is a broad-spreading deciduous tree with a rounded crown. Leaves composed of seven to seventeen leaflets are up to ten inches long and a lustrous bright green. Mildly fragrant creamy white flowers are borne in terminal panicles that can reach a foot in height and width. Blossoming occurs in July and August, when few other plants are in bloom. In October, pods of bright green seeds change to yellow and then yellow brown. The tree is invaluable in the urban setting, and wherever the soil is poor. It is fine for lawns, parks, golf courses, and street plantings.

Beautiful lawn specimen of the Japanese pagoda tree at Mt. Auburn Cemetery.

Texas Mountain Laurel
Sophora secundiflora
15–25' x 20'   Zones 8–9

The Texas mountain laurel is one of the best evergreens for an arid, calcareous soil. The native tree's leaves of a medium green color come in groups of three to five pairs with silky hairs beneath. Wisteria-like panicles of slightly fragrant violet blue flowers appear in spring. Woody seedpods are eight inches in length, and the bony bright red seeds inside are sometimes strung as necklaces.

Texas mountain laurel in spring flower in San Antonio

American Mountain Ash
Sorbus americana
Rosaceae
15–25' x 15'   Zones 2–6

A shrubby and very hardy deciduous species, the American mountain ash can thrive in relatively dry soil. Leaves to ten inches long are compound, with

Foliage of the Japanese pagoda tree

American mountain ash in flower in Anchorage, Alaska

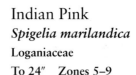

Indian Pink
Spigelia marilandica
Loganiaceae
To 24″   Zones 5–9

Found in small colonies and not abundant, the Indian pink likes moist soil and full sunlight or partial shade. Erect stems to two feet tall bear dark green, sessile leaves up to four inches long. Trumpet-shaped flowers, gradually widening to five-pointed cups, are red outside and yellow inside. Bloom is in April and May, and flowers open from the top to the bottom of the stems. This native perennial is suitable for naturalistic settings, where it combines well with other small perennials.

American mountain ash in fruit in the Great Smoky Mountain National Park, Tennessee and North Carolina.

a dark green upper surface and a paler lower surface. White flowers appear in late spring in flat-topped clusters up to six inches across. Orange red berrylike fruit ripens in autumn, to be eaten by birds. In the more southerly part of the plant's region of adaptation, this native of cold climates is most successfully grown at high altitudes. Even there, it is relatively short-lived.

Colony of native Indian pinks

European Mountain Ash
Sorbus aucuparia
20–30′ x 20′
Zones 3–6/7

The European mountain ash performs best at high altitudes if it is grown in the southerly part of its range of adaptation. A deciduous tree from abroad, it mounts an impressive display of red berrylike fruit in autumn. The clustered berries do not last long, since more than a dozen species of birds devour them. The small white late-spring blossoms are borne in flat-topped clusters three to five inches in diameter. The tree has an oval shape when young and a graceful open canopy when mature. It is susceptible to a host of insects, from borers to aphids, and diseases, from fire blight to crown gall. The available cultivars differ in form, leaf, and fruit color.

Fruit of the European mountain ash in summer.

Fruit of the European mountain ash, red in autumn.

THE SPIREAS

Rosaceae

In the genus of the spireas there are several spring-flowering deciduous shrubs that grow in gardens in most sections of the United States. Flower color varies with the species and the cultivar of the species but is most often white, pink, or red. The shrubs are generally low, with twiggy growth. Most flowering occurs in early spring, although some of the newer cultivars bloom well into summer. Spirea is not fussy about soil but performs best in good garden loam in full sunlight or partial shade. Most of the available selections are long-lived, but to keep them in bounds and encourage flowering it is necessary to prune them each year after flowering. One-third of the oldest and tallest nonproductive canes or stems may be cut to within two or three inches of the ground. The plants are valued in the landscape for their spring bloom, fine texture, ease of culture, and interesting form. They may be used in shrubbery borders, on sloping embankments, in mass plantings, and as single specimens.

'Anthony Waterer' Bumald spirea flowering in late spring

Bumald Spirea
Spiraea × bumalda
2–3′ x 3–5′   Zones 3–8

Fast-growing, the Bumald spirea has erect branches and a flattish top but often also a mounded form. Young leaves, one to three inches long, are at first pinkish red but turn dark bluish green when mature. White to pink flowers are abundant in late spring, with a sporadic blooming for several weeks thereafter. Flat-topped flower heads are four to six inches across, and clipping them off when they are spent gives the plant a more pleasing appearance. 'Anthony Waterer', with deep pink flowers, is one of the older and more popular cultivars of this hybrid.

Reeve's Spirea
Spiraea cantoniensis
5′ x 5–10′   Zones 6–9

Native to Japan and China, the Reeve's spirea has somewhat wedge-shaped blue green leaves from one inch to two and a half inches long. Dense clusters of white flowers an

Reeve's spirea, a reliable spring-flowering shrub for a large part of the nation

inch and a third across decorate the graceful stems in early spring. This spirea has a medium-fine texture and a mounding form with arching branches. The cultivar 'Lanceata' has double flowers and is widely grown in the south.

'Shirobana' Japanese spirea, which may have flowers of three different colors on the same plant.

Japanese Spirea
Spiraea japonica
2–3′ x 4′   Zones 3–8

Variations in flower color and size, leaf shape and color, and plant form make it impractical to try to describe the typical Japanese spirea. Flower clusters to a foot in diameter vary in color from white to red. One cultivar, 'Shirobana', has white, pink, and deep rose flowers on the same plant.

Bridal Wreath Spirea
Spiraea prunifolia
5–8′ x 5′   Zones 4–9

With many upright stems arising from a tight central crown, bridal wreath spirea forms a dense vase-shaped plant. Glossy dark green leaves an inch long are pointed at both ends. There are sometimes autumn colors of yellow

and red. Buttonlike white double flowers appear before the leaves in early spring. Blooms are thickly set along the stem, more thickly in colder regions.

Lacy-textured specimen of baby's breath spirea

Baby's Breath Spirea
Spiraea thunbergii
3–5′ x 5′   Zones 4–8

The thin, feathery light green leaves of the baby's breath spirea are up to two inches long. They turn golden yellow in autumn. This spirea is a profuse bloomer, but the flowers are dainty and measure only about a third of an inch in diameter. The form is rounded, sometimes irregularly, with twiggy, arching branches and a dense mass.

Close-up of flowers of the Vanhoutte spirea

Vanhoutte Spirea
Spiraea × vanhouttei
4–6′ x 8′   Zones 3–8

The Vanhoutte spirea is a hybrid with graceful upright-arching branches and slightly ginkgolike blue green foliage that is pointed at the tip and up to an inch in length. Orange red

Rocketlike sprays of bridal wreath spirea

foliage adorns the shrub in autumn. Prominent two-inch flat-topped clusters of white flowers are on the branches after most other spireas have bloomed. Flowering is sporadic where winters are mild.

Flowers and foliage of the silky camellia

Silky Camellia
Stewartia malacodendron
Theaceae
6′ x 6′   Zones 7–9

A native deciduous shrub with broad-spreading horizontal branches, the silky camellia grows in deep fertile, well-drained soil that has a pH of 4.5 to 5.5, especially in partial shade. Its membranous leaves are two to four inches long and about half as wide. Downy white silky-textured flowers with prominent dark purple stamens are borne singly in the leaf axils. Blossoms four inches across, with five crimped-edge petals, continue from April through June. Sometimes refered to as the wild camellia, the plant, in its finickiness, poses a challenge that only the expert gardener is likely to meet.

Butterfly Vine
Stigmaphyllon ciliatum
Malpighiaceae
Vine to 20′   Zones 8/9–10

Attractive yellow flowers to an inch accross are borne in clusters on the butterfly vine during the warm months. The vine is listed in some references as *Mascagnia macroptera*.

Yellow flowers and chartreuse butterfly-like seedpods of the butterfly vine.

Unique seedpods, resembling large butterflies, are chartreuse for two or more weeks and turn tan when mature. Slender, evergreen, and twining, the vine flowers poorly in shade and prefers full sunlight. It often dies back to the ground after a freeze but will return in spring. It cannot be recommended north of the lower quarter of zone 8.

Bird-of-Paradise
Strelitzia reginae
Strelitziaceae
4–5′ x 4′   Zones 9–10

Exotic eight-inch yellow orange flowers with cobalt blue tongues and purplish bracts are produced intermittently throughout the year

Exotic flower of the bird-of-paradise

by the bird-of-paradise. The tropical perennial's gray green paddle-shaped leaves are up to a foot and a half long and six inches wide. The plant will grow in partial shade but prefers full sunlight. It will not flower for a year after a freeze kills the foliage to the ground. Best flowering occurs once the clumps become crowded. *S. nicolai* is similar but larger, with bigger leaves and nearly white flowers that have a reddish spathe.

Giant bird-of-paradise, with white flowers.

Flowers of the styrax in early spring

Styrax, Snowbell
Styrax americanus
Styracaceae   Zones 5–9
8–15′ x 8′

Moist, porous woodland soil, where there is sunlight or partial shade, is ideal for the styrax. The native large deciduous shrub or small tree bears bright green leaves three inches long on zigzagged stems. Clusters of fragrant white bell-shaped flowers with narrow reflexed petals appear in April and May. The fruit is a roundish dry capsule. The plant is useful in naturalistic settings where a multiple-stemmed plant of upright form is desired. *S. japonicus*, the Japanese snowbell, is a larger tree, has more prominent flowers, and is better adapted to cold climates.

Horse Sugar, Sweetleaf
Symplocos tinctoria
Symplocaceae   Zones 7–9
10–20′ x 15′

Foliage and fruit of the horse sugar.

A native small semievergreen tree, the horse sugar grows near rivers and streams in sandy soil. The slender, spreading branches give it an open appearance. Its glossy, leathery medium green leaves are five to six inches long and an inch or two wide. They turn purple before falling. Sap from the leaves is sweet to the taste. The tree has a wilted appearance, as if under water stress. Clusters of fuzzy, fragrant yellowish flowers appear on the bare stems from late winter through early spring. The fruit is an elongated drupe that matures to an orange brown in late summer. *S. panicu-*

lata, the sapphireberry or Asian sweetleaf, is a related species that has bright turquoise blue fruit attractive to birds as it ripens in fall.

Common Lilac
Syringa vulgaris
Oleaceae
8–10′ x 8′   Zones 3–7/8

Extremely fragrant flowers perfume the spring air near the common lilac. Its cultivars, of which there are hundreds, have blossoms in white, pink, lilac, blue, magenta, or purple. The bluish green leaves up to five inches in length are about half as wide. An upright grower, the deciduous shrub has few lower branches when mature. Its fruit is a half-inch capsule. It grows in full sunlight or partial shade and prefers a soil that is nearly neutral but contains some organic matter. Pruning, if desired, should be done

Lilac specimen in flower

Lilacs on Lilac Hill at the Arnold Arboretum on Lilac Sunday

immediately after flowering; if not, the spent flower heads should be removed. *Syringa × persica*, the Persian lilac, is a graceful hybrid that produces a profusion of fragrant pale lilac flowers in spring.

Salt Cedar
Tamarix gallica
Tamaricaceae
10–20′ x 10′   Zones 5–6

A large shrub or small tree, the salt cedar thrives in a sunny location where the soil is well-drained, sandy, and alkaline. Very tolerant of salt spray, the plant is good for coastal areas. Its feathery foliage is silvery blue and juniper-like. The trunk is often contorted and has reddish brown bark. Panicles four to six inches long are held above the foliage, each composed of racemes of tiny white to pink blossoms. Interesting branching, summer flower color, salt and drought tolerance, and an ability to control erosion all contribute to the value of the plant.

alt cedar in spring bloom near the seashore

Bald Cypress
Taxodium distichum
Taxodiaceae
50–100′ x 60′   Zones 4–9

Lumber from the mature bald cypress can last for over a century, and the tree itself can endure even longer. This native conifer grows rapidly for the first ten years, whether in water, near water, or in highland soil. It needs full sunlight. The young tree has a conical form, with short, stiff horizontal branches; the mature tree is highly irregular. Soft, delicate featherlike foliage is emerald green in spring and russet brown in fall. The leaves are compound, with leaflets up to three-quarters of an inch long and a sixteenth of an inch wide. The tree's summer flowering is of no ornamental value. The round green seed cones, about an inch in diameter,

Foliage of the bald cypress in spring.

Mature bald cypress

Autumn color of the bald cypress

turn purplish when mature. The swollen basal trunk and stumplike knees may be a nuisance in refined landscape maintenance.

THE YEWS

Taxaceae

One taxonomist has said, "A species is what a good taxonomist says it is." So much confusion attaches to this genus that the expertise of several good taxonomists would be required to place the many cultivars in rational species. To the lay person, most appear to be the same except in form and size. Still, yews are the most widely planted evergreen trees and shrubs from zone 8 northward, few species growing south of that. The leaves, borne on spreading and ascending branches, are glossy or dark green, flat and needlelike, and pointed or tapering at the end. They may turn yellow or brown during winter, particularly when exposed to drying winds. Plants are ordinarily dioecious, with male and female flowers on separate plants. The flowers are of little or no ornamental value. Yews vary widely in habit, size, growth rate, and textural character. Most culti-

vars are dense and compact, even in advanced age. Excellent drainage and a moist, fertile soil are a requirement. Grow the plants in full sunlight or partial shade. Most cultivars can be kept in bounds easily by an early-spring pruning. Clipping during the late spring and through the summer is necessary to maintain the desired form and avoid the appearance of a bad hair day. Older, overgrown specimens can be cut back to a foot or two above ground level to rejuvenate them and reduce their size. The genus is liable to few insects and diseases capable of doing serious damage. Too frequently the shrubs are clipped to geometrical forms, ending up looking like spheres, hemispheres, and rectangles of green Styrofoam. In the landscape, yews are suitable as single specimens and in screens, hedges, and mass plantings. The fleshy, jelly-bean-like red fruit, an aril, is the only part of the yew that is not toxic, and ingesting small amounts of leaves, stem, or bark can kill human beings, pets, and farm animals.

English Yew
Taxus baccata
20–50′ x 15–25′
Zones 6–7/8

The English yew is a large evergreen shrub to medium-sized tree. It has a broad, rounded form with dense, spreading branches. Not as hardy as others species, this yew will grow in a wide range of soils, including those that are calcareous. Leaves up to an inch and a quarter long and a quarter inch wide are spirally arranged on erect shoots. They are shiny and almost

English yew

black green, adding to the beauty of the plant's dense, dark pyramidal form. In Europe, there are specimens over a hundred years old. The age of one in Ireland is more than four hundred years.

Japanese Yew
Taxus cuspidata
10–30′ x 10′   Zones 4–7/8

The best of the yews for shade, the Japanese yew has a form varying from broad to narrow, with the crown erect or flattened and the branches spreading or upright and

Low, spreading Japanese yew in the Tower Hill Botanic Garden, in Worcester, Massachusetts.

Anglojap Yew
Taxus × media
5–15' x 2'   Zones 5–8

The growth habit of the Anglojap yew, a hybrid (*Taxus cuspidata × Taxus baccata*), varies widely. The plant is similar to other members of the genus except for the olive green of the foliage on branches more than two years old. It is a shrub or medium-sized tree, typically of broad-spreading pyramidal form. 'Hatfieldii' and 'Hicksii' are cultivars having a columnar or pyramidal form that seldom

spreading. On the older plant, the exfoliating bark is reddish brown. This species is reported to withstand the smoke, dust, and air pollution of industrial cities. There are several cultivars, the most common being 'Capitata', which is pryamidal in form. 'Repandens' is a dwarf selection that is two to six feet tall and may spread up to fifteen feet.

Dwarf Japanese yew at the National Arboretum

Large pyramidal Japanese yew at Cave Hill National Cemetery, Louisville, Kentucky.

Columnar Anglojap yew at the Morton Arboretum

225

'Hicksii' Anglojap yew, showing typical yew foliage

exceed twenty feet in height and are generally kept to a height of four to six feet. 'Densiformis' is one of the best selections having a low, dense shrublike form. It grows from three to four feet tall and twice as broad. 'Halloran' has a broad, compact form and after twenty years seldom exceeds a six-foot height and spread.

Cleyera
Ternstroemia gymnanthera
Theaceae
8–15' x 8'
Zones 7–9

Cleyera's foliage

The cleyera's glossy, leathery dark green foliage is up to four inches long and an inch wide. The new spring foliage is coppery red, and in freezing temperatures the evergreen shrub's leaves may

The fruit of the cleyera, colorful in late summer and in autumn

turn purple. Fragrant white flowers about a half inch across appear in late spring. Globose red fruit can be showy in late summer or in autumn. The plant grows in full sunlight or partial shade and needs a well-drained sandy, loamy soil that is slightly acid. It may be single- or multitrunked, with an upright oval form and upright branches. It lends itself to pruning and is excellent as an accent plant in small places. It is also good in screens and hedges.

Rice-Paper Plant
Tetrapanax papyriferus
Araliaceae
4–8' x 4'   Zones 8/9–10

In its native Taiwan, the stem of the rice-paper plant was at one time used in making paper. In the Lower South, it is fast-growing and can become nearly treelike if it is in a fer-

Rice-paper plant

tile moist, well-drained soil. Under less favorable conditions, the plant is smaller. Its very large fuzzy light green leaves are a foot or two across and heart-shaped at the base. Its flowers, in late fall or early winter, are an inch in diameter and creamy white. Rounded clusters of the flowers form panicles three feet tall. An abundance of small black fruit follows in areas without frost. The plant will grow in full sunlight or partial shade. Its roots sucker freely, and it can become invasive if not confined. Ornamentally, the plant's value lies in its coarse texture and tropical character.

Golden Oriental arborvitae, of the same genus as the American arborvitae.

American Arborvitae
Thuja occidentalis
Cupressaceae
40′ x 10′   Zones 2–8

The frondlike evergreen foliage of the American arborvitae is borne on branches that are mainly horizontal. This native species thrives in a variety of soils but does best in well-drained ground. Given the plant's fast rate of growth, it soon becomes a large conical tree unsuited to its familiar placement on small sites. The egg-shaped seed cones are of no landscape value. The plant does not like poor drainage and is very susceptible to bagworms, spider mites, and leaf and stem blight. 'Emerald', with a narrow, compact pyramidal form, is one of the most popular of the numerous cultivars.

Bengal Clock Vine, Sky-Flower
Thunbergia grandiflora
Acanthaceae
Vine to 30′   Zones 8/9–10

The Bengal clock vine is an evergreen perennial that is sometimes planted as an annual, since it is a rapid grower. It is appropriate for arbors, trellises, and the walls of buildings. The vine produces a large number of bell-shaped light blue flowers to three inches across. Flowering begins in summer and continues until killing frost. A hard freeze kills the vine to the ground, but if the roots are heavily mulched, it will resume rapid growth in spring.

Flowers of the Bengal clock vine.

Princess flower, a herbaceous perennia

Princess Flower, Glory Bush
Tibouchina urvilleana
Melastomataceae
3′ x 2′   Zones 9–10

The princess flower is a shrubby perennial that can attain a height of fifteen feet but is commonly pruned to a much smaller size. Pruning increases flowering, which occurs through most of the year in warm climates. The rosy purple to violet blooms are up to two inches across. The dark green leaves are up to four inches long and two inches wide. The plant grows best in a fertile, well-drained soil and likes full sunlight or partial shade. It will withstand light frost, but a hard freeze kills it completely.

Emerald' American arborvitae in Louisville, Kentucky

American Linden, Basswood
Tilia americana
Tiliaceae
60–80' x 40–60'   Zones 4–8

American linden's heart-shaped leaves and its pale yellow flowers hanging from bracts.

The American linden has pointed, heart-shaped leaves up to eight inches long and nearly as wide. The fragrant pale yellow flowers that are borne in hanging clusters of five to ten in late spring are a good source of nectar for bees. Grayish nutlike fruit, to a half inch, does not have ornamental value. A broad, rounded crown on a tall, straight trunk and horizontal branching are typical for the tree, which is tolerant of most conditions and grows in soils from dry to moist. This species is subject to a number of insect and disease problems. Several cultivars are available that differ in size, form, and leaf color.

Littleleaf Linden
Tilia cordata
40–70' x 50'   Zones 3–8

The width of the leaves often exceeds their length, which is usually not more than three inches, on the littleleaf linden. The foliage of this native deciduous tree is a lustrous dark

Littleleaf linden, a reliable tree for urban settings

green on top, sometimes changing to yellow in autumn. Fragrant yellow flowers are present in drooping clusters in late spring. The tree's fruit is similar to that of the American linden. Excellent as a street tree and in many other roles as a landscape specimen, this linden grows well in moist, well-drained soil and prefers full sunlight. It performs well in soils from slightly acid to alkaline. Aphids, Japanese beetles, and other insects can be a problem for it, as can a number of diseases. Twenty or more cultivars have been introduced.

Asian Jasmine
Trachelospermum asiaticum
Apocynaceae
Vine to 25'   Zones 7–10

Asian jasmine covering a large part of a garden, accented with aspidistra

Introduced from China, the Asian jasmine is one of the best evergreen ground covers in the South. The vine grows in full sunlight or shade and in many soils, from moderately wet to fairly dry. The glossy dark blue green leaves are about an inch long and half as wide and become leathery at maturity. The plant is a fast grower and forms a mat up to two feet deep if left untrimmed. Use either a lawn mower, set at a high cutting height, or a monofilament weed trimmer to maintain a lower ground cover. Trim in late winter, just before spring growth. Trimming may be done again later in the season, but never after August. The vine will overpower low-growing shrubs and herbaceous plants. A variegated variety, with white leaf margins, is good for open, sunny locations.

White flowers of the Confederate jasmine

Confederate Jasmine
Trachelospermum jasminoides
Vine to 20′   Zones 8/9–10

The Confederate jasmine is prized for its fragrant white spring flowers, fast growth, and evergreen foliage. A native of Asia, the vine grows in full sunlight or partial shade if it is in a fertile, well-drained soil. Extremely fragrant creamy white star-shaped flowers an inch across cover the plant in May, and a few blooms may open in early summer. The glossy blue green leaves on short petioles are two to four inches long. Stems are green when young but turn brown as they age. Leaves and stems exude a white latex when they are broken. The vine is a fine choice for a trellis, arbor, or fence or as a coarse ground cover. Although this species is more likely than the Asian jasmine to be damaged when an early freeze occurs, it generally returns from the root system. Mulch will help protect roots from freezing.

Trilliums, Wake-Robins
Trillium species
Liliaceae
6–10″   Zones 3–8

Shady woodlands with deep topsoil and a thick layer of humus are the natural habitat of the trilliums, which are native to Asia and North America.

One of many native trilliums

Whorled leaves, either three-spotted or mottled, are borne on stems two to five inches long. Plants emerge between February and May, depending on location and species. Solitary flowers appear in the center of three leaves at the top of three- to six-inch stalks. The color of the flower varies with the species and may be white, pink, maroon, or purple. The plants are not easy to cultivate, for the natural growing conditions must be duplicated exactly. Where they can be grown, they can be considered for naturalistic settings, as ground covers in small areas, and as coarse-textured accents. *T. recurvatum* thrives in the Lower South; *T. ludovicianum* and *T. sessile* grow best farther north.

Canadian hemlock of weeping form

Canadian Hemlock
Tsuga canadensis
Pinaceae
30–50′ x 25′   Zones 3–7

The Canadian hemlock is the most widely planted of the hemlocks. Its short needles are a lustrous dark green on top, with two whitish bands on the underside. Cones about an inch in length are light to medium brown at maturity. The male flowers, or catkins, are light yellow. The graceful pyramidal evergreen tree ages beautifully, maintaining its form throughout its life. It grows well in full sunlight or partial shade but will not withstand poor drainage, drought, or a windswept exposure. In the landscape, it can be attractive as a specimen or in screens or mass plant-

ings. Many cultivars are available, including a large number that grow compactly.

Garden Tulips
Tulipa species
Liliaceae
To 28″   Zones 3–8

Tulips have had a place in gardens for over four hundred years. Introduced from Turkey, they are now in gardens around the world. Constituting a large and complex genus, they are among the most highly researched of bulbous spring-flowering perennials. Flowers vary from the classic tulip shape to shapes with twisted and pointed elongated petals, as in the lily and acuminata types. Plants vary in height from the three or four inches of the polychroma species to the twenty-eight-inch stems of the Darwin hybrids. The entire spectrum of colors is found in tulips, and there are both solids and bicolors. The flowers can be single or double, with their petal margins smooth, ruffled, fringed, or scalloped. In the coastal South, bulbs must receive a chilling at approximately 40 degrees Fahrenheit for six to eight weeks prior to their winter planting. Without that, flower stems do not elongate and flowering is erratic. In colder climates, planting should be in October. In the Deep South, the plants do not propagate additional bulbs large enough to flower. Grow in a well-drained soil, preferably in raised beds, in full sunlight. Where the soil freezes, plant five to six inches deep, and in warmer climates to half that depth.

Spring tulips at Monticello

Spring tulips at Williamsburg

Cattail
Typha latifolia
Typhaceae
4–6′   Zones 5–10

The cattail grows in ditches, marshes, and other standing
water, and at the edge of ponds. Scattered throughout the
southern states, it forms dense clumps and spreads by
creeping rootstock until the clumps unite in one gigantic
mass. The flat almost evergreen foliage is four to six feet
tall with parallel veins. Hundreds of unisexual flowers are
crowded in dense terminal spikes, the tails for which the
plant is named. They are cinnamon brown in May and
June, turning darker brown and then, in late autumn, almost black. In autumn and winter, the heads break up and
the seeds disperse. The plant is a good choice for bogs and
other poorly drained areas, but keep in mind that it is aggressive and will crowd out other plants at the water's
edge.

American elm, with upward-sweeping branches

Cattails in the Chicago Botanic Garden

Winged Elm
Ulmus alata
Ulmaceae
30–50′ x 30′
Zones 6–9

The winged elm is a
rapidly growing
deciduous tree native
from Virginia to
Florida and east

Winged elm in autumn color

Texas. Small branches that are at least three years old have
two corky wings on each side. The tree has a spherical
crown, similar to the American elm's. Dark green leaves an
inch or two in length with roughened upper surfaces turn
yellow in autumn. Greenish red flowers appear in late winter, and seeds, with a hairlike covering and tipped at the
end with two curving bristles, ripen in May and June. The
tree is easy to grow and is good as a street or shade planting. It deserves greater acceptance and is an outstanding
choice where a medium-sized tree is wanted.

American Elm
Ulmus americana
60–80' x 60'   Zones 3–9

The American elm, a stately native deciduous tree, is found from the Rocky Mountains to the Atlantic Ocean and from Florida into Canada. Moist, fertile soil and full sunlight are optimal for growth, but the tree is tolerant of widely various growing conditions. Leaves three to six inches long and one to three inches wide are a lustrous dark green. Bright red stamens highlight the late winter flowers, and the countless green to reddish green papery seeds turn brown by late spring. The upward sweep of the branches gives the tree a vaselike shape. Dutch elm disease has devastated a large portion of the fine elms in New England and the Midwest. The Lower South's trees have been less affected, possibly because of the lower density of the species there. Several other insects and diseases pose a serious threat for the American elm. The cultivars that are available differ in form, growth rate, leaf characteristics, and resistance to Dutch elm disease.

Bark of a Chinese elm at Busch Gardens, Tampa.

Cedar elm, similar to the American elm in form.

Close-up of the leaves of the Chinese elm.

Cedar Elm
Ulmus crassifolia
40–50' x 40'
Zones 7–9

The cedar elm is a deciduous tree well disposed to the moist soil of bottomlands. It is especially common in east Texas and tolerates the slightly alkaline soil around San Antonio. This elm resembles the American elm, except that the canopy is rounded and the ends of the branches are slightly pendulous. Foliage is up to two inches long and three-quarters of an inch wide, and it is dark green with a leathery texture. Flowers appear from late summer into early autumn, and fruiting follows, but neither is of much consequence. Fast-growing and clean, this species makes a good street tree, with considerable drought tolerance. It is, however, susceptible to Dutch elm disease.

Chinese Elm
Ulmus parvifolia
20–40' x 70'   Zones 5–8

The Chinese elm, a magnificent species from Japan and China, is one of the best possible tree selections for landscapes. It is fast-growing for about its first decade. It does well in slightly acid to alkaline soils that are moist, fertile, and loamy. Glossy dark green leaves up to three inches in length remain into autumn. Flowering and fruiting occur in late summer and autumn, as with the cedar elm. The tree is rounded to oval, with wide-spreading branches and a comparatively short trunk. After a few years the exfoliating bark of the trunk and older branches makes them look like patchwork etchings in green, orange, gray, and brown. The available cultivars are distinguished by their form, cold hardiness, and period of leaf retention.

Siberian Elm
Ulmus pumila
20–40' x 30'   Zones 4–9

A fast-growing tree from Asia, the Siberian elm does poorly in the Lower South, where it is short-lived and keeps its attractiveness for only about fifteen years. It is much more

Siberian elm, here at the LBJ Ranch, in Texas, a good tree for a drier climate

Tree Huckleberry
Vaccinium arboreum
Ericaceae
15′ x 8′   Zones 7–9

Tree huckleberry with autumn fruit

The tree huckleberry is a native semievergreen shrub of irregular upright form that may be handsome either single- or multiple-trunked. Leaves are dark green on top, paler underneath. Their length rarely exceeds an inch and a half. Small bell-shaped flowers, constricted at the end, are white to pinkish white. Flowering is in April and May, and small black many-seeded fruit matures from August to November. The dry, mealy berries are edible and seem to be a treat for resident and migratory birds. A slow grower, the plant likes a moderately acid soil and full sunlight or partial shade.

Highbush Blueberry
Vaccinium corymbosum
6–12′ x 8′   Zones 3–7

Moderately acid soil (pH 4.5–5.5) is needed for best growth and fruit production in the highbush blueberry. The native shrub's leaves, dark green on their upper side, are from one to three inches long and a third as wide. Their yellow to red autumn color can be outstanding. Small pink-tinged white flowers appear in great number in spring as the deciduous plant leafs out. Round, coarse-fleshed blue black fruit is eaten by birds as it ripens in summer. The upright, multi-stemmed plant is easy to grow, requiring little more than well-drained soil, full sunlight or partial shade, generous mulch around the roots, and annual pruning. The cultivars

Puls

Fruit of the blueberry

satisfactory for dry climates similar to those of west Texas. Some of the cultivars have characteristics that make them more desirable than the original species. Dark green leaves up to three inches long and an inch wide are borne on rather open ascending branches. Flowers are greenish and appear before the leaves. Neither the flowers nor the fruit that follows is of ornamental interest. This species is often sold as Chinese elm, though it is far inferior to the true Chinese elm. In its favor are quick growth, drought tolerance, and cold hardiness.

available can produce berries of higher quality, and some adapt to different climate ranges. Many can be successfully grown even in zones 8 and 9.

Wild verbena

Wild Verbena
Verbena rigida
Verbenaceae
To 12″   Zones 6–10

Wild verbena is a native plant that produces lavender-colored flowers in spring and summer. A herbaceous perennial well adapted to dry soil of low fertility in locations receiving full sunlight, it spreads freely. It cannot compete with herbaceous plants that grow taller and shade it out. The four-angled stem and the rough, sandpaper-like surface of the foliage distinguish it from the garden verbena. It self-seeds in large colonies, and it makes an interesting ground cover along roadsides and in meadows. *Verbena* × *hybrida,* the garden verbena, has flower clusters up to four inches across and comes in colors that include white, yellow, pink, red, and purple, and in bicolors. It needs a good garden soil for best performance.

THE VIBURNUMS

Caprifoliaceae

The Eighteen Twelve Overture performed without percussion could be a simile for a landscape without viburnums. The evergreen and deciduous shrubs of this genus contribute interest to the garden over many months: in spring, lovely fragrant flowers; in summer, luxuriant medium- to bold-textured foliage; and then for many species in autumn, beautiful leaf coloration and an abundance of fruit appealing to birds. To ensure fruiting, plant two or more species in close proximity, so that cross-pollination can occur. At least one species is adapted to each hardiness zone in the United States, and some have outstanding cold hardiness. For best growth and flowering, give viburnums a well-drained slightly acid soil and full sunlight or part shade. Prune after spring flowering. The scorching of leaves is likely to be a problem when viburnums are planted in wet or poorly drained soil. Whiteflies may bring on sooty mold, which is a fungus that feeds on the whitefly's sugary excrement, or honeydew, and covers the leaves with a black film. There are over a hundred species and many cultivars in the genus.

Burkwood Viburnum
Viburnum × *burkwoodii*
6–8′ x 6′   Zones 5–7/8

Hemispherical clusters of fragrant white flowers appear on the Burkwood viburnum in early spring. This hybrid's foliage is a lustrous dark green. It is semievergreen in the South and turns reddish purple in autumn in the North. Fruiting is not heavy. The fruit is red, changing to black at maturity.

Fragrant Viburnum
Viburnum × *carlcephalum*
6′ x 6′   Zones 5/6–8

Sweet-smelling pink flowers that fade to white are on the fragrant viburnum in five-inch clusters during spring. This hybrid is the best of the snowball flowering viburnums. The fruit changes from red to black in autumn but is not very showy. The foliage is dark green and somewhat lustrous. It changes to reddish purple in fall.

Fragrant viburnum's snowball-like flower heads

Outstanding foliage of the David viburnum

David Viburnum
Viburnum davidii
3–5′ x 5′   Zones 8–9

The David viburnum forms a beautiful low, compact mound of dark green foliage. This evergreen species does well along the coast of the Pacific Northwest and in similar climates. In spring, clusters of pink flower buds open into dull white flowers. Oval blue fruit to a quarter inch long may be on the shrub from late summer into fall. Fruit is rare, though, since cross-pollination is necessary for it to be set.

Arrowwood viburnum with autumn fruit

Arrowwood Viburnum
Viburnum dentatum
6–15′ x 8′
Zones 4–9

A native deciduous shrub or small tree with many upright-arching branches growing from a central base, the arrowwood viburnum forms an umbrella-like crown. Flowering in April and May, the shrub has flat clusters of creamy white blossoms four or five inches across. Those are followed in late summer by clusters of metallic blue black fruit. The foliage may be a splashy red in autumn. *V. ashei* is closely related, but its leaves are more elongated, its canopy is more open, and its overall texture is finer.

Fruit of the Ash's arrowwood under pine tree

Linden Viburnum
Viburnum dilatatum
6–10′ x 8′   Zones 4/5–7

The versatile linden viburnum is appropriate in borders, mass plantings, and screens. A prolific bloomer, the native shrub makes a bold statement with its flat clusters of creamy white flowers in late spring. In September, bright red fruit is conspicuous. It often remains into winter. Some cultivars, notably 'Erie', have superior fruiting qualities. The lustrous medium-textured foliage assumes various colors in autumn, among them yellow, red, and reddish purple.

Fruit of the 'Erie' linden viburnum

Japanese viburnum specimen

Japanese Viburnum
Viburnum japonicum
8–15′ x 8′   Zones 8–10

Glossy, leathery dark blue green foliage is the major attraction of the stiff Japanese viburnum, an evergreen. The mildly fragrant white flowers in spring do not make a deep impression. Red fruit is occasionally produced in summer, but it too makes little impact. The shrub's density, upright growth, and coarse texture make it a possibility for screening and mass planting.

Judd Viburnum
Viburnum × juddii
6–8' x 6'   Zones 4–7

One of the best viburnums for the northern zones, the Judd viburnum has wonderful fragrant white flowers that are followed by glistening reddish black fruit. The deciduous plant is a hybrid of *V. carlesii* and *V. bitchiuense*, inheriting its fragrance from the former and its shrubby form from the latter. It is reported to be superior to either parent and is resistant to bacterial leaf spot, a disease affecting many viburnums.

Flower heads of the Judd viburnum, the constituent blooms of which can range from white to light pink.

Wayfaring Tree
Viburnum lantana
10–15' x 15'   Zones 4–7

The wayfaring tree's leathery leaves are a dull dark green until they turn reddish purple in autumn. Creamy white spring flowers appear in flat clusters three to five inches in diameter. In August and September, the fruit turns yellow,

Fruit of a wayfaring tree on Kings Island, near Cincinnati

then red, with both colors on the same plant at times. This species is fine for screens, hedges, mass plantings, and shrub borders. Because of its coarse winter texture, it is effective in naturalistic settings.

Nannyberry, Sheepberry
Viburnum lentago
10–18' x 8'
Zones 3–7

The fruit of the nannyberry runs through an appealing sequence of colors. Starting out green, it gradually changes to light yellow, then pinkish, and finally blue black with a lustrous bloom. Over twenty species of birds relish it. In May, flowers in flat clusters about four and a half inches in diameter last for ten to twelve days. The erect growth habit of the native deciduous shrub makes it ideal for naturalistic plantings.

Unusual colored fruit of the nannyberry

Chinese snowball in Natchez

Chinese Snowball
Viburnum macrocephalum 'Sterile'
15–8'   Zones 6–9

The Chinese snowball is the only snowball viburnum to grow and flower well in the Deep South, where it is semi-evergreen. It grows slowly for the first year or two but rapidly thereafter, and plants reach their full height in a few years. Large globular clusters of spectacular white flowers bedazzle the eye for a two- or three-week period. The plant is sterile, producing no fruit. Leaves are medium green and coarse textured. Allow plenty of room for this viburnum, and prune carefully after flowering.

Swamp Viburnum
Viburnum nudum
8–15′ x 6′   Zones 6–9

A native deciduous to semievergreen shrub best grown in a sandy soil, the swamp viburnum tolerates a wide range of soils. It often has multiple upright stems forming an oval canopy, and its young leaves have a reddish cast. Flat clusters of off-white flowers are abundant in spring, and a few may appear in autumn. Wildlife eat the clusters of blue fall fruit. This species is serviceable as a specimen in a naturalistic setting and as an understory tree in a small space. The dried flowers are foul-smelling.

Sweet Viburnum
Viburnum odoratissimum
10–20′ x 15′   Zones 8–10

A huge shrub with a dense broad, oval form and upright branching, the sweet viburnum becomes treelike as it matures. Leaves of a medium green four to six inches long and two inches wide have an unpleasant odor when crushed. Mildly fragrant white flowers are sometimes followed by red fruit that turns black in autumn. Whitefly seriously affects this viburnum, which is also subject to winterkill in the upper part of zone 8.

Sweet viburnum

European Cranberry Bush
Viburnum opulus
8–12′ x 10′
Zones 4–8

Dark green leaves resembling those of the maple, two to four inches long and wide, are a medium-textured background

European cranberry bush in fruit

for the outstanding flowers and fruit of the European cranberry bush. Two- to three-inch clusters of white flowers appear in May on this deciduous species, an outer ring of sterile flowers surrounding a center of fertile blooms. Bright red translucent berrylike fruit ripens in September and October. If wildlife do not eat it, it will survive through winter, acquiring the look of raisins. The cultivar 'Compactum' is half the size of the species, and its fruit and flowers make a brilliant display.

Double-File Viburnum
Viburnum plicatum var. **tomentosum**
8–10′ x 10′   Zones 4–8

Probably the most exquisite of the viburnums, the double-file viburnum is a deciduous species that leafs out early in the season. The foliage, which is borne on pronounced horizontal branches, is dark green with prominent veins. In April and May there are parallel paired rows of flat-topped clusters of white flowers, the outer ring sterile. Brilliant red berries a third of an inch long are pleasing against the backdrop of reddish purple autumn foliage. Of the out-

Summer fruit of the 'Mariesii' double-file viburnum

standing cultivars on the market, 'Mariesii', 'Shasta', and 'Shoshoni' are popular.

Dark green flowers and foliage of the lantanaphyllum viburnum

Lantanaphyllum Viburnum
Viburnum × *rhytidophylloides* 'Willowwood'
8–10′ x 8′   Zones 5–8

The lantanaphyllum viburnum's creamy white spring flowers complement its excellent leathery dark green foliage. The flat flower clusters are three to four inches in diameter. Red fruit changes to black as it ripens in late summer and early fall. This viburnum is semievergreen in the lower part of its range of adaptability. It is outstanding in mass plantings.

Understory specimen of the rusty blackhaw viburnum

Rusty Blackhaw Viburnum
Viburnum rufidulum
20′ x 15′   Zones 6–9

The rusty blackhaw viburnum is a small native tree with glossy dark green foliage on stiff, spreading branches. Creamy white flowers appear in late spring. Clusters of dark blue fruit, each as large as a half inch in diameter with a powdery white sheen, become especially visible after leaf fall. Over a dozen species of resident and migratory birds compete for the fruit, which is fairly sparse.

'Shasta' double-file viburnum in the National Arboretum

239

Fruit of the 'Seneca' Siebold viburnum

Siebold Viburnum
Viburnum sieboldii
15' x 15'
Zones 4–7

Fast-growing and with a year-round rugged, coarse texture, the Siebold viburnum has prominently veined lustrous dark green leaves two to five inches long and half as wide. This deciduous species is grown as a large shrub or small tree, and is especially appreciated for its abundant clusters of white flowers in late spring and its attractive red fruit in autumn. The fruit, up to a half inch long, is a favorite of birds from late summer into fall. The rose red fruit stems remain for up to a month after the fruit is gone.

green leaves, two to four inches long, have a rough upper surface and a strong, almost unpleasant odor when crushed. The fragrant white to pinkish flowers are borne in dense semiglobose panicles in early spring. The red fruit is seldom prominent.

Laurustinus Viburnum
Viburnum tinus
8' x 5'   Zones 8–10

An evergreen blooming in late winter and early spring, the laurustinus viburnum has white to pinkish white flowers in flat clusters two to three inches in diameter. Metallic blue black fruit stays on the shrub for long periods. The glossy dark blue green foliage that is up to three inches long and half as wide enhances the plant's appeal. This species will withstand medium shade and has some tolerance of salt spray. An early or prolonged freeze can severely damage or kill the plant.

Flowers and fruit of the laurustinus viburnum in late winter.

Sandankwa viburnum hedge

Sandankwa Viburnum
Viburnum suspensum
6–8' x 6'   Zones 8–10

The Sandankwa viburnum, a broad-spreading evergreen, is a regular in southern gardens but probably should not be chosen in zone 8 because of its liability to freeze injury. The thick dark

Maplelike leaves and fruit of the American cranberry bush.

American Cranberry Bush
Viburnum trilobum
8–12' x 10'   Zones 3–7

The American cranberry bush resembles the European cranberry bush in foliage and fruit. Its lustrous dark green maplelike leaves are two to five inches long. The plant has flat-topped white flower clusters. Edible red fruit matures in fall and remains into late winter, available for making jellies and jams. Large-growing, this species can be appropriate as a flowering accent or for creating a hedge or screen.

Wright viburnum

Wright Viburnum
Viburnum wrightii
6–8′ x 5′   Zones 6–8

An attractive deciduous shrub, the Wright viburnum produces six-inch clusters of white flowers in spring and comparably sized clusters of deep red to maroon berries, a quarter of an inch across, in fall. It is probably the best-fruiting species for the Deep South. Upright, rounded plants have shiny green leaves that can turn red during autumn, though they will not do that every year.

Vinca, Periwinkle
Vinca major
Apocynaceae
10–18″   Zones 7–9

Vinca is a viny ground cover for naturalistic settings where refinement is not critical. It has lustrous dark green leaves that may be up to three inches long and half as wide. Its lilac blue flowers, about an inch in diameter, are present in spring

Variegated periwinkle ground cover

and summer, with the heaviest flowering in spring. The plant has excellent shade tolerance and likes a moist, well-drained soil. It can look as if it is going to die during hot, dry weather, and good waterings are necessary for its survival in the southern part of its range of adaptability. Raise the blades of the lawn mower high, and give it a good shearing in early spring. It is also handsome in containers, window boxes, and beds where cascading foliage is desired.

Dwarf Periwinkle, Myrtle
Vinca minor
4–8″   Zones 5–9

The dwarf periwinkle is a common evergreen ground cover in the North, although several insects and diseases may trouble it. Leaves are about an inch long and three-quarters of an inch wide. When they are mature, they are a lustrous dark green. Lilac blue flowers about an inch in diameter appear in spring, with a few still opening in summer. The dense, low-growing ground cover spreads rapidly and is best suited to shady locations in the South and full sunlight or partial or full shade in the North. It will grow in most garden soils. Cultivars are available with flowers of different colors and with variegated foliage.

Dwarf periwinkle ground cover

Violet
Viola odorata
Violaceae
6–10″ x 12″ clump   Zones 6–9

Many romantic associations attach to the violet, but even apart from them, the plant deserves a place in the garden for its ease of culture, early bloom, and beautiful foliage. In moist, fertile slightly acid soil it will spread rapidly and disperse seed to form an appealing ground cover. It performs best in partial shade but can tolerate full sunlight and adverse conditions. Flowering is in early spring. The sweet-scented deep violet flowers, three-quarters of an inch in diameter, last for several weeks. The plant is good in borders, naturalistic settings, and containers. Other popular garden species include *V. pedata,* the bird's-foot violet;

Bird's-foot violet

V. primulifolia, the primrose-leafed violet; and *V. affinis*, the Brainerd violet.

Vitex, Lilac Chaste Tree,
Vitex agnus-castus
Verbenaceae
15' x 15'   Zones 6–9

Sometimes referred to as the southern lilac, the vitex is a deciduous tree with aromatic five-inch compound leaves resembling those of marijuana. According to legend, Roman maidens made their beds of the tree's foliage during the feast of Ceres to keep themselves chaste. Five- to eight-inch terminal spikes of lavender flowers rise above the foliage in May and June. Sandy soil and full sunlight are ideal for the plant, but it grows well under many conditions. It will tolerate high heat and withstand

Vitex blooming in June in south Georgia

urban adversities, but cercospora leaf spot often causes defoliation by midsummer. Cultivars are available with white or pink flowers. *V. negundo* is a more cold hardy species, but it does not flower as profusely.

Grape Vines
Vitis **species**
Vitaceae
Vine over 30'   Zones 4–9

Muscadine grapes, often turned into jellies and wines.

Grape vines may be grown for ornamental or commercial use. Sunlight to partial shade and a soil that is moist and well-drained are best for growing grapes. The leaf size and shape of the climbing and fruiting vines vary. The clusters of greenish flowers are of little ornamental value. Edible fruit, the size and color dependent on the variety, is highly prized for fresh consumption and processing into jellies, juices, and wines. Careful pruning is necessary while the plants are dormant to keep them in bounds and promote fruiting. They can make handsome coverings for fences, arbors, and trellises when a dense mass is desired.

Ground cover of wedelia

Wedelia
Wedelia trilobata
Compositae
12–15'   Zones 8/9–10

Gaining popularity as a ground cover in the coastal South, wedelia thrives in a loose, well-drained soil. The native of tropical America grows well in full sunlight or partial shade. Somewhat thick yellow green leaves with a rough upper surface are borne on trailing stems. Yellow daisylike flowers up to two inches in diameter continue blooming from early spring until the first killing frost. The salt-tolerant perennial is difficult to confine, but it can be trimmed with a lawn mower or a monofilament weed trimmer. Cold tender in zone 8, it may be killed to the ground some years, particularly when an early freeze occurs. It can make a beautiful specimen in a hanging basket.

Weigela
Weigela florida
Caprifoliaceae
6–9′ x 8–12′   Zones 4–8

Weigela has had a place in American gardens for many years. The hardy deciduous shrub has a medium to fast growth rate when planted in a fertile loose, well-drained soil with a sunny exposure. There are over forty cultivars, and in late spring or early summer, according to the selection, they produce trumpet-shaped flowers in white, yellow, pink, or red. Some have variegated foliage, and some grow compactly. The shrub flowers sparsely in the Deep South,

probably because the temperatures are not cold enough to initiate much development of flower buds. Prune weigela immediately after spring bloom. It is appropriate in mass plantings and screens, and as a specimen plant.

Chinese wisteria on a small cottage arbor in Colonial Williamsburg

Chinese Wisteria
Wisteria sinensis
Fabaceae
Vine to 100′   Zones 4–9

The Chinese wisteria's fragrant lavender blue flowers in racemes up to a foot long perfume the early spring air. Scattered blossoming may continue until late summer. The rampant deciduous vine from China can be kept in bounds by two annual prunings, one in summer and the other in winter. To encourage flowering, root pruning may be advisable in late spring. This wisteria is the best one for the southern half of the United States. A seedling may not flower until it is eight years old, or older. The long-lived plant has leaves with seven to fifteen leaflets. It grows in full sunlight or partial shade in a wide range of soils. Requiring a large, sturdy structure on which to grow, it can quickly cover a small trellis. With lots of work, it can be trained into a tree form. Cultivars include 'Alba', with white flowers; 'Caroline', with lavender flowers; 'Plena', with double flowers; and 'Jako',

Mature weigela specimen

Close-up of weigela flower and new leaves.

Rambling white wisteria on an overhead arbor

Standard or tree wisteria

Spanish Bayonet
Yucca aloifolia
Agavaceae
4–8′ x 5′   Zones 7–10

Stiff, erect unbranched trunks with daggerlike leaves that are two to three inches wide and more than two feet long give the Spanish bayonet—a native plant—its sculptural quality in the landscape. Like all yuccas, this one prefers a well-drained soil and full sunlight. The white flowers, four inches in diameter and borne in stout, erect panicles to two feet above the foliage in late spring and summer, are frequently tinged with purple. Two cultivars with variegated foliage are available. Leaf diseases, borers, and scale insects are a serious problem with yuccas.

with very fragrant large white flowers. *W. floribunda*, the Japanese wisteria, is best suited to areas with cool summers. It has violet blue flowers, and its cultivars have flowers ranging from white to light blue and reddish purple in clusters as long as twenty inches. There is one cultivar with double flowers.

Spanish bayonet on the grounds of Rosalie, an antebellum house in Natchez.

Xylosma
Xylosma congestum
Flacourtiaceae
10–20′ x 15′   Zones 8–10

Foliage of the xylosma

Similar to cherry laurel and ligustrum, and sometimes called the rich man's ligustrum, xylosoma has some features superior to either. The form of the evergreen native of China is from upright to rounded, with irregular branching that varies from nearly vertical to horizontal. The glossy yellow green leaves are about an inch in length. In full sunlight and a well-drained soil, the plant is fast-growing and makes an excellent screen, espalier, container specimen, or small tree that is insect- and disease-free and drought-tolerant. It can be killed by a hard freeze.

Adams needle

Adam's Needle
Yucca filamentosa
3′ x 3′   Zones 5–10

The Adam's needle, a slow-growing evergreen native, is nearly stemless, and its gray green swordlike leaves are two to four inches wide and up to two feet long. The leaf margins have curly, threadlike filaments to three inches long that give the plant its species name. The plant should have a sunny location where the soil is well drained. In spring and summer, it is glorious, with bounteous two- to three-inch off-white flowers in panicles three to six feet high. Its salt tolerance, low mass, rosette form, prominent flowers, and adaptability to dry locations are among its advantages. A variegated cultivar is available.

Mound lily yucca

Mound Lily Yucca, Gloriosa Yucca
Yucca gloriosa
4–8' x 5'   Zones 6–9

In the South, the mound lily yucca is widely planted and does particularly well in well-drained, sandy loam and full sunlight. The foliage of the evergreen native is gray green, sword-shaped, and about two feet long and two inches wide. The lower leaves are soft, and not dangerously rigid and sharp like those of other yuccas. Thick, erect panicles of white cup-shaped flowers to three inches across are three feet tall and bloom in summer and early fall. This clump-forming yucca is easy to grow, particularly in dry places, where its rosette form can be an accent adding year-round interest.

Trecul Yucca
Yucca treculeana
8–12' x 4'   Zones 7–10

The trecul yucca grows well in full sunlight if the soil is well drained and sandy, as in its native habitat in south Texas and Mexico.

Trecul yucca in Mexico

Its upright form and coarse texture make it a commanding specimen. The dark green spine-tipped leaves two and a half feet long are thick and daggerlike. Do not place where the leaves may cut people. Terminal flower stems up to three feet tall produce numerous white flowers, generally in summer and early fall. Dead leaves stay on the plant and should be removed yearly to keep it attractive.

Coontie
Zamia floridana
Zamiaceae
2' x 3'   Zones 9–10

The coontie is an evergreen native to the sandy, slightly acid soil of the hammocks of north and central Florida. Dark green compound leaves about a foot long arise at or near ground level. Plants are dioecious, with both sexes having conelike reproductive structures. Shiny bright orange red seeds, sometimes more than twenty of them in each female cone, are evident when the cones mature. It has been reported that a desirable nitrogen-fixing bacterium thrives around the plant's roots. Indians are said to have obtained an arrowroot starch from the large underground stems.

Ground cover of coontie

Spring flowers of the calla lily

Calla Lily
Zantedeschia aethiopica
Araceae
2′ x 2′   Zones 8–10

The calla lily's pure white waxy spathes, three to five inches across and four to eight inches long, are borne among arrow-shaped leaves that can reach a height of three feet. Spring and early-summer flowering is best once the plant is established for two years. It likes a cool location protected from afternoon sun and a soil that is moist and slightly acid. Sometimes grown in a container as far north as zone 7, it will require protection, however, above zone 9. Cultivars and other species produce pink or yellow flowers, and some have variegated foliage.

Prickly Ash
Zanthoxylum clava-herculis
Rutaceae
20–30′ x 20′   Zones 5–7

Spine-tipped corky bark on the trunk of a prickly ash.

Inconspicuous but pungent flowers appear on the prickly ash in April. The native deciduous tree's brown seedpods mature in fall, when they open to expose black seeds. The tree tolerates salt spray and will grow on gravel and shell bars. The leaves are seven to fifteen inches long and are composed of five to nineteen leaflets apiece, each about three inches long. Numerous pyramidal, spine-tipped corky growths punctuate the bark of the trunk and larger branches.

Foliage of the Japanese zelkova

Japanese Zelkova
Zelkova serrata
Ulmaceae
40–60′ x 40′   Zones 5–8

When Dutch elm disease killed off American elms through entire regions, the Japanese zelkova offered itself as a replacement. It has many of the excellent characteristics of the American elm, including its form and its leaf texture and shape, as well as its rapid rate of growth when young and its long life. The tree has an amazing ability to stand up against the pressures of the modern environment, including air pollution, and it has heat and drought tolerance. It is both an excellent tree in the residential landscape and an ideal street tree. It grows well in a wide range of soils but most rapidly in one that is fertile and well drained. The luxuriant green foliage turns bronze in autumn and, in some selections, acquires red hues late in the season.

White Rain Lily
Zephyranthes candida
Amaryllidaceae
8–12″   Zones 7–10

Argentina is the home of the white rain lily. A number of white star-shaped flowers two and a half inches across may be produced by a single bulb during the flowering period, which is in late summer and in autumn. In large clumps, the easily grown plant adds seasonal brightness. Its evergreen foliage makes it an excellent choice as a border plant. It may be dug and the bulbs divided almost anytime bulbs

are needed elsewhere. Other species of merit for the garden include *Z. atamasco*, with white flowers that have a pink edge; *Z. citrina*, with yellow flowers; and *Z. drummondii*, with white flowers. Hybrids come in pink, rose, red, and orange.

White rain lilies, a surprise bloomer in late summer and in autumn

GLOSSARY

ACCENT PLANT. A plant used to give special emphasis to a part of a landscape through color, form, or texture.

ACIDITY. Soil reaction, with a pH of 7.0 being neutral, a pH below 7.0 acid, and a pH above 7.0 alkaline. Most ornamental plants grow in a pH range of 4.0 to 8.0.

AGGREGATE FRUIT. A cluster of ripened ovaries such as is found in the mulberry, the strawberry and the kousa dogwood.

ALKALINITY. Soil reaction, low ACIDITY.

ANNUAL. A plant that completes its life cycle from seed through flowering to seed again in a single growing season.

ANTHER. The male, pollen-bearing portion of a flower.

APEX. A tip or terminal end.

ARCHING. Upward- and outward-curving, as stems or branches, achieving a graceful, fountainlike effect.

AROMATIC. Having scent or fragrance in a plant part, particularly when crushed or broken. Anise, camphor, rosemary, and sassafras have aromatic parts.

AWL-SHAPED. Tapering from the base to a slender and stiff point like a needle. The shore juniper has awl-shaped foliage.

AXIL. The angle on the upper side between a leaf and the stem that bears it or between a stem or branch and the AXIS from which it diverges.

AXILLARY BUD. A bud positioned in a leaf AXIL.

AXIS. The main stem or trunk of a plant; alternatively, the linear center of some portion of a plant.

BARRIER. An obstruction that hinders movement. A hedge is a barrier.

BASAL. At the bottom of a plant or plant part. Leaves at or near ground level, as in the bird-of-paradise, are basal leaves.

BERRY. A pulpy or fleshy FRUIT with one or more seeds. Grapes and huckleberries are berries.

BIPINNATE. PINNATE and with the pinnately disposed parts themselves pinnate. The goldenrain tree is bipinnate.

BRACT. A modified leaf. Dogwoods, dove trees, and poinsettias have bracts.

BRISTLE. A stiff, pointed hairlike appendage. The leaf tips of many red oaks have bristles.

BULB. A modified underground stem surrounded by fleshy, scalelike leaves. Daffodils and tulips are grown from bulbs.

CALCAREOUS. High in lime or calcium content and alkaline, as soil.

CANOPY. The spread of the overhead portions of a tree.

CAPSULE. A seed case or seedpod. Capsules form on the witch hazel.

CATKIN. Spikelike male flower that contains pollen. Catkins are found on birches, pecans, and oaks.

CLIMAX SPECIES. The various SPECIES in the final ecological collection of plants on a site.

COLONY. A group of the same plants growing together. Devil's-walking-stick and Chinese privet are often in colonies.

COMPOUND LEAF. A leaf composed of two or more LEAFLETS.

CONCAVE. Curved like the inner surface of a hemisphere.

CONE. A dense collection of woody, leathery, or fleshy scales attached to a core, each bearing one or more seeds. Pines, magnolias, spruces, and firs have cones.

CONICAL. CONE-shaped. The young cypress and the 'Nellie Stevens' holly are of conical form.

CONIFER. A CONE-bearing plant. Pines, spruces, and firs are conifers.

CONIFEROUS. Of or relating to CONIFERS.

CONVEX. Curved like the outer surface of a hemisphere. The Burford holly leaf is convex.

CORDATE. Heart-shaped. The redbud and tung oil tree's leaves are cordate.

CORM. A solid underground bulblike stem. Gladioli are grown from corms.

CORYMB. A more or less flat-topped flower head. The flowers of many viburnums and verbenas are corymbs.

CROWN. The upper mass or head of a tree or other plant.

CULTIVAR. A cultivated variety. The 'Pride of Mobile' azalea is a cultivar of *Rhododendron indicum.*

DECIDUOUS. Dropping foliage at one season of the year, generally in autumn.

DIOECIOUS. Having male and female flowers on separate plants. Hollies are dioecious, and berries will form on female plants only if there is a fertilizing male plant nearby.

DISK FLOWER. One of the closely packed tubular flowers at the center of an INFLORESCENCE. Disk flowers are at the center of the flower heads of chrysanthemums and daisies.

DORMANT. In a state of rest with little or no noticeable vegetative growth, generally during winter.

DRUPE. A fleshy fruit the seed of which is enclosed within a stony layer. Cherries are drupes.

ENTIRE. Smooth, as a leaf margin.

EPIPHYTE. A plant that grows on another plant but does not derive its nourishment from the plant on which it is growing. Some bromeliads are epiphytes.

ESPALIER. A plant trained in a flat plane against a wall or other structure.

EVERGREEN. Having green FOLIAGE throughout the year. Pines and yews are evergreen.

EXFOLIATE. To peel in thin layers, as bark. The river birch exfoliates its bark.

FILAMENT. A thread or threadlike organ, such as the STALK that bears the ANTHER.

FLORET. A minute flower that is part of a larger INFLORESCENCE.

FLORIFEROUS. Flowering abundantly.

FOLIAGE. The leaves of plants.

FRUIT. A ripened ovary. An apple is a fruit.

GENUS. A group of SPECIES differing only in a few minor characteristics and so closely related that they indicate common parents.

GLABROUS. Not hairy but generally smooth. The surface of a philodendron leaf is glabrous.

GLAUCOUS. Covered with a waxy white bloom that rubs off easily. Grapes and plums are glaucous fruit.

GLOBOSE. Having a spherical or round form.

GROUND COVER. A carpetlike spread of low-growing plants. English ivy and pachysandra often serve as ground covers.

HABITAT. The surroundings to which a plant is adapted and in which it grows.

HERB. A plant valued for its medicinal or aromatic qualities. Rosemary is an herb.

HERBACEOUS. Having no persistent, woody stems above ground. Day lilies and Shasta daisies are herbaceous plants.

HIP. A FRUIT or seedpod, as of a rose or gardenia.

HYBRID. A plant that results from crossing two or more closely related plants.

INFLORESCENCE. The flowering part or parts of a plant.

JUVENILE. In an early phase of plant growth, usually vigorous and nonflowering.

KEEL. A boat-shaped structure formed when two front petals unite to enclose the reproductive parts of a flower.

KNEE. An upright to dome-shaped appendage formed from the roots of bald cypress and pond cypress trees and rising above ground or water level.

LEADER. The primary or terminal shoot or trunk of a tree or SHRUB.

LEAFLET. A segment of a COMPOUND LEAF. Katsura, locust, and hickory foliage is formed of leaflets.

LOBED. Having prominent divisions separated by fissures, as leaves. The leaves of the red oak are lobed.

LUSTROUS. Shiny or with a metallic surface gloss.

MARGIN. Edge, as of a leaf.

MASS PLANTING. A grouping of a large number of plants of the same species.

MATURE. In a later phase of plant growth, usually with increased flowering and fruiting and a reduction in vegetative development.

MIDRIB. The central vein of a leaf.

MONOECIOUS. Having male and female flowers on the same plant. Pecans and oaks are monoecious, and a tree in isolation from others will yield nuts.

MOUND. A vegetative unit having a domed CROWN and continuing full to the ground.

NARROW-LEAF. Having long, slender pinelike needles; alternatively, having leaves in which the length is much greater than the width. Spruces are narrow-leaf evergreens. Willows and Jerusalem thorns are narrow-leaf deciduous trees.

NATIVE. A plant indigenous to an area.

NATURALISTIC. Having the character of spontaneous growth.

NEMATODE. A microscopic wormlike organism that attacks plant parts, particularly roots.

NODE. A thickened joint of a stem, where buds and leaves arise. Many grasses have nodes.

NUTLET. A hard nutlike structure with a thickened wall.

OBOVATE. Having a shape with the broad end at the top. The leaves of pyramidal magnolias are obovate.

OPPOSITE. Occurring two at a NODE, directly across from each other. The leaves of most viburnums are opposite.

OVAL. Twice as long as wide, with the widest portion being in the center, as leaves. Silverbells' leaves are oval.

PALMATE. Fan-shaped, with leaf parts originating at a common point. Buckeyes and Virginia creepers are palmate.

PANICLE. A branching INFLORESCENCE. Crape myrtle and lilacs have their blooms in panicles.

PENDULOUS. Having a hanging or weeping form.

PERENNIAL. A plant, normally HERBACEOUS, that persists for three or more seasons. Day lilies, peonies, and hostas are perennials.

PETAL. A unit of INFLORESCENCE that normally is colorful and showy.

PETIOLE. A leafstalk or leaf stem.

pH: The measure of the ALKALINITY or ACIDITY of a soil.

PHOTOPERIODIC. Responding to the duration of light exposure in development and reproduction. Chrysanthemums and poinsettias are photoperiodic in that they flower when the length of days is shorter than the length of nights.

PINNATE. Featherlike, with leaves or other segments on either side of a common AXIS.

POD. A structure enclosing a fruit or seeds. Most members of the pea or legume family have pods.

POWDERY MILDEW. A fungus disease evidenced by a powdery white coating on leaves and other plant parts.

PROLIFERATION. The production of offshoots in an unusual fashion. Day lilies and walking irises multiply by proliferation.

PROSTRATE. Lying close to or flat on the ground. Blue rug juniper and some cotoneasters are prostrate-growing.

PUBESCENT. Having soft, hairlike surfaces, as leaves. The leaves of paper mulberries are pubescent.

RACEME. An unbranched flower head. Nandina and wisteria have have their blooms in racemes.

RACHIS. The AXIS of a leaf or an INFLORESCENCE.

REFLEXED. Bent backward or downward. The leaves of Chinese holly plants are reflexed.

RHIZOME. An underground stem that differs from roots in having NODES. Irises grow from rhizomes.

ROSETTE. A tight cluster of leaves or flowers originating from a central point. The sago palm grows in a rosette.

RUNNER. A slender stem that grows along the surface of the ground. Ardisia and many of the ornamental grasses spread by runners.

SCAPE. A leafless stemlike structure arising at the BASAL portion of a plant and bearing flowers. Amaryllises and crinums are plants with scapes.

SELF-SEEDER. A plant that normally produces many seeds capable of germinating freely. Privets, pines, and grasses are self-seeders.

SEMIEVERGREEN. Holding some foliage during dormancy. Sweet-bay magnolias and cross vines are semievergreen.

SERRATE. Having toothed margins, with the teeth pointed forward, as leaves. The leaves of elms and cherries are serrate.

SESSILE. Attached directly to a twig, rather than by means of an intervening stalk or leaf stem.

SHRUB. A plant that remains relatively low and produces several shoots from or near its base.

SPECIES. A group of closely related plants or animals that produce similar offspring.

SPECIMEN PLANT. An ACCENT PLANT.

SPIKE. An unbranched, elongated flowering stem. The liatris grows in spikes.

SPORE. A tiny seedlike reproductive body such as is found on the underside of fern leaves.

STALK. A supporting structure for a leaf, flower, or FRUIT.

STAMEN. An ANTHER and its FILAMENT taken together.

STANDARD. A plant that has been pruned or trained into a treelike form. Ligustrums, cleyeras, and Indian hawthorns can be maintained as standards.

STERILE. Incapable of producing seeds. The flowers of some hydrangeas and viburnums are sterile.

STOLON. A stem that runs along the ground, a new plant forming at the tip. Strawberry begonias and ajuga spread by stolons.

SUCCULENT. A plant having juicy soft, fleshy tissue. Cacti are succulents.

TAXONOMIST. A professional whose concern is with the classification and naming of plants and animals.

TENDRIL. An aerial structure of a plant by which the plant can attach itself to a surface.

TERMINAL. A tip or top end.

TOMENTOSE. Having a dense woolly or hairy surface.

TRIFOLIATE. With leaves arranged in groups of three. The wild orange and Boston ivy are trifoliate.

TUBER. A short, thickened stem that is usually underground. Caladiums grow from tubers.

UMBEL. An INFLORESCENCE that is usually umbrella-like. Fatsia may bear umbels.

UNDERSTORY. Plant growth under the canopy of larger SPECIES. Dogwoods are often in an understory.

UNISEXUAL. Having male or female parts but not both, as flowers.

VARIEGATED. Having two or more colors in the same parts, as leaves, flowers, or FRUIT.

VARIETY. A subdivision of a SPECIES in which the individuals share some characteristic distinguishing them from others in the species.

VENATION. The arrangement of veins in a leaf.

WHORL. An arrangement of three or more structures in a circlelike pattern and arising from a central point like a NODE.

XERISCAPE. A landscape or a grouping of plants that grows with a minimum amount of water.

REFERENCES

Durr, Michael A. *Manual of Woody Landscape Plants: Their Identification, Ornamental Characteristics, Culture, Propagation, and Uses.* 4th ed. Champaign, Ill., 1990.

Fell, Derek. *The Essential Gardener.* New York, 1990.

Heriteau, Jacqueline, and H. Marc Cathey. *The National Arboretum Book of Outstanding Garden Plants.* New York, 1990.

Jones, David L. *Encyclopaedia of Ferns.* Melbourne, 1987.

Liberty Hyde Bailey Hortorium staff. *Hortus Third.* New York, 1976. Initially compiled by Liberty Hyde Bailey and Ethel Zone Bailey.

Odenwald, Neil, and James Turner. *Identification, Selection, and Use of Southern Plants.* Baton Rouge, 1987.

Ogden, Scott. *Garden Bulbs for the South.* Dallas, 1994.

Pope, Thomas, Neil Odenwald, and Charles Fryling, Jr. *Attracting Birds to Southern Gardens.* Dallas, 1993.

Still, Steven M. *Manual of Herbaceous Ornamental Plants.* 4th ed. Champaign, Ill., 1994.

Taylor, Norman. *Taylor's Encyclopedia of Gardening.* Boston, 1948.

Vines, Richard A. *Trees, Shrubs, and Woody Vines of the Southwest.* Austin, Tex., 1960.

Welch, William C. *Perennial Garden Color.* Dallas, 1989.

Whitcomb, Carl E. *Know It and Grow It.* Tulsa, 1976.

Wyman, Donald. *Wyman's Gardening Encyclopedia.* 2nd ed. New York, 1986.

INDEX OF COMMON NAMES

INDEX OF SCIENTIFIC NAMES